Posthuman Legalities: New Materialism and Law Beyond the Human

Posthuman Legalities

New Materialism and Law Beyond the Human

Edited by

Anna Grear

Professor of Law and Theory, Cardiff University, UK

Emille Boulot

PhD Candidate, Natural Resource Sciences, Leadership for the Ecozoic Program, McGill University, Canada

Iván Darío Vargas-Roncancio

Postdoctoral Researcher, Natural Resource Sciences, Leadership for the Ecozoic Program, McGill University, Canada

Joshua Sterlin

PhD Candidate, Natural Resource Sciences, Leadership for the Ecozoic Program, McGill University, Canada

A SPECIAL ISSUE OF THE JOURNAL OF HUMAN RIGHTS AND THE ENVIRONMENT

Edward Elgar
Cheltenham, UK • Northampton, MA, USA

© Edward Elgar Publishing 2021

All rights reserved. No part of this publication may be reproduced, stored in a retrieval system or transmitted in any form or by any means, electronic, mechanical or photocopying, recording, or otherwise without the prior permission of the publisher.

Published by
Edward Elgar Publishing Limited
The Lypiatts
15 Lansdown Road
Cheltenham
Glos GL50 2JA
UK

Edward Elgar Publishing, Inc.
William Pratt House
9 Dewey Court
Northampton
Massachusetts 01060
USA

For further information on the *Journal of Human Rights and the Environment* see www.elgaronline/jhre or email sales@e-elgar.co.uk

A catalogue record for this book is available from the British Library

Library of Congress Control Number: 2021947587

This book is available electronically in the **Elgar**online
Law subject collection
http://dx.doi.org/10.4337/9781802203349

Printed on elemental chlorine free (ECF) recycled paper containing 30% Post-Consumer Waste

ISBN 978 1 80220 333 2 (cased)
ISBN 978 1 80220 334 9 (eBook)
Printed and bound in the USA

Contents

Editorial

Posthuman legalities: New Materialism and law beyond the human
Emille Boulot, Anna Grear, Joshua Sterlin and Iván Darío Vargas-Roncancio   1

Articles

Re-forming property to address eco-social fragmentation and rift
Margaret Davies   13

'For the trees have no tongues': eco-feedback, speech, and the silencing of nature
Matt Harvey and Steve Vanderheiden   38

Climate change, environmental justice and the unusual capacities of posthumans
Nick J Fox and Pam Alldred   59

Posthuman international law and the rights of nature
Emily Jones   76

Response-abilities of care in more-than-human worlds
Marie-Catherine Petersmann   102

Alter-transitional justice; transforming unjust relations with the more-than-human
Danielle Celermajer and Anne Therese O'Brien   125

The practice of multispecies relations in urban space and its potentialities for new legal imaginaries
Teresa Dillon   148

Editorial

Posthuman legalities: New Materialism and law beyond the human

In 2020, a single virus changed many of the *worlds* in which humans live. From restrictions on immigration, movement and gatherings, to changes to public health policy, through to economics and housing, the SARS-CoV-2 virus restructured laws and lives. It also changed our more-than-human siblings' worlds: some took the opportunity to roam into the quiet of the relatively human-free spaces produced by lockdown, some provided company to their humans working from home, and some, too, were susceptible to the virus.

The dense entanglement of the material and the semiotic and of human and more-than-human worlds evident in this contemporary example has always been the actuality of the lively ecological communities that support life. And, as Indigenous, feminist and materialist scholars have argued, the 'human' always comes about through entanglement with other beings. As the *Feral Atlas* project puts it, '[e]veryday human life is always a multispecies effort' and '[o]ther species, as well as non-living things, make it possible to be human'.[1] The concept of the 'human' is a far more complex, interdependent and entangled actuality than is presented/represented by the autonomous, bounded individual assumed by Western legal systems.[2]

In this sense, 'we' are what de la Cadena calls, a 'complex we': 'a shared condition from which "self" and "other" emerge relationally as intra-acted assertions of divergence', both an 'us' and a 'them',[3] or what anthropologist Deborah Bird Rose has called a 'domain of entanglement'.[4] By far the most productive comparative partner in such relational thinking has been, and at the behest of, Indigenous, black, peasant and other communities.[5] An example is provided by the Yolngu people in northern

---

1. AL Tsing, J Deger, A Keleman Saxena and F Zhou, *Feral Atlas: The More-Than-Human Anthropocene* (Stanford University Press, Redwood City 2021) <https://www.feralatlas.org/>.
2. See for example, Bawaka Country including S Suchet-Pearson, S Wright, K Lloyd and L Burarrwanga, 'Caring as Country: Towards an Ontology of Co-becoming in Natural Resource Management' (2013) 54(2) Asia Pacific Viewpoint 185; D Haraway, *Staying with the Trouble* (Duke University Press, Durham 2016); C Merchant 'Reinventing Eden: Western Culture as a Recovery Narrative' in W Cronon (ed), *Uncommon Ground: Toward Reinventing Nature* (W.W. Norton, New York 1995); V Plumwood, *Feminism and the Mastery of Nature* (Routledge, London 2993); A Grear, '"Anthropocene, Capitalocene, Chthulucene": Re-encountering Environmental Law and its "Subject" with Haraway and New Materialism' in L Kotzé (ed), *Environmental Law and Governance for the Anthropocene* (Hart Publishing, Portland 2017).
3. M de la Cadena, 'An Invitation to Live Together: Making the "Complex We"' (2019) 11(2) Environmental Humanities 477, 478.
4. D Rose, 'An Indigenous Philosophical Ecology: Situating the Human' (2005) 16(3) The Australian Journal of Anthropology 294, 303.
5. It is important to recognize here however that it is not the responsibility, nor some would argue, the concern, of Indigenous peoples whether or not settler and Western populations can

Australia, who describe co-becoming, a presupposition that sees all life, including humans, as coming into being through relationships.[6] Yolngu people view their wellbeing and that of country as an interconnected relationship of mutual care, one in which the human is decentred, while recognizing that Bawaka Country cares not only for itself but also for the nonhuman world.[7] This 'complex we' is evident not only in the example of Covid-19 but also in the shifting climate and its auguring of the collapse of the imagined binary relations between humanity and the wider community of life. As multiple beings and communities experience ecological collapse, lawyers and those from other related and concerned disciplines must ask: what is the purpose, description and function of the legal and ethical systems that are supposed to regulate and guide relations in ecological communities? Can existing legal orders help posthuman beings, borrowing from Donna Haraway, to 'stay with the trouble'[8] so as to chart a path away from present defuturing conditions?

Although there has been significant work (and some progress in legal systems worldwide) on such issues, the apparently relentless road to ongoing extraction seems to be paved with the best intentions of existing environmental law and governance models. Legal responses remain systems of norms and procedures that independently regulate the 'human' use of an external and agentless 'natural world', specifying allowable harm rather than encouraging responsibilized relations between beings of all kinds. In attempts to restructure relations with the more-than-human worlds in which humans live, many scholars, lawyers and activists have turned to extending legal rights for nature in order to re-define/reject the human-nature dualism, and to facilitate a deeper and more mutually beneficial relationship between realms currently constructed as distinct.[9] This movement has been heavily influenced by, and has been predominantly inspired and driven by, Indigenous peoples the world over – from Ecuador and Colombia to New Zealand/Aotearoa – informed by their legalities, lifeways and ontologies. National and transnational legislations, court decisions and governance models across the world have increasingly recognized the legal subjectivity of animals, rivers and forests, among other beings and relations, as a legal avenue whereby to extend protection and standing to more-than-human lives and lively systems.[10] The rights of nature (RoN) approach is a growing legal response not only to the 'inter-related global crises of climate, food, energy, [and] poverty, [but also to a crisis of] meaning'.[11]

---

come to some level of relationality that may sustain the world, or a legal order that truly accounts for the living: see K Whyte, C Caldwell and M Schaefer 'Indigenous Lessons about Sustainability Are Not Just for "All Humanity"' in J Sze (ed), *Sustainability: Approaches to Environmental Justice and Social Power* (University Press Scholarship Online 2019). See also Z Todd, 'An Indigenous Feminist's Take on the Ontological Turn: "Ontology" is Just Another Word for Colonialism' (2016) 29(1) Journal of Historical Sociology 4, 9.

6. Bawaka Country et al. (n 2) 187.
7. ibid 192.
8. Haraway (n 2).
9. M Maloney and P Burdon, *Wild Law in Practice* (Routledge, Abingdon, UK 2014); C Cullinan, *Wild Law: A Manifesto for Earth Justice* (2nd edn, Chelsea Green Publishing, White River Junction VT 2017); DR Boyd, *The Rights of Nature: A Legal Revolution That Could Save the World* (ECW Press, Canada 2017).
10. I Vargas-Roncancio, 'Forest on Trial: Towards a Relational Theory of Legal Agency for Transitions into the Ecozoic' in CJ Orr, K Kish and B Jennings (eds), *Liberty and the Ecological Crisis: Freedom on a Finite Planet* (Routledge, New York 2020).
11. A Escobar, 'Thinking-Feeling with the Earth: Territorial Struggles and the Ontological Dimension of the Epistemologies of the South' (2016) 11(1) Revista de Antropología Iberoamericana 13.

RoN certainly have the potential to express the interdependence between ecological and social systems. However, the legal discipline is still deeply informed by the mindsets, practices and institutions casting nature as a limitless source of goods and services to meet ever-expanding human needs. Can the RoN movement facilitate a more relational complex 'we' under a legal system that so pervasively casts nature as mere 'resource'? Environmental law, however radical, continues to work within the binary categories central to Modernist thought, seemingly unable satisfactorily to register nonhumans as selves, apparently incapable of adequately capturing the lively and vibrant more-than-human materiality and/or the agency that nonhumans possess beyond legal modes of representation.[12] Perhaps the best Modernist attempts at broadening the horizon for the legal participation of other-than-human beings in legal systems have granted at most a gesture towards 'subjectivity' (i.e. 'territory as victim' or nature as 'witness').[13] Such attempts have not, however, gone so far as to truly reckon with the forms of agency aspired to in the RoN framing. Environmental law, in seeking to find the exits from the ontologically Modern room, as anthropologist Philippe Descola has noted, finds them blocked.[14]

The ontological discontinuity constructed between humans and nonhumans and the forms of juridical and other relations that follow from this binary continue to lie at the root of the socio-ecological devastation of the planet. The task ahead is that of seriously attending to and cultivating the necessary 'nation to more-than-human nation' relationships[15] while re-embedding social institutions and systems within the broader community of life and its ways. When it comes to law, the task of probing new epistemological and 'ontological openings'[16] for legal thought and practice in these times of planetary crisis is urgent. A legal ontological turning[17] is required, wherein the fundamental categories, concepts and conceptions on which Western law is based are interrogated and reimagined/replaced.[18] It is vital to question the very grounds upon which legal orders are based, interrogating, in a metaphysical register, their basic conceptual foundations, from bounded individuals to earth systems articulated by positivist science, and more besides.

Any legal system, as Anishinaabe legal scholar Aaron Mills has explored, is embedded in, and is an expression of, a lifeway.[19] It is clear that the contemporary

---

12. E Kohn, *How Forests Think: Toward an Anthropology Beyond the Human* (University of California Press, Berkeley 2013).
13. D Ruiz-Serna, 'El territorio como víctima. Ontología política y las leyes de víctimas para comunidades indígenas y negras en Colombia' (2017) 53(2) Revista Colombiana de Antropologia 85–113.
14. P Descola, *Beyond Nature and Culture* (University of Chicago Press, Chicago 2013) 192–200.
15. E Boulot and J Sterlin, 'Steps Towards a Legal Ontological Turn: Proposals for Law's Place Beyond the Human' (2021) Transnational Environmental Law 1–26, doi: 10.1017/S2047102521000145.
16. M de la Cadena, 'Runa: Human but Not Only' (2014) 4(2) HAU: Journal of Ethnographic Theory 253.
17. S Vermeylen, 'Materiality and the Ontological Turn in the Anthropocene: Establishing a Dialogue Between Law, Anthropology and Eco-philosophy' in L Kotzé (ed), *Environmental Law and Governance for the Anthropocene* (Hart Publishing, Oxford 2017); Boulot and Sterlin (n 15).
18. W Grant, H Greene and T Zelle (eds), *Earth Law: Emerging Ecocentric Law – a Guide for Practitioners* (Wolters Kluwer Legal & Regulatory, New York 2021).
19. A Mills, 'Miinigowiziwin: All That Has Been Given for Living Well Together: One Vision of Anishinaabe Constitutionalism' (2019) PhD Thesis, University of Victoria.

mainstream, growth-oriented and deracinated neoliberal lifeway is untenable and that contemporary legal systems are but expressions of such worldview commitments. The now-questions are: what directions and what sources might be drawn upon in order to transform such legal orders and that which underwrites them? How might the gap between imagination, methodology and adjudication be mapped in a 'new' dimension of law that can be called 'ontological'? How can the legal 'activation of relationality' (that is, the activation of relational thinking in concrete scenarios of legal adjudication, teaching and learning) *be itself activated*?[20]

It is in response to such now-questions that this Special Edition of the *Journal of Human Rights and the Environment* has brought together scholars under the mantle of the ongoing creation and articulation of posthuman legalities.

Further questions emerge. By attending to the agential properties of matter as examined by New Materialism might it be possible to grasp the always-already entangled nature of more-than-human relations so that it might register in the space, and in the structures, called 'the law'? How can the unexpected and lively properties of seemingly inert matter come to animate praxes of doing 'law-otherwise'?[21] Might it be possible to discern legalities that are participated in and expressed in non-symbolic terms – such as 'eco-feedback'? By looking towards critical thinking that not only 'decentres the human',[22] but deconstructs its very meaning, might it be possible to speak both beyond, and in excess of, the human so as to hold open a vital space for multi-being entanglement in the legal field more generally?

The invitation embodied in a 'law beyond the human' more broadly seeks a multiplicity of approaches, including those influenced by biosemiotics, artistic practices, posthuman/New Materialist thinking and, crucially, 'Indigenous legalities'.[23] Might rethinking multispecies entanglements from the perspective of an animate 'political ontology'[24] aid in reworking the precautionary principle, the notion of a more-than-human transitional justice, or RoN?

This Special Issue, recruited via an open, international call, reflects an invigorating variety of perspectives and experiments at the interface between the more-than-human world and ecocentric legal approaches. Drawing broadly on the insights of posthuman scholarship, the authors in this edition integrate leading insights and critical thought from the legal and social sciences and environmental humanities in order to interrogate environmental law as it currently stands – and to ground alternative legalities. The authors set out avenues for law's future, and potential possibilities for the future of earthly life. Despite differing foundations for their arguments, some of which might be incommensurable with each other, the articles offer a multiplicity of reflections beyond the horizon of present legal imaginaries.

---

20. A Escobar, *Designs for the Pluriverse* (Duke University Press, Durham 2018).
21. This concept builds on Eduardo Restro and Arturo Escobar, 'Other Anthropologies and Anthropology Otherwise: Steps to a World Anthropologies Framework' (2005) 25(2) Critique of Anthropology 99.
22. A Grear, 'Deconstructing Anthropos: A Critical Legal Reflection on "Anthropocentric" Law and Anthropocene "Humanity"' (2015) 26(3) Law and Critique 225.
23. K Anker, P Burdon, G Garver, M Maloney and C Sbert (eds), *From Environmental to Ecological Law* (Routledge, London and New York 2021); Mills (n 19).
24. M Blaser, 'Political Ontology: Cultural Studies Without "Cultures"?' (2009) 5–6 Cultural Studies 873.

Authors in this issue examine the ways in which myriad nonhumans – from rivers, forests and the multiple forms of life teeming in oceans, to the soil that is the material substrate for all Earthly life – can be made legally present. The question of how such forms of liveliness might 'speak' for themselves, rather than being represented by a form of human ventriloquism,[25] while their personhood remains a mere juridical fiction, remains an area of unfinished collective work to which this Special Issue hopes to contribute. Whether in urban, rural or 'wild' settings, how might legal registers shift towards goals imagined not *within* (constrained by) but *after* – analytically and temporally – the so-called Anthropocene[26] and its many epithets and alternative formulations: for example, the Capitalocene,[27] Plantationocene,[28] Civilicene?[29]

If the all-encompassing concepts of 'nature' and 'environment' do not exist outside of the ontologies of Modernity, what happens to *environmental* law and the Rights of *Nature*? Perhaps the answer lies in the kinds of complex, lively relations that Anishinaabe legal scholar Aron Mills[30] has noted – the kind of 'rooted law' of which the normative relations of Indigenous peoples have been the most notable and enduring examples – a 'rooted law' open to all/every 'thing'.

This Special Issue, we hope, takes up in multiple ways the possibility of a law that finds itself 'rooted' in soils, oceans and forests, and issues an invitation to reflect on rights, responsibilities, agreements and other legal concepts and practices in an entirely different way in the light of the fundamental question: what is law *beyond* the 'human' and *after* 'nature'?

The contributions of the authors of this Special Issue broadly fall into three themes, running from the legal-theoretical, to the practical-juridical, on to the affective-restorative. These are as follows:

1. Posthuman/New Materialist legal theory;
2. More-than-human international law; and
3. Environmental response-ability: justice, art and relationalities.

POSTHUMAN/NEW MATERIALIST LEGAL THEORY

In the first article in this edition, Margaret Davies explores the connections between social and environmental justice and the implications of a posthuman, eco-social materiality for the legal concept of private property. Davies begins by setting out a relational move away from a Western, extractive and colonial perspective of human society and its relationship to land towards a co-becoming eco-society, inter-reliant on integrated eco-social networks, communities and habitat(s). Using the concepts of fragmentation and rift, Davies explores the material disintegration

---

25. Vermeylen (n 17).
26. P Crutzen and E Stoermer, 'The Anthropocene' (2000) 41 IGBP Glob. Chang. Newsl: 17–18.
27. J Moore, *Capitalism in the Web of Life* (Verso, London 2015).
28. D Haraway, SF Noboru Ishikawa, KO Gilbert, AL Tsing and N Bubandt 'Anthropologists Are Talking – About the Anthropocene' (2016) 81(3) Ethnos 535.
29. J Sterlin, 'The Civilicene and its Alternatives: Anthropology and its Long Due Durée' in CJ Orr, K Kish and B Jennings (eds), *Liberty and the Ecological Crisis: Freedom on a Finite Planet* (Routledge, New York 2020).
30. A Mills, 'The Lifeworlds of Law: On Revitalizing Indigenous Legal Orders Today' (2016) 61(4) McGill Law Journal/Revue de droit de McGill 847.

of biological, physical and cultural entanglement – a process that has resulted in ongoing environmental injustice, ecological degradation, appropriation and disconnection from the very conditions of existence. Davies then turns her attention to private property, which she argues 'enshrines both the rift between human and nonhuman and the fragmentation that characterizes eco-society', a system that requires radical rethinking towards a more relational, responsible and integrated understanding. Using the concept of habitat, Davies argues that a relational form of property with obligations owed to human and nonhuman life will ensure a system more equal and inclusive for owner and non-owner alike.

The second article in this edition considers the legal representation of the nonhuman. Using the guardianship model as developed by Christopher Stone and the concept of eco-feedback, Matt Harvey and Steve Vanderheiden investigate communication between human and nonhuman. Drawing upon both law beyond the human legalities and New Materialist theory on nonhuman subjectivity, Harvey and Vanderheiden explore the 'Lorax problem' – that is, the problem of whether a legal guardian can ever truly communicate the needs and interests of their nonhuman charge. Drawing upon New Materialist scholarship, the authors conceptualize a vibrant materiality in order to illustrate the potential for nonhuman forms of agency, challenging the guardianship model's restriction of subjectivity to the human realm, and extending agency from the atomistic human individual to what the authors call 'swarms' or conglomerates of human and nonhuman actants. This signalling of vital materiality, they argue, is a form of communication that challenges the exclusionary human/nature, subject/object binary found in law.

MORE-THAN-HUMAN INTERNATIONAL LAW

Nick J Fox and Pam Alldred open their contribution, and the contributions on the theme of a more-than-human international law, by offering a theorization and development of 'a posthumanist and new materialist approach to sustainable development policy'. To this end, their contribution to the Special Issue charts a pathway between humanism and anti-humanism to establish a posthumanism of the environment and an understanding of 'posthumans' that challenges both environmental anthropocentrism and the model of the human as white, male and from the global North. Thus, while 'posthumans' are 'a fully integral element within the environment', they should no longer be considered to be an amorphous category as is sometimes implied by concepts such as the 'human species'. To be sure, '"posthumans" gain a diverse range of context-specific capacities as they interact with other matter' and some of these capacities – for example, empathy, altruism, conceptual thinking and modelling futures – are very unusual. Yet, these 'unusual capacities' might be key 'to addressing the current crises of environmental degradation and anthropogenic climate change'.

In the fourth contribution, Emily Jones continues the focus upon international law and suggests that both posthuman theory and the RoN movement have the potential to challenge the anthropocentrism of international environmental law. Scholars, she argues, have begun to document transformative shifts that could occur through the application of posthuman legal theory to international environmental law, but these theories have yet to be applied to law in practice. While RoN have been applied in domestic law, they have been applied comparatively little in international law, while the question of what RoN includes and excludes remains contested. Jones brings posthuman theory and RoN together, reflecting on how posthuman legal theory might contribute to the framing of RoN, with a focus on challenging the anthropocentrism of international environmental law. She argues that the next step for posthuman legal theory will be its application to existing law and, noting convergences between posthuman legal theory and the RoN, contends that those seeking to apply posthuman legal theory might find alliances by turning to RoN. Meanwhile, using posthuman theory to frame RoN could help to ensure that RoN live up to their transformative potential.

Marie-Catherine Petersmann embraces the disorienting and destabilizing rupture of the Anthropocene/s with respect to international environmental law and the Modernist onto-epistemology upon which it is 'grounded'. She sees in this moment a generative opportunity to rethink the animating forces and motivations of environmental jurisprudence. Living amidst Modernist ruins, both physically and metaphysically, provides Western-descended legal orders with the prospect of reformulating fundamental assumptions. Drawing on a variety of New Materialist, relational and posthuman literatures – and informed by critiques of them by decolonial, Indigenous and black scholars – Petersmann seeks to bring environmental law into line with these literatures and their emphasis on the necessity, and inescapability, of more-than-human relations. Rather than deploying responsibility and protection as focal organizing concepts (which presuppose a separation between human beings, their Liberal States, and the nonhumans they command and control), Petersmann advocates for response-ability and care. This is not, however, care *for* but rather care *with*, which acknowledges human always-already entanglement and earth-boundedness, and seeks an open-ended moral exploration from a position of humility and vulnerability. Being *involved*, rather than in charge, being relationally embedded in the materiality of the world, requires an orientation that is in excess of the rigidity of environmental law as it is currently practised, she argues.

MULTI-SPECIES JUSTICE, ART AND RELATIONALITIES

Danielle Celermajer and Anne O'Brien seek, in their article, to extend the conceptual framing of transitional justice beyond the bounds of the human. By applying transitional justice (which focuses entirely on how wrongs committed between human beings can be repaired) to the alterity of soil as a moral agent, the authors pursue the possibilities that such a shift affords to alter the underlying assumptions of transitional justice itself. By shifting away from reflexivity and subjectivity as assumed preconditions for transitional justice, and aways from its concomitant emphasis upon victim and perpetrator, Celermajer and O'Brien focus upon the relation itself as the fundamental ontological unit. This focus opens space for a non-hierarchical transformation in practices and embodied relationships, and facilitates a reassessment of the systemic wrongs between human and more-than-human. This ambitious task of re-encountering the 'limit case' that is soil – something of which Western society seems to have an overwhelmingly utilitarian and instrumental vision – as morally considerable thus requires new forms of attentiveness, and the humility to acknowledge epistemic limits. The authors conclude their article by exploring the ways in which artistic work has already begun to rework these conceptions and relations, hoping to see how these kinds of practices might aide in generating the forms of publics necessary for the more-than-human social order to be repaired.

Teresa Dillon uses art practices as a generative site of focus in order to explore the enactment of multispecies relations within the context of urban environments. She examines multiple artistic installations and works which seek to bring into presence nonhuman animal cultures, histories, rituals and justice so as to create living frameworks for living otherwise. Affective confrontation with these other-than-human lives destabilize the categorizations of 'animal' and 'nature' upon which present anthropocentric lawscapes are built. To foster multispecies justice, Dillon argues, constant, public, educational and social rehearsals can be called upon in decentring the human and destabilizing the particular form of liberal individualism that law presently promulgates. In so doing, these rehearsals might forge ontological openings that create more equitable conditions for all. For an increasingly city-bound species, beset by climate emergencies and biodiversity loss, a more expansive vision of the urban commons is required if we are to have urban futures at all.

CLOSING REFLECTIONS: ALTERITY, POWER AND THE CHALLENGES OF RELATIONALITY

As the authors of this Special Issue have eloquently communicated, conventional models of environmental law and governance in the West particularly, but exported throughout the world through colonization and globalization, continue to insist on the separation of law, society and Earth systems. This ontology of separation affords a limited capacity to respond to the pressing social-ecological challenges of the age: climate change, biodiversity loss and the profusion of differing forms of social-ecological injustice. As these challenges so starkly illustrate, the nonhuman can no longer be considered to be a mute object of conventional normative description, of appropriation, or of protection in need of human ventriloquism.

Foregrounding the need to pay attention to forms of life beyond the human in legal thought and practice, the contributors to this Special Issue have offered a sophisticated range of posthuman approaches and conceptual devices, including: the need to re-centre response and care in international environmental law (Petersmann); thinking-with soils as moral agents in the context of transitional justice (Celermajer and O'Brien); learning what it means to enact multispecies relations in urban space and earth-bound legalities (Dillon); probing posthuman theory and the RoN movement to challenge the anthropocentrism of international environmental law (Jones); learning how 'posthumans' as agents gain a diverse range of context-specific capacities to face different environmental global challenges (Fox and Alldred); asking what it means to speak for the trees (Harvey and Vanderheiden) and reconsidering property as relational habitat (Davies).

As these authors have identified, much of this work has its antecedents in Indigenous legalities, cosmologies and intellectual labour. And while it may be possible, and aspirational, to consider Indigenous legalities as a site of generative friction, of competing cosmologies, such reflection raises not only questions of alterity but also significant questions of researcher positionality, agency and power.

Mills writes that there is a fundamental incommensurability between legal orders based upon differing forms of constitutionalism, which themselves are rooted in differing lifeways or outgrowths of differing ontological arrangements.[31] Contemporary

---

31. Mills (n 19).

power remains heavily weighted towards liberal idealism and marketization, and gives force to Mill's fears of constitutional capture. There is a genuine question concerning the extent to which theorization and scholarship can contribute to the broader decolonial undertaking without simply continuing a form of colonialism by appropriating and/or pilfering from Indigenous legal orders. How might scholars and researchers seeking a new paradigm, a more life-affirming onto-vision, avoid such trespassing? Here, appropriative risks attach to questions of translation and capture. Much work has been put into trying to honour Indigenous 'law as law' and there is much to laud here.[32] This same orientation is visible in legal anthropology and the old cultural relativist injunction to see the cultural elaborations of all human beings as being on the same level and as equivalent in categorization. However, (neo-)Structuralist questions aside, this approach still results in the effacement of, as Bateson put it, 'differences that make a difference'.[33] Indeed, there remains a sense in which the incommensurability between legal orders observed by Mill problematizes the very basis of traditional legal anthropology: is it even possible to compare law across ontologies, or is equivocation uncontrollable?[34] And with what implications for power relations? These questions will not be answered here, but they remain ever relevant, central to an ongoing posthuman research agenda, and they must be addressed in order to achieve the transformative potential of the agenda itself. Relationality is not without its challenges.

The authors in this special edition largely agree that law requires a paradigm shift towards relational thinking. But we ask, as anthropologist Arturo Escobar does as he works with Afro-descendant and Indigenous collectives in the Colombian Pacific region, how might it be possible to 'activate relationality' in legal theory and practice?[35] Again, questions abound. Is speaking on behalf of nonhumans an insurmountable limit to a posthuman legal agenda? What kind of theoretical and methodological tools does a law beyond the human offer in concrete scenarios of education, decision-making and adjudication? Can Davies' concept of property as habitat be operationalized in current legal systems? How? Will eco-feedback as set out by Harvey and Vanderheiden be sufficient to engage and represent eco-communities in law? Beyond the RoN approach, how does a law that is entangled with local territorial practices challenge anthropocentric and colonial concepts of justice, agency and value? These fundamental questions of relationality and its activation remain potential limitations of a posthuman legal agenda.

Here, as editors, we identify four particular challenges for a posthuman law, law beyond the human, that for us are signalled by the contributions to this edition.

First, (i) *an over-reliance on human representation* as the only way to engage with the legal: law is conventionally defined as a system of normative statements, that is, as language, or a form of symbolic representation. However, law, as our authors have made clear, can also be defined as a non-symbolic system comprising material dynamics, ecological relations, lived experience, artefacts and dreams,

---

32. H Friedland and V Napoleon, 'Gathering the Threads: Developing a Methodology for Researching and Rebuilding Indigenous Legal Traditions' (2015) 1(1) Lakehead Law Journal 43.
33. G Bateson, *Steps to an Ecology of Mind* (University of Chicago, Chicago 2000) 459.
34. In the vein of E Viveiros de Castro, 'Perspectival Anthropology and the Method of Controlled Equivocation' (2004) 2(1) Tipití: Journal of the Society for the Anthropology of Lowland South America 3–22.
35. Escobar (n 20).

among other sources. Harvey and Vanderheiden pursue this line of approach in their article when they frame eco-feedback as a necessary basis for reformulating environmental law. Building on their work, and extrapolating from it in combination with a broader range of approaches, it is possible to imagine re-grounding law in a bold ontological and methodological assumption that humans are not the only thinking selves in the world.[36] More broadly, this means that 'life thinks', or that 'life is semiotic'[37] – that soils, oceans, beetles, plants, fungi, fish and mammals are not only sentient but meaning-making selves.

Second, expanding the notion of representation (and even more so, materio-semiotic agency) to more-than-human beings and collectives has profound (ii) *methodological implications* for legal thinking and justice in Western legal systems. More-than-human beings, given onto-epistemic significance in law, open out alternative ways of perceiving law – new expressions of law as entanglement, law as materiality. This kind of law seems to exceed propositional form (language) and thus to require non-propositional methodologies, as gestured towards by Celermajer and O'Brien's article in this collection. Such a broad, attentive definition of law would be untenable unless 'we', *humans*, become perceptually open to modes of socio-legal agency that exceeds *us*. Law would thus become a mode of, for example, making decisions or adjudicating justice for which 'human' perspectives and textual methodologies are understood to be but one among *many* ways of meaning-making in a larger cosmological meshwork of life forces and ways of doing and acting in the world.

The challenge of 'hearing', however, remains. How can humans 'listen' to the 'law of a territory' or the 'laws of habitats' where human and more-than-human lifeways are deeply entangled?[38] Reckoning with the limits of human representation brings us to the third challenge for a law beyond the human: the possibility of (iii) *formally incorporating – with some degree of analytical precision – non-representational methodologies* into legal decision-making: How can law listen to non-propositional kinds of law that exceed – and yet inform – legal language in specific contexts and at different scales (local and global)? Translating across worlds – of the forest or ocean, for example – into a legal world of symbolic language will require sensing, minimally, into worlds of non-symbolic language (ie, image, corporality, ritual, dreams), and might require multiple and different techniques. As Petersmann has argued in this collection, the only way for a law worthy of the environment to proceed is for such law to emerge from *within* human always-already entangled relationalities – legal, bodily, affective, and otherwise – in the more-than-human world. Does a 'law beyond the human' need a methodology beyond the law?

Dillon's work in this edition gestures towards at least one answer: by exploring what it might mean to enact multispecies relations in urban spaces through contemporary art practices. These, as she shows, can create living frameworks for encountering nonhuman animal cultures, histories, rituals and justice, with which she interrogates conventional legal methodologies from the vantage point of these artistic practices. She eloquently summarizes the promise of such methodologies: 'This

---

36. Kohn (n 12).
37. ibid 9.
38. I Vargas Roncancio, 'Conjuring Sentient Beings and Relations in the Law: Rights of Nature and a Comparative Praxis of Legal Cosmologies' in K Anker, P Burdon, G Garver, M Maloney and C Sbert (eds), *From Environmental to Ecological Law* (Routledge, London and New York 2021).

is the power that art holds. It provides possibilities for conjuring up worlds, which even if they fail, still "work" as imagery scaffolds through which we can collectively grip onto the ontological changes that are at stake'.

This brings us to the fourth challenge: (iv) the challenge of *imagining a law beyond the human while necessarily engaging with the very categories* of thought and language that at present continue to sustain conventional legal thinking and action: languages of nature, rights, property, etc. Contributors to this edition 'de-centre the human' and aim to 're-centre the posthuman' in law by proposing ways in which legal fields such as international environmental law and property law can be pushed beyond conventional modern frameworks into networks of relationship and care, as Jones and Davies both suggest. However, a question remains concerning the degree to which a radical posthuman/New Materialist agenda can be truly transformative while law still deploys its current categories and scholarship is necessarily forced to engage with its dominant constructs.

A LAW BEYOND 'THE ENVIRONMENT'?

While we have signalled some of the existing difficulties of cross-ontological comparison and engagement, it is nevertheless our hope that this collection gestures towards a potential transformation of law. Such transformation, it seems, is nascent in multiple ways, and would imply a shift away from individual rights towards relational being and responsibility; from an extractive and appropriative legal system towards an integrated eco-social legality embracing norms of non-oppressive restorative responsibility. Breaking open the binary division between nature and culture transforms the onto-epistemic underpinnings of law, diversifying its participants, re-imagining its subjects, transforming its modes of emergence, relationality, operations and performance while inviting 'other kinds' of legal thinking and practice. A law beyond the human is also a law beyond symbolic representation alone – an acknowledgement that already exists to some degree in legal anthropology and Indigenous legal theories. While attention to the other-than-symbolic forms of legal reckoning and nonhuman non-symbolic communications populate these fields, such modes of meaning-making are ignored by mainstream legal theory and liberal legality. These remain fixated with the analysis of (exclusively inter-human) social relations and are overwhelmingly sociocentric.

This Special Issue has been an invitation to readers to appreciate *other kinds of law* that emerge from non-modern ontologies, from Indigenous cosmologies, from nonhuman voices 'in their own right' and from posthuman and New Materialist theoretical perspectives, as applied through legal theoretical analysis and – here too – reflections on artistic practice. Law can *also* be – as our authors have shown – an outgrowth, a co-emergence, of 'something else'. Law expresses relationalities, between kinds of beings, assemblages and 'things' (as Bennett would put it[39]) with their own ingenious communicative modes and abilities (as many of the authors collected here point towards). If it is indeed the case that other-than-human beings are as agential as the RoN aspirationally describes, as posthuman theory and New Materialism insists, and as animist Indigenous peoples attest to the world over, then the notions of *nature* and

---

39. J Bennett, *Vibrant Matter: A Political Ecology of Things* (Duke University Press, Baltimore 2010).

therefore of *environment* must be reassessed and perhaps even abandoned entirely unless they can be reformulated in ways that do not preclude the very possibility of agency in the other-than-human world. In a sense, then, in this edition, as editors, we seek to encounter law anew and otherwise, both *beyond* the human, and *after* 'the environment', offering the potential for a re-grounding of law that *exceeds* (Modernist) 'nature'.

Emille Boulot
Leadership for the Ecozoic Doctoral Fellow, McGill University, Canada
Anna Grear
Professor of Law and Theory, Cardiff University, UK
Joshua Sterlin
Leadership for the Ecozoic Doctoral Fellow, McGill University, Canada
Iván Darío Vargas-Roncancio
Leadership for the Ecozoic, Postdoctoral Researcher, McGill University, Canada

Re-forming property to address eco-social fragmentation and rift

Margaret Davies*
Matthew Flinders Distinguished Professor, Flinders University

Two concepts that bridge the nature-human divide may help to diagnose and address some of the present and future problems of eco-social change in a legal context. 'Fragmentation' refers to loss and degradation of the habitat of nonhuman life. It is also a useful concept for understanding the fracturing of the material conditions for human life in a modern globalised world. The notion of 'metabolic rift', derived from Marx by John Bellamy Foster, refers to a break in the human-nonhuman circulation of natural materials, brought on by industrial agriculture and urbanisation. These related ideas provide a frame for exploring the connections between social and environmental justice and the role played by legal forms such as private property. In keeping with the imperative to re-form legal concepts to account for eco-social existence, the article presents a view of property as human and nonhuman habitat. This approach aims to use law to help recreate the conditions for the constructive inter-dependence of social and environmental goods.

Keywords: *property, metabolic rift, fragmentation, habitat, environmental justice*

1 INTRODUCTION

Across all scholarly disciplines and all fields of human activity commentators and activists are now finding ways to reintegrate what have often, in the scholarly traditions of the modernist and postmodernist West, been understood as separate natural and human spaces. The trend towards – and indeed necessity of – starting with the embeddedness of the human species in an extended physical reality is equally beginning to drive legal scholarship. Western ideas of law throughout the modern era have been structured by the mythologies of human separateness from nature and by

---

* Orcid.org/0000-0003-1546-7204. This research has been funded by the Australian Research Council DP190101373 'Property as Habitat'. Many of the ideas developed in this paper are the product of collaborative thinking and I am indebted to my co-investigators on the project, Lee Godden and Nicole Graham, for their individual and joint input. See eg, Nicole Graham 'Dephysicalized Property and Shadow Lands' in Robyn Bartel and Jennifer Carter (eds), *Handbook on Space, Place, and Law* (Edward Elgar, Cheltenham UK 2021); Lee Godden 'Legal Geography – Place, Time, Law and Method: The Spatial and Archival in Connection to Country' in Tayanah O'Donnell, Daniel Robinson, and Josephine Gillespie (eds), *Legal Geography: Perspectives and Methods* (Routledge, Abingdon 2020). Earlier forms of this paper were delivered as the Annual Lecture in Law and Social Justice, Leeds University October 2019 and a plenary lecture at the Law and Society of Australia and New Zealand, December 2019, Southern Cross University. I would like to thank the audiences on these occasions for their helpful questions and comments. Finally I'd like to thank the anonymous referees and the Editor-in-Chief Anna Grear for their many comments and, in particular, for helpful suggestions about strengthening the argument.

universalism – mythologies relying on abstraction from everyday materiality. These mythologies stand in sharp contrast to the older place-emergent legal narratives of Indigenous peoples, which are now providing inspiration and some guidance for mainstream legal scholarship. One symptom of the turn towards ecological materiality is the emergence of new terms that bridge the traditional divisions typical of Western thought: these terms include natureculture, socionature, bioculture, eco-society, bio-legality, and eco-legality.

The project of bending law towards a less abstract and more materially integrated understanding of the world is neither simple nor short-term. What is needed is a collective and widespread regeneration of legal concepts. The critical legal project of the twenty-first century and beyond will involve both deployment of the techniques and insights of past critique as well as an ontological rebuilding towards what might for the moment be characterized as posthuman law or as eco-legality.[1] This project has commenced and I believe it will continue to strengthen over the coming decades in response to a new consciousness of planetary and ecological imperatives.[2] It is an extensive undertaking involving nothing less than the complete reconceptualization of fundamental legal concepts for an eco-social future.

In this article, I consider the relationship between eco-social materiality and the idea of property as it has been developed and practised in the capitalist world. In Western economies, property is (as was once said of liberalism[3]) the 'air we breathe' and it is therefore especially important to understand its role in the ecological destruction we are currently witnessing. Re-forming property as an idea, a practice, and an institution in a way that is materially responsive and (for land) situated in space[4] is one of the most significant adjustments required for a more resilient and sustainable social-ecological future. This is no simple task, as the thought and practice of property engages an entire ontological landscape for which subjects are separate from objects and human individuals control 'external' things.[5] In Australia, where I live and work, this colonial and Eurocentric ontology is in constant conflict with the

---

1. These terms are placeholders, signifying a transition away from twentieth-century abstract and separate notions of law, but not yet entirely matched to whatever is to come.
2. See, for instance, Anna Grear, 'The Vulnerable Living Order: Human Rights and the Environment in a Critical and Philosophical Perspective' (2011) 2(1) Journal of Human Rights and the Environment 23–44; Anna Grear, 'Deconstructing Anthropos: A Critical Legal Reflection on "Anthropocentric" Law and Anthropocene "Humanity"' (2015) 26 Law and Critique 225–229; Andreas Philippopoulos-Mihalopoulos, '"…the Sound of a Breaking String": Critical Environmental Law and Ontological Vulnerability' (2011) 2(1) Journal of Human Rights and the Environment 5–22; Astridis Niemanis, 'Alongside the Right to Water, a Posthumanist Feminist Imaginary' (2014) 5 Journal of Human Rights and the Environment 5–24; Daniel Matthews, 'Law and Aesthetics in the Anthropocene: From the Rights of Nature to the Aesthesis of Obligations' (2019) Law, Culture, and the Humanities (online), DOI: 10.1177/1743872119871830.
3. Anthony Arblaster, *The Rise and Decline of Western Liberalism* (Basil Blackwell, Oxford 1984) 6.
4. Nicole Graham, *Lawscape: Property, Environment, Law* (Routledge, Abingdon 2011).
5. Bradley Bryan, 'Property as Ontology: On Aboriginal and English Understandings of Ownership' (2000) 13 Canadian Journal of Law and Jurisprudence 3–31; on the issue of plural ontologies see Maria Lugones, 'Playfulness, "World-Traveling", and Loving Perception' (1987) 2 Hypatia 3–19; Annemarie Mol, 'Ontological Politics: A Word and Some Questions' (1999) 47 (supplement to issue 1) Sociological Review 74–89; Marisol de la Cadena and Mario Blaser (eds), *A World of Many Worlds* (Duke University Press, Durham 2018).

much older ontologies of Aboriginal peoples. Similar conflicts are repeated throughout the colonized world, taking many localized forms. Two related imperatives for the legal theory of Australia, of the Anglosphere, and more generally of the capitalist West, are first to develop an openness to alternative ontologies and second to specifically cultivate the theoretical resources of European thought and its derivatives so that material interconnection is understood to be fundamental to existence rather than a secondary process performed by entities that are naturally distinct. This article is directed at the furtherance of the second of these imperatives. It consolidates and to some extent reframes extensive analysis already conducted in the scholarly literature and argues for a conception of property that recognizes the co-emergence of subject and object in complex and ecologically open locations.

Before turning to consider property, however, some groundwork is needed. The first part of the article briefly outlines transitions in politics and consciousness concerning the relationship between human society and the ecological sphere: in essence this shift consists of a move from a view of society as human to an integrated eco-social consciousness. In the second and third parts of the article I use two images – fragmentation and rift – as explanatory devices for the multiple axes of material disintegration that have led the capitalist West to this historical moment. As I will explain, 'fragmentation' and 'rift' are composite terms: they are concepts that describe ongoing material-historical ruptures in ecological processes. To be fragmented and riven from environmental conditions are also onto-epistemological modes of being human that are produced by Euro-colonial cultures. The language of fragmentation and rift is intended, therefore, to capture processes across intersecting biological, physical, and cultural planes, and therefore to communicate the need to imagine remedies and reforms that are practical co-becomings of the human and nonhuman.[6] In the final two parts, I turn to property and habitat. As presently imagined and practised, the institution of private property is strongly implicated in – we might even say responsible for – ecocide, meaning that property's justification needs to be questioned and its form radically changed.[7] We need to reimagine it as a relational form that that could improve rather than destroy the biosocial conditions for life.

1.1 From society to eco-society

In much mainstream and politically neoliberal commentary, environmental protection continues to be seen as an impediment to economic development and improvement,

---

6. See generally, eg, Donna Haraway, *The Companion Species Manifesto: Dogs, People, and Significant Otherness* (Prickly Paradigm Press, Chicago 2003); Bawaka Country et al., 'Caring as Country: Towards an Ontology of Co-Becoming in Natural Resource Management' (2013) 54(2) Asia-Pacific Viewpoint 185–97; Vito de Lucia, 'Re-embodying Law: Transversal Ecology and the Commons' in Ruth Thomas-Pellicer, Vito De Lucia and Sian Sullivan (eds), *Contributions to Law, Philosophy and Ecology: Exploring Re-Embodiments* (Routledge, Abingdon 2016).

7. On the justifications for property see Margaret Davies, 'Can Property be Justified in an Entangled World?' (2020) 17(7) Globalizations 1104–17; on change to the form of private property see, among many others, Nin Tomas, 'Maori Concepts of Rangatiratanga, Kaitiakitanga, the Environment and Property Rights' in David Grinlinton and Prue Taylor (eds), *Property Rights and Sustainability: The Evolution of Property Rights to Meet Ecological Challenges* (Martinus Nijhoff, Leiden 2011); William Lucy and Catherine Mitchell, 'Replacing Private Property: The Case for Stewardship' (1996) 55 Cambridge Law Journal 566–600.

and therefore as an impediment to social well-being. Through this lens, environmental harms are framed as being necessary for the social good, which in turn is seen to rely on employment and economic growth.[8] The extractive narrative that dominated the twentieth century erases or downplays the long-lasting harms of environmental damage that accrue to both human and nonhuman communities. By contrast, in the twenty-first century, environment-related harms are now more widely understood as harming particular human communities, humanity at large (albeit unevenly), and planetary ecosystems.

The distributional impacts of harm to nature can be and are increasingly understood to be both intra-human and ecological.[9] It is widely accepted that, within human society, it is marginalized and vulnerable communities that suffer first and most severely from environmental injustices.[10] There are many shocking examples of industry externalizing its costs to the detriment both of ecosystems and marginalized human communities.[11] Moreover, much environmental injustice is not accidental but rather deliberate: highly polluting industries are co-located with poor communities, who might also be forced to follow such industries for work; national and global 'sacrifice zones' are created so that environmental harms such as open-cut mines and waste dumps are concentrated in specific locations;[12] relatively wealthy industrialized countries export waste to less developed parts of the world.[13] There also exist other seemingly endless, multiply situated,[14] eco-social harms that are not necessarily directly intended but are rather the result of policy failures.

---

8. Critiques of neoliberal fundamentalism are now widespread: see, for instance, Jonathan D Ostry, Prakash Lougani, and Davide Furceri, 'Neoliberalism: Oversold?' (2016) 53(2) Finance and Development: A Quarterly Magazine of the IMF 38–41; Chystia Freeland, *Plutocrats: The Rise of the New Global Super-rich and the Fall of Everyone Else* (Penguin Books, London and New York 2013).

9. Christie Parris et al., 'Justice for All? Factors Affecting Perceptions of Environmental and Ecological Injustice' (2014) 27 Social Justice Research 67–98.

10. As I write, historically unprecedented bushfires are destroying large areas of the Australian landscape. The intensity and extent of the bushfires are much worse because of human-induced climate change. In some senses, it appears that the relatively wealthy communities of Australia are at the forefront of the climate crisis. However, it must be noted that widespread devastation is less visible in poorer areas of the world, that relative wealth brings a level of resilience to crisis, and that indeed such wealth has come from full participation in the environmentally exploitative practices of industrialism and industrial agriculture.

11. Several thousand high-profile examples are documented in the *Environmental Justice Atlas* (ejatlas.org) but this is presumably a small fraction of the environmental injustices worldwide. See also Ryan Holifield, Jayajit Chakraborty, and Gordon Walker (eds), *The Routledge Handbook of Environmental Justice* (Routledge, Abingdon 2018).

12. Julia Fox, 'Mountaintop Removal in West Virginia: An Environmental Sacrifice Zone' (1999) 12(2) Organization and Environment 163–83; Drew Cottle, 'Land, Life, and Labour in the Sacrifice Zone: The Socio-Economic Dynamics of Open-Cut Coal Mining in the Upper Hunter Valley, New South Wales' (2013) 22(3) Rural Society 208–16; Neera Singh, 'Environmental Justice, Degrowth, and Post-capitalist Futures' (2019) 163 Ecological Economics 138–42.

13. Silpa Kaza, Lisa Yao, Perinez Bhada-Tata, and Frank van Woerden, *What a Waste 2.0: A Global Snapshot of Solid Waste Management to 2050* (World Bank Urban Development Series, 2018); Val Plumwood, 'Shadow Places and the Politics of Dwelling' (2008) 44 Australian Humanities Review 139–50.

14. Gordon Walker, 'Beyond Distribution and Proximity: Exploring the Multiple Spatialities of Environmental Injustice' (2009) 41(4) Antipode 614–36.

For instance, poorly mitigated climate change underpins disasters that are more frequent and more intense because of global warming, whether these are bushfires or inundations, storms or droughts, resulting in numerous impacts on health, food, water, infrastructure, and economies.[15] Some environmental harms affect people indiscriminately but it is still clear that the poorest populations are also the most vulnerable to and the least resilient in the face of environmental destruction.[16] The terms 'environmental racism', 'environmental injustice', and 'toxic colonialism' were coined decades ago to describe these global transfers of environmental damage from the wealthy to the poor,[17] transfers that are one form of continuing racial and colonial politics responsible for the devastation both of peoples and ecological systems. That those who are the least responsible for ecosystem collapse and climate change suffer the most means that environmental harms are legible as a form of social injustice aligned with inequities in procedure, distribution, and recognition:[18] environmental harm both intensifies injustices that already exist in the distribution of resources and creates entirely new forms of injustice.

Environmental destruction can therefore be understood as having a direct, but external, relationship to the material conditions of human social life. In the extractive narratives it is regarded as necessary for the advancement of society, while in certain environmental justice narratives it is understood as causing harm to specific human communities. Both the discursive framing of environmental issues through paradigms of, on the one hand, economic growth and, on the other, social justice, discrimination, and inequality can easily separate nature from human society. The environment – the entire nonhuman sphere – is thus seen as something other than humanity: human society shapes and acts upon the environment and has the capacity to continue in its destructive ways or to desist. This framing that perceives effects on human society as qualitatively different from harms to the nonhuman sphere draws upon the default framework of Western and colonial culture, the one which many of us trained in this tradition frequently revert to in trying to understand contemporary problems. Alternative worldviews that do not so sharply divide the human from the nonhuman remain common, however, outside the traditions of Western Europe, particularly among

---

15. Camilo Mora et al., 'Broad Threat to Humanity from Cumulative Climate Hazards Intensified by Greenhouse Gas Emissions' (2018) 8 Nature Climate Change 1062–71.

16. In the midst of the Australian bushfire crisis one commentator wrote 'In a matter of weeks Canberra – a city known for its crisp sunny skies and eucalyptus smell – has shown us how every aspect of climate change disproportionately impacts those who have the least social and economic resources. The city has air inequity, where those with high incomes can purchase thousand dollar air purifiers, while those who do not sit in their homes marinating in particulate counts that are known to be beyond hazardous.' Gemma Carey, 'Being Pregnant in a Climate Emergency was an Existential Challenge. Miscarriage has Brought a New Grief', Guardian Australia (10 January 2020).

17. Robert Bullard, *Dumping in Dixie: Race, Class, and Environmental Quality* (Westview Press, Boulder CO 1990); Robert Bullard (ed), *Confronting Environmental Racism Voices from the Grassroots* (South End Press, Cambridge, MA 1993); Paul Mohai and Bunyan Bryant, 'Environmental Injustice: Weighing Race and Class as Factors in the Distribution of Environmental Hazards' (1992) 63 University of Colorado Law Review 921–32; Susan Cutter, 'Race, Class, and Environmental Justice' (1995) 19(1) Progress in Human Geography 111–22; Robert Bullard, *Environment and Morality: Confronting Environmental Racism in the United States* (UN Research Institute for Social Development 2004); Susan Buckingham and Rakibe Kulcur, 'Gendered Geographies of Environmental Justice' (2009) 41(4) Antipode 659–83.

18. Gordon Walker, 'Beyond Distribution and Proximity: Exploring the Multiple Spatialities of Environmental Injustice' (2009) 41(4) Antipode 614–36.

Indigenous peoples[19] whose thoroughly relational ontology perceives the emergence of living entities in their ecological and continuously lived connections.[20] Yet, throughout Western history, there have also been counter-narratives to the view that human society is above nature. The separation of human from nonhuman that has led to a human-centred or anthropocentric default position is now widely challenged in order to account for several critical facts: first, humans are physical beings, not abstract individuals; second, human life has emerged, and continues to emerge, from the biosphere and is entirely entwined with it (indeed the production of life forms occurs as energetic-material flows through a dense multi-scalar network, from atoms to organisms, to groups);[21] and third, like all life, humans are wholly dependent on the physical world and in particular the soil, vegetation and everything that supports it. These observations seem staggeringly obvious – making it necessary to see harms to the biosphere as constituting harm to humanity as a whole, since we are collectively reliant on the biosphere for our existence.

Extending this appreciation of inter-reliance, it is undeniable that social networks are not only networks between people, but also between people and place, people and things, people and ecological processes.[22] The physical world of nature and of artificial objects plays a significant role in *all* social relationships: place, material things, food, animals, microbes, soil fungus, air, fish, water, all co-exist ecologically and form an extended social network. 'Society' must therefore be understood as eco-society.[23] On this basis, the concept of 'society' can be seen to include even the components of the soil – the nematodes, funghi, protozoa, and bacteria, as well as non-living nutrients, and even sand, clay and dirt: after all, the earth is circulated through our own bodies and is essential for our existence. The same is of course true of other elements identified by the ancients – wind, air, or atmosphere; fire or energy;

---

19. See, for instance, Irene Watson *Aboriginal Peoples, Colonialism and International Law* (Routledge, Abingdon, 2015); Ambelin Kwaymullina and Blaze Kwaymullina, 'Learning to Read the Signs: Law in an Indigenous Reality' (2010) 34 Journal of Australian Studies 195; Bradley Bryan, 'Property as Ontology: On Aboriginal and English Understandings of Ownership' (2000) 13 Canadian Journal of Law and Jurisprudence 3–31; Nin Tomas, 'Maori Concepts of Rangatiratanga, Kaitiakitanga, the Environment and Property Rights' in David Grinlinton and Prue Taylor (eds), *Property Rights and Sustainability: The Evolution of Property Rights to Meet Ecological Challenges* (Martinus Nijhoff, Leiden 2011).
20. Arturo Escobar, 'Thinking-Feeling with the Earth: Territorial Struggles and the Ontological Dimension of the Epistemologies of the South' (2016) 11(1) AIBR Revista de Antropologia Iberoamericana 11–32.
21. As explained in exquisite biochemical detail by Samantha Frost in *Biocultural Creatures: Toward a New Theory of the Human* (Duke University Press, Durham 2016); see also Scott Gilbert, Jan Sapp, and Alfred Tauber, 'A Symbiotic View of Life: We Have Never Been Individuals' 2012 Quarterly Review of Biology 87(4) 325–41; Marc de Leeuw and Sonja van Wichelen, *Personhood in the Age of Biolegality: Brave New Law* (Palgrave Macmillan, Cham, Switzerland 2020).
22. Donna Haraway, *The Companion Species Manifesto: Dogs, People, and Significant Otherness* (Prickly Paradigm Press, Chicago 2003); Bruno Latour, *Reassembling the Social: An Introduction to Actor-Network Theory* (Oxford University Press, Oxford 2005); Jane Bennett, *Vibrant Matter: A Political Ecology of Things* (Duke University Press, Durham 2010); Joanna Latimer and Mara Miele, 'Naturecultures? Science, Affect, and the Nonhuman' (2013) 13 Theory, Culture, and Society 5–31.
23. Since law is intrinsically social, we should also say that law is eco-legal, that is, emergent from eco-sociality.

and above all water.[24] This is not to suggest either that this crude division of nature into four categories is exhaustive *or* that life is composed mechanically from elements. It is simply a heuristic for some of the essential conditions of human life. The human is first and foremost a physical and ecologically-connected *being*. Being human is not primarily about 'our' rationality, as so much commentary over the centuries has asserted (though that is not to say that rationality of a sort has nothing to do with being human). Both human cognition and embodied presence are reliant on material-semiotic engagements in an extended network formed by relationships.[25] The term 'posthumanism' has been coined to describe approaches that start from the position that the human is a distributed and interconnected being rather than rational and self-contained.[26]

Western legal theory urgently needs the conceptual resources to encompass the co-emergence of the human and the nonhuman. Legal theorists need such concepts for the purposes both of analysis of the past and present and in order to promote change. We also need them in order to promote an attitude of openness to Indigenous and other non-hegemonic knowledges, an attitude that involves decentring the onto-epistemic commitments of Eurocentric and colonial mainstream law and legal theory. As many have argued, the challenge is to reorient thought in such a way that human society is regarded as being a dimension of an ecological world which has ethical and ontological primacy. It is for this reason that I use the term eco-society to emphasize that 'human society' is part of the biosphere. Environmental injustice is eco-social injustice (or 'socio-ecological injustice'[27]) because it harms the conditions for human existence and it harms the extended socio-ecological networks that are shared by all living beings. Distributional inequities exist across eco-society understood in this sense, and not just in the imagined human sphere.

In order to connect the human to the nonhuman in the material world and in Western philosophical worldviews, it is important first to understand how their constructed onto-epistemic disconnection is manifested across existence and what its symptoms and causes are. In the following two sections of the article I focus on two critical ideas, each of which represents an assemblage of processes associated with European colonial interventionism and the extractive engagements with nature encouraged by Western political and philosophical thought. 'Fragmentation' and 'rift' are composite terms that place historical processes into a common framework with both ecological damage and the conceptual architecture of Western thought. As images or narratives, 'fragmentation' and 'rift' aggregate thoughts and practices that connect philosophy, social existence, and human-induced ecological change. The purpose of deploying these ideas here is primarily analytical and critical. Having sketched

---

24. David Macauley, *Elemental Philosophy: Earth, Air, Fire and Water as Environmental Ideas* (SUNY Press, Albany 2010).
25. Lambros Malafouris, *How Things Shape the Mind* (MIT Press, Cambridge, MA 2013); Lambros Malafouris, 'Metaplasticity and the Primacy of Material Engagement' (2015) 8(4) Time and Mind 351–71.
26. N Katherine Hayles, *How We Became Posthuman: Virtual Bodies in Cybernetics, Literature, and Informatics* (University of Chicago Press, Chicago 1999); Karen Barad, 'Posthumanist Performativity: Toward an Understanding of How Matter Comes to Matter' (2003) 28(3) Signs: Journal of Women in Culture and Society 801–31; Rosi Braidotti, *The Posthuman* (Cambridge, Polity 2013).
27. Donna Houston, 'Crisis is Where We Live: Environmental Justice for the Anthropocene' (2013) 10 Globalizations 439–50; Louis Kotzé, 'The Anthropocene, Earth System Vulnerability and Socio-Ecological Injustice in an Age of Human Rights' (2019) 10 Journal of Human Rights and the Environment 62–85.

these ideas, I turn to the concept and practice of private property, which in its present form provides not only *a*, but arguably *the* archetypal legal technique of fragmentation and rift. The critique and analysis of property facilitated by the ideas of fragmentation and rift lays bare the need for a reconstructive approach that allows for a legal reconnection of life to its conditions of existence. Reimagining property as part of our habitat is a more relationally embedded possibility, and in the final section of the paper I sketch this as an alternative legal form.

2 FRAGMENTATION

'Fragmentation' is a term that can be used to describe a reduction and fracturing of the material conditions of life for both human beings and animals. In ecology, 'fragmentation' refers to destructive changes in the ecosystems that provide a habitat for non-human life – 'the division of habitat into smaller and more isolated fragments separated by a matrix of human-transformed land cover'.[28] Habitat fragmentation is the result of land clearance for roads, agriculture, urban expansion, mines, and other industries. Increasingly, it is also the result of natural disasters that are worse as a result of human activities, as we have seen in the Australian bushfires of 2019–2020. These human-intensified disasters caused the destruction of millions of hectares of habitat and the deaths of potentially hundreds of millions of animals and can no longer be regarded, as they have so often been in the past, only as unfortunate natural occurrences.[29] Habitat fragmentation is characterized by a loss of connectivity between areas of habitat, the shrinking sizes of the patches of land that constitute habitat, and a loss of habitat quality. It is also clearly associated with a reduction in biodiversity, as the resources needed to maintain a healthy level of redundancy in any ecosystem are reduced. Unsurprisingly, habitat fragmentation has also been associated with a loss of connection in animal social networks.[30]

Habitat fragmentation, loss, and degradation, though not always named as such, have also been a common feature of human history in the West: enclosures, clearances, colonization, urbanization, and gentrification have displaced large numbers of people and seriously downgraded their living conditions.[31] These uprootings of people from places they had inhabited for generations (and in some cases millennia) were pursued in the name of 'improvement' of the land.[32] Far from improving the

---

28. Nick Haddad et al., 'Habitat Fragmentation and its Lasting Impacts on Earth's Ecosystems' (2015) 1(2) Science Advances, DOI: 10.1126/sciadv.1500052. A vast literature on habitat fragmentation has accumulated since the 1960s: even the earliest literature warned about the effects of fragmentation on biodiversity.
29. Estimates have varied, from several hundred million to a billion. What is not in doubt is that the fires have destroyed a large amount of habitat and that some species will move closer to extinction as a result.
30. Sam C Banks et al., 'Sex and Sociality in a Disconnected World: A Review of the Impacts of Habitat Fragmentation on Animal Social Interaction' (2007) 85 Canadian Journal of Zoology 1065–79.
31. Karl Polanyi, *The Great Transformation: The Political and Economic Origins of Our Time* (first published 1944, Beacon Press, Boston 1957), in particular ch 3, 'Habitation versus Improvement'; Nicole Graham, *Lawscape: Property, Environment, Law* (Routledge, Abingdon 2011) 51–133.
32. Laura Brace, 'Husbanding the Earth and Hedging out the Poor' in AR Buck, John McLaren, and Nancy Wright (eds), *Land and Freedom: Law, Property Rights, and the British Diaspora*

land, however, the result was often degradation of the soil and of biodiversity, as complex and integrated systems of agricultural management were replaced by monocultures and the use of artificial fertilizers.[33] Whilst living conditions improved as a result of these changes for many people throughout the twentieth century, for many others improvement was too rapid and hence problematic, with excessive consumption replacing other forms of social connectedness. In developing nations, 'progress' has been much more patchy and is highly contingent upon the multiple ways in which value has been extracted from the poor by global capitalism.[34] Precarious employment and material fragility across the world have in recent times been further exacerbated by the global financial crisis, austerity policies, and now a pandemic.

In addition to describing change in human and nonhuman conditions of subsistence, fragmentation is also a powerful description for many aspects of liberal and neoliberal human society. The term 'social fragmentation' is well established and such fragmentation has been studied for well over a century, though not always under that name.[35] In the theoretical domain, fragmentation has been identified in the distinguishing or alienation of human individuals from an experience of community, in their inability to self-actualize, and in the separation of human society from nature.[36] In applied scholarship, 'social fragmentation' is used to refer to a matrix of factors such as isolation, housing insecurity, and population instability in geographical areas.[37] Social fragmentation is set up in this context as being the opposite to social cohesion, and is associated with a dissolution of social norms.[38] Social fragmentation may or may not be associated with poverty and is also often studied for its influence on mental health.[39] Meanwhile, non-geographical networks forged

---

(Ashgate, Dartmouth 2001); J Weaver, 'Concepts of Economic Improvement and the Social Construction of Property Rights: Highlights from the English-Speaking World' in John McLaren, AR Buck, and Nancy Wright (eds), *Despotic Dominion: Property Rights in British Settler Societies* (Cambridge University Press, Cambridge 2005); Brenna Bhandar *Colonial Lives of Property: Law, Land, and Racial Regimes of Ownership* (Duke University Press, Durham 2018), ch 3.

33. See, eg, Nicole Graham, *Lawscape: Property, Environment, Law* (Routledge, Abingdon 2011) 128–30. Graham reports that two methods used to 'improve' forests in colonial Australia were fire and ringbarking. See also Bruce Pascoe, *Dark Emu* (Magbala Books, Broome 2014).

34. Maria Mies, *Patriarchy and Accumulation on a World Scale* (Zed Books, New York 1986); David Harvey, *The New Imperialism* (Oxford University Press, Oxford 2001); Saskia Sassen, 'A Savage Sorting of Winners and Losers: Contemporary Versions of Primitive Accumulation' (2010) 7(1) Globalizations 23–50.

35. Émile Durkheim developed the concept of anomie to describe the disconnection of individuals from social norms. See, eg, É Durkheim, *Suicide: A Study in Sociology* (Free Press, New York 1951). Interestingly, he identified wealth – and wealthy communities – as risk factors for anomie: see pp. 213–14.

36. See, for instance, Axel Honneth's discussion of Georg Lukács' early writings in A Honneth, *The Fragmented World of the Social: Essays in Social and Political Philosophy* (SUNY Press, Albany 1995), in particular 51–3.

37. Social fragmentation or anomie indices have been used for some decades to measure such social fragmentation factors, particularly in urban neighborhoods. See G Davey Smith, E Whitley, D Dorling, and D Gunnell, 'Area Based Measures of Social and Economic Circumstances: Cause Specific Mortality Patterns Depend on the Choice of Index' (2001) 55 Journal of Epidemiology and Community Health 149–50.

38. See, eg, Émile Durkheim, *Suicide: A Study in Sociology* (Free Press, New York 1951) 207–15.

39. See, for instance J Allardyce et al., 'Social Fragmentation, Deprivation and Urbanicity: Relation to First-Admission Rates for Psychoses' (2005) 187 British Journal of Psychiatry

through the internet and social media complicate the study of cohesion and fragmentation,[40] although such hybrid geographical-cyber spaces also provide the backdrop for new scholarship in both.[41]

Human society is fragmented in multiple, intersecting and sometimes indescribable ways, even for those of us who are relatively secure in a material sense. In addition to the fragmentation of the means of survival, established political systems have become notoriously fragmented and now appear – even to the relatively privileged – to be increasingly unreliable. For colonized and vulnerable peoples, state political systems have always been dangerous and disconnected from their material lives, while the fractures of colonialism papered over by imposed solutions are constantly re-forming.[42] Looking to an even more abstract layer of existence, it was frequently observed throughout the twentieth century that knowledge had become fragmented or compartmentalized: from the 'two cultures' of science and the arts noted by CP Snow in 1959,[43] scholarship has become divided into increasingly narrow (one might even say 'micro') specializations that do not communicate well with each other and are highly protective of the boundaries of their field. Critical and interdisciplinary interventions have destabilized some of the foundations of these epistemologically gated communities, but critique has also shown itself to be susceptible to a similar level of protectionism, with closed niches forming around father figures and specific disciplinary combinations.[44] Despite these complexities, shifts, and fragmentations, disciplines still persist in a traditional form and obstacles to removing traditional (and newer) boundaries remain. Eurocentric knowledge thus broadly remains suspicious of outsiders and entrapped in its history.

Fragmentation is far from being the only consequence of intersecting historical processes of colonialism, industrialization, and individualization. Nor is such change always negative as far as every segment of human society is concerned: in many instances, the dissolution of old truths and structures is necessary for constructive transformations to occur. The appearance and perception of fragmentation can thus be highly situational and subjective. Ecological change is, however, overwhelmingly driving loss of habitat and hence of biodiversity on a once thriving planet. And while it might seem that the fragmentation of social existence is a different issue from the

---

401–6; James Fagg et al., 'Area Social Fragmentation, Social Support for Individuals and Psychosocial Health in Young Adults: Evidence from a National Survey in England' (2008) 66 Social Science and Medicine 242–54; Sigrid Mohnen et al., 'Neighbourhood Social Capital and Individual Health' (2011) 72 Social Science and Medicine 660–67; David Coburn, 'Income Inequality, Social Cohesion, and the Health Status of Populations: The Role of Neoliberalism' (2000) 51 Social Science and Medicine 135–46.
40. Leila Hedayatifar et al., 'US Social Fragmentation at Multiple Scales' (2019) 16(159) Journal of the Royal Society Interface.
41. Matt Reed and Daniel Keech, 'Gardening Cyberspace – Social Media and Hybrid Spaces in the Creation of Food Citizenship in the Bristol City-Region, UK' (2019) 44(7) Landscape Research 822–33.
42. For a recent discussion, see Stewart Motha, 'A "Dred Scott Moment" – But Not Only for the UK Supreme Court' (2019) <http://criticallegalthinking.com/2019/09/20/a-dred-scott-moment-but-not-only-for-the-u-k-supreme-court/?fbclid=IwAR0bkgGqV4FiF8P8UdEx8cCdtIRh9tKLj_wRQ2Z0oXajg3P8xyzkRhHO4mA>.
43. CP Snow, 'Two Cultures' (1959) 130(3373) Science.
44. Anders Karlqvist, 'Going Beyond Disciplines' (1999) 32 Policy Sciences 379–83; Andrew Barry, Georgina Born and Gisa Weszkalnys, 'Logics of Interdisciplinarity' (2008) 37(1) Economy and Society 20–49.

fragmentation of arctic sea ice, this perception of difference is itself a product of the separatist – or to use the Marxist term, alienated – epistemology of Western thinking. The matrix of factors that constitute the liberal-capitalist-rationalist worldview and that are responsible for these multiple layers of disconnection between the biophysical world and human society, and between body and mind, have been much discussed:[45] these factors include individualism, the subject-object distinction, the ideology of mastery over nature, and the associated extractive mentality. Fragmentation is therefore a useful analytical frame for understanding certain types of historical change and in particular, as I will explain, especially those motivated by highly individualized and highly fungible practices of private property.

3 RIFT

The second idea that is useful in understanding the property-driven fractures in eco-society is the notion of 'rift'.[46] This is another concept that both creates and crosses the divide between physical and cultural processes. Until recently, Karl Marx was not much studied for his ecological thinking, pre-dating as he did, the major environmental movements of the twentieth century. Twenty years ago, however, John Bellamy Foster developed from Marx the notion of the 'metabolic rift', an idea that has now become popular in social-ecological thought.[47] Early in *Capital* Marx speaks of labour as an 'eternal natural necessity which mediates the metabolism between man and nature, and therefore human life itself'.[48] The term 'metabolism' [*Stoffwechsel* in German] refers to the material exchange that takes place between human society and nature: human labour mediates that exchange for instance in the acts of collecting or growing food for consumption. Typically, labour for Marx involves the transformation of a raw material by the input of human energy.[49] As an aside, I would point out that Marx's focus on *human* labour as the basis for value sidelines what Western thinking has rather belatedly discovered to be the agency of the soil, indeed the Earth's labour.[50] The role of microbes, bacteria, and nutrients in growing things far

---

45. See, for instance, Val Plumwood, *Feminism and the Mastery of Nature* (Routledge, London 1993).
46. I am indebted to Nicole Graham for drawing my attention to the scholarship on metabolic rift. See in particular Nicole Graham, 'Dephysicalized Property and Shadow Lands' in Robyn Bartel and Jennifer Carter (eds), *Handbook on Space, Place, and Law* (Edward Elgar, Cheltenham UK 2021).
47. John Bellamy Foster, 'Marx's Theory of Metabolic Rift: Classical Foundations for Environmental Sociology' (1999) American Journal of Sociology 105(2) 366–405; see also John Bellamy Foster, *Marx's Ecology: Materialism and Nature* (Monthly Review Press, New York 2000); Nathan McClintock, 'Why Farm the City? Theorizing Urban Agriculture through a Lens of Metabolic Rift' (2010) 3(2) Cambridge Journal of Regions, Economy, and Society 191–207; Mindi Schneider and Philip McMichael, 'Deepening, and Repairing, the Metabolic Rift' (2010) 37(3) Journal of Peasant Studies 461–84.
48. Karl Marx, *Capital: A Critique of Political Economy*, Ben Fowkes (trans) (Penguin Books, London 1976) 133.
49. Ted Benton, 'Marxism and Natural Limits: An Ecological Critique and Reconstruction' (1989) 178 New Left Review 51–86, 66.
50. Teresa Brennan, 'Economy for the Earth: The Labour Theory of Value Without the Subject/Object Distinction' (1997) 20 Ecological Economics 175–85. As Morgan Robertson explains, Marx in fact describes 'a unified metabolism between humans and material nature', but insists

outweighs any human contribution as yet: humans can modify life, but not produce it, and to that extent everything productive is generated by the Earth.

Foster highlights several passages in *Capital* that form the basis for the notion of a rift in this metabolic exchange. Foster notes, for example, that Marx was drawing on the work of a German chemist, Liebig.[51] For instance, at the end of Chapter 15 of Volume I, Marx argues that, because of urbanization,

> Capitalist production ... disturbs the metabolic interaction between man and the earth, *i.e.* it prevents the return to the soil of its constituent elements consumed by man in the form of food and clothing; hence it hinders the operation of the eternal natural condition for the lasting fertility of the soil.[52]

Further, Marx says that 'all progress in capitalistic agriculture is a progress in the art, not only of robbing the worker, but of robbing the soil; all progress in increasing the fertility of the soil for a given time is a progress towards ruining the more longlasting sources of that fertility'.[53] Under capitalist conditions, human-nature transactions are not an exchange, but rather an appropriation. 'Natural resources' transformed by labour into value for a human economy are not returned to nature, or at least not within a time frame whereby they can be naturally recycled and reused. This rupture in the processing of materials is the basis of human societies that are unsustainable. One result of this rupture was an agricultural demand for artificial phosphate fertilizers, a demand that was at one time addressed by the extensive devastation of Pacific Islands such as Nauru and Banaba through phosphate mining.[54] As feminist ecophilosopher Val Plumwood argued, the costs of beautiful landscapes and forests close to the homes of the relatively privileged, as well as the costs of these comfortable private homes, are often outsourced to what she calls 'shadow places'[55] – those areas of the world too impoverished to insist on clean air, clean waterways and pollution-free habitat.

---

that it is human labour that is the source of capitalist value; M Robertson, 'Measurement and Alienation: Making a World of Ecosystem Services' (2012) 37 Transactions of the Institute of British Geographers NS 386–401, 389. The extensive literature on ecosystem services that has flourished over the past three decades or so brings the contributions of nature into economic equations in an instrumental fashion – as services for humanity. See below.

51. See John Bellamy Foster, '"Robbing the Earth of its Capital Stock" An introduction to George Waring's Agricultural Features of the Census of the United States for 1850' (1999) 12(3) Organization and Environment 293–7; George Waring, 'Agricultural Features of the Census of the United States for 1850' [1855] (1999) 12(3) Organization and Environment' 298–307.

52. Karl Marx, *Capital: A Critique of Political Economy*, Ben Fowkes (trans) (Penguin Books, London 1976) 637.

53. ibid 638.

54. Katerina Teaiwa, 'Ruining Pacific Islands: Australia's Phosphate Imperialism' (2015) 46(3) Australian Historical Studies 374–91; see also Jimmy Skaggs, *The Great Guano Rush: Entrepreneurs and American Overseas Expansion* (St Martin's Press, New York 1994); Brett Clark and John Bellamy Foster, 'Ecological Imperialism and the Global Metabolic Rift: Unequal Exchange and the Guano/Nitrates Trade' (2009) 50(3) International Journal of Comparative Sociology 311–44.

55. Val Plumwood, 'Shadow Places and the Politics of Dwelling' (2008) 44 Australian Humanities Review 139–50; see also Nicole Graham 'Dephysicalized Property and Shadow Lands' in Robyn Bartel and Jennifer Carter (eds), *Handbook on Space, Place, and Law* (Edward Elgar, Cheltenham UK 2021).

It is extremely interesting to think that Marx explicitly connected the exploitation of workers with the exploitation of the soil. It is good – reassuring even – from an academic perspective to have a term of art like 'metabolic rift' that identifies the interruption in the circulation of matter between human and nonhuman systems. However, it is dispiriting to note that the damaging effects of industrial agriculture were so well known in the nineteenth century that a prominent agricultural chemist from the United States, George Waring, could refer to 'earth butchery and prodigality',[56] stating that 'Man is but a tenant of the soil and he is guilty of a crime when he reduces its value for other tenants who are to come after him'.[57] The broad direction of metabolic rift has thus been known for well over a hundred and fifty years, but it is only in recent decades that the principles of sustainable and regenerative farming have seriously challenged the industrial mindset.

The problem of metabolic rift, however, remains. Underlining its extent is the following statement from a group of 800 scientists, published in *The Australian* newspaper in 1971:

> It is very difficult to find in Australia one industrial process which, when traced through all its ramifications, is in balance with the supply of raw materials and with the ability of the environment to repair the damage which essential parts of most processes cause. Grazing and farming in much of our vast arid regions are reducing the capacity of the land to reproduce.[58]

And further, 'The web of life which nurtured man for a million years and on which man depends for his survival is falling to pieces'. There is now nothing at all remarkable about this statement or its message, though it is notable that it was published 50 years ago, when the rift observed by Liebig and theorized by Marx had already become critical. The Australian scientists were far from alone: there are many examples of scientists of the mid-twentieth century making similar observations. In the late 1960s, an informal thinktank, the Club of Rome, commissioned research into the 'predicament of mankind', resulting in a remarkable report, *The Limits to Growth* (1972). The authors argued that if exponential growth in 'population, industrialization, pollution, food production, and resource depletion' was not controlled then 'the most probable result will be a rather sudden and uncontrollable decline in both population and industrial capacity'.[59]

The rift inherent in industrial agriculture and the consequential damage to soil fertility is of course only one aspect of a great divide that modern humanity has established between human systems and earth systems.[60] Rift is also a social and

---

56. George Waring, 'Agricultural Features of the Census of the United States for 1850' [1855] (1999) 12(3) Organization and Environment' 298–307, 306.
57. ibid. See generally John Bellamy Foster, '"Robbing the Earth of its Capital Stock": An introduction to George Waring's *Agricultural Features of the Census of the United States for 1850*' (1999) 12(3) Organization and Environment 293–7.
58. Thank you to Rob Fowler, who mentioned this statement in the talk 'Sustainability and the Law', Hawke Centre, 10 September 2019.
59. Donella Meadows et al., *The Limits to Growth: A Report for The Club of Rome's Project on the Predicament of Mankind* (Universe Books, New York 1972) 23. See also Graham Turner, 'A Comparison of *The Limits to Growth* with 30 Years of Reality' (2008) 18 Global Environmental Change 397–411; Graham Turner, *Is Global Collapse Imminent?* (Melbourne Sustainable Society Institute, 2014).
60. Johan Rockström et al., 'Planetary Boundaries: Exploring the Safe Operating Space for Humanity' (2009) 14(2) Ecology and Society, article 32 (online).

conceptual attitude and worldview based on the prevalent cultural narrative that divides human society from the natural environment and treats our human interests as greater than the interests of the planet. The onto-epistemological division of human from nonhuman is not universally held, but it is universally destructive because of the global reach of capitalism. In this sense, the idea of a rift between nature and culture is nothing new to scholarship: feminists and many others have discussed the dualisms that dominate thought concerning a separation between nature and society, and the gendered and racialized meanings that attach to each.[61] Which is cause and which is effect – the rift in the circulation of matter or the more abstract rift in cultural worldview – is indeterminate.[62] Suffice it to say that these rifts are mutually reinforcing dimensions of a collective disposition and set of behaviours characterizing the preponderance of post-Enlightenment European and colonial interactions with the physical world.

The fragmentation and rift that were witnessed throughout the twentieth century were exacerbated by capitalism, but have also produced the conditions in which neoliberal capitalism has been able to accelerate eco-social degradation. Neoliberalism has removed the fetters from private accumulation, for instance through the privatization of public resources, by reduced government control, and by an emphasis on self-interest and aggressive individualism. Fragmentation has reduced individual and collective resilience to these trends as well as our ability to resist; while rift encourages a complete disconnection of human society from its own conditions of existence.

4 THE ROLE OF PRIVATE PROPERTY

> The hoarding drive is boundless in its nature.[63]

> Overweening ambition always exceeds the results obtained, great as they may be …[64]

I have described the interconnected problems of social and environmental injustice as being characterized by widespread material and conceptual fragmentation and rift. This is a simplified overview of a complex terrain. My first objective has been to collect an apparently disparate set of issues under two broad narratives that bring the human and the nonhuman into a common analysis concerning the causes of ecocide. My second objective, outlined in this section, is to frame private property within these narratives. In its legal form private property is constituted by the conceptual fragmentation of the world and the rift between human and nonhuman. In turn, property facilitates eco-social fragmentation and rift as processes intrinsic to capitalist-colonial economies. Finally, in the next section, I offer some observations about how property might be reimagined in order to promote more constructive human-nonhuman engagements.

---

61. Carolyn Merchant, *The Death of Nature: Women, Ecology, and the Scientific Revolution* (Harper and Rowe, New York 1980); Val Plumwood, *Feminism and the Mastery of Nature* (Routledge, London 1993); Val Plumwood, *Environmental Culture: The Ecological Crisis of Reason* (Routledge, Abingdon 2002); Anna Grear, 'The Vulnerable Living Order: Human Rights and the Environment in a Critical and Philosophical Perspective' (2011) 2 Journal of Human Rights and the Environment 23–44.
62. But see the discussion in Mindi Schneider and Philip McMichael, 'Deepening, and Repairing, the Metabolic Rift' (2010) 37(3) Journal of Peasant Studies 461–84.
63. Karl Marx, *Capital: A Critique of Political Economy*, Ben Fowkes (trans) (Penguin Books, London 1976) 230.
64. Émile Durkheim, *Suicide: A Study in Sociology* (Free Press, New York 1951) 214.

As noted in the previous section, the process of metabolic rift was attributed by Marx to capitalist agriculture that robbed both workers and nature. In the present day, and along the same lines, the cause of environmental destruction is frequently said to be the expectation that economies always deliver growth:[65] this insistence on growth has been described as a ponzi scheme or a pyramid scheme. The centrality of growth as ideology means that while there is a limit to sustainable accumulation and a limit to planetary resources, there is no agreed political limit to economic growth. This growth mentality is clearly extremely destructive, but simply blaming economic growth begs the question of what it is that motivates and permits growth. While there are many factors that make up the social-ideological system that fixates on the view that growth is progress and drive the consequential destruction this causes when pursued unthinkingly,[66] the most critical factor, and the focal point for this article, is private property. The capitalist system permits and even promotes unlimited accumulation of private property together with the personal power that property brings, allowing the costs of that accumulation to be outsourced via the extraction of value from both human and nonhuman spheres. Both the form and the practice of property are troubling because of the role of property both in producing huge social disparities and in facilitating environmental damage. Structurally and conceptually, private property has very few built-in restraints, meaning that – when pursued individually and collectively – it feeds accelerating accumulation and an associated acceleration in ecocide.

Private property enshrines both the rift between human and nonhuman and the fragmentation that characterizes eco-society. The rift between human and nonhuman processes is co-extensive with private property as it is understood by Western law. In its modern legal form, private property is based on a division between owner and owned, subjects and objects.[67] Humans are owners and property-holding subjects, while things – land, animals, consumer goods – are all objects of property. Regardless of any emotional, psychological or existential connection that a person may have to their 'objects of property', the division of subject from object, and the dominance of human owners over the nonhuman world, is basic to property's legal form. However, the subject and the object are categories constituted by law, philosophy, and a Euro-colonial narrative of fundamental 'human' difference from 'nature'.[68] These categories have shifted over time: the history of slavery shows, for instance, that it took many centuries for the line between subject and object to be formally drawn to include all humans.

A system that divides the world into subjects and objects is intrinsically hierarchical, meaning that all of the things classified as objects are ontologically debased, can

---

65. See, for instance, the New Economics Foundation Report, *Growth Isn't Possible* (2010); Herman Daly, *Beyond Growth: The Economics of Sustainable Development* (Beacon Press, Boston, MA 1996); Herman Daly, 'A Further Critique of Growth Economics' (2013) 88 Ecological Economics 20–24; Donella Meadows et al., *The Limits to Growth: A Report for The Club of Rome's Project on the Predicament of Mankind* (Universe Books, New York 1972).
66. See JK Gibson-Graham, *The End of Capitalism as We Knew It: A Feminist Critique of Political Economy* (University of Minnesota Press, Minneapolis 2006).
67. James Penner, *The Idea of Property in Law* (Clarendon Press, Oxford 1997) 105–27; Margaret Davies 'Material Subjects and Vital Objects – Prefiguring Property and Rights for an Entangled World' (2016) 22(2) Australian Journal of Human Rights 37–60.
68. See, eg, Alain Pottage and Martha Mundy (eds), *Law, Anthropology, and the Constitution of the Social: Making Persons and Things* (Cambridge University Press, Cambridge 2004); Margaret Davies and Ngaire Naffine, *Are Persons Property? Legal Debates About Property and Personality* (Ashgate, London 2001).

be treated as mere commodities for exchange, and treated as equals in economic exchanges. Land, for example, becomes abstract in real estate transactions so that it can participate fully in capitalist circulation.[69] Aboriginal connections to country based on continuity between peoples and place are disrupted by the legal techniques of native title and translated into objectified formalities.[70] A patch of land that supports ecological diversity can be exchanged via the medium of money for a specified number of plastic buckets. Ecologically valuable land can be reductively measured within the same system of value as can 'shares', 'followers', or 'likes' in the 'attention economy'.[71] Private property thus has a strong tendency to reduce things to a fungible form in which items can be exchanged for each other through what Marx called the universal commodity of money.[72] All manner of things that really ought to be beyond monetary value are drawn into the process of exchange and have their distinct characteristics and wider value flattened:[73] Marx called money 'the radical leveller', precisely because it 'does away with all distinctions'. This reduction is problematic for eco-social justice: in many instances the unique qualities of an item are levelled in the process of accumulation in the form of private property – and in a context where the fungibility of land is legally paramount, development driven by a profit outcome can all too easily reduce human and environmental safety to mere regulatory costs that need to be minimized. It seems perverse that resources that are critical to life on earth and to human well-being can be quantified according to the same measures as things that are entirely unnecessary and even destructive.

The economy constituted by the circulation within human society of money and privately owned resources is not the only economy that exists.[74] It is however the

---

69. See, generally, Nicole Graham, *Lawscape: Property, Environment, Law* (Routledge, Abingdon 2011); Robyn Bartel and Nicole Graham, 'Property and Place Attachment: A Legal Geographical Analysis of Biodiversity Law Reform in New South Wales' (2016) 54(3) Geographical Research 267–84; Kenneth Vandevelde, 'The New Property of the Nineteenth Century: The Development of the Modern Concept of Property' (1980) 29(2) Buffalo Law Review 325–67.

70. Lee Godden, 'Legal Geography – Place, Time, Law and Method: The Spatial and Archival in Connection to Country' in Tayanah O'Donnell, Daniel Robinson, and Josephine Gillespie (eds), *Legal Geography: Perspectives and Methods* (Routledge, Abingdon 2020); see also Kathleen Birrell, Lee Godden, and Maureen Tehan, 'Climate Change and REDD+: Property as a Prism for Conceiving Indigenous Peoples' Engagement' (2012) 3(2) Journal of Human Rights and the Environment 196–216.

71. See eg, Alice Marwick, 'Instafame: Luxury Selfies in the Attention Economy' (2015) 27(1) Public Culture 137–60.

72. Also money: 'Just as in money every qualitative difference between commodities is extinguished, so too for its part, as a radical leveller, it extinguishes all distinctions.' Karl Marx *Capital: A Critique of Political Economy*, Ben Fowkes (trans) (Penguin Books, London 1976), 229.

73. Bartel et al., call such items 'notionally fungible commodities that are grown in non-fungible conditions', see R Bartel et al., 'Legal Geography: An Australian Perspective' (2013) 51(4) Geographical Research 339. Margaret Radin's provocative title also makes the point: 'What, If Anything, Is Wrong with Baby Selling?' (1995) 26(2) Pacific Law Review 135–46. See also M Radin, 'Property and Personhood' (1982) 34 Stanford Law Review 957–1015; Kenneth Vandevelde, 'The New Property of the Nineteenth Century: The Development of the Modern Concept of Property' (1980) 29(2) Buffalo Law Review 325–67.

74. JK Gibson-Graham, *The End of Capitalism (As We Knew It): A Feminist Critique of Political Economy* (2nd edn, University of Minnesota Press, Minneapolis 2006).

dominant one and has the power to consume other economies and alternative forms of property. Scholarly and activist efforts to revitalize and strengthen the commons[75] activate these alternatives but are also a symptom of the loss of the significant value once accorded to the public interest, public space, and publicly-owned goods.[76] (This is not to suggest that political economy is moving inevitably in the direction of destruction: many practical resistances and more constructive narratives also exist.) A critical feature of the economic, material, and ontological rift between human society and the rest of the biosphere is that the ecosystem in itself has no value in the economic systems of the capitalist West. It is only seen to be of value for the raw materials it can provide and is otherwise fully external to society and the dominant economy. This logic means that one of the most legible remedies for environmental destruction has been to monetize environmental goods through mechanisms such as carbon trading or ecosystem services accounting.[77] These approaches commodify nature and attach a monetary value to it so that it can be exchanged in the market, just like other goods. Such mechanisms and approaches have the merit of making 'the environment' visible to the most powerful system of value accounting that exists for global capitalism, but remain ontologically problematic precisely because they work via the levelling process associated with money.[78] As Nicole Graham has explored in detail,[79] the commodification of nature dephysicalizes it and alienates human beings further from the natural material connections we are formed from.

Fragmentation is also intrinsic to property, and to property relations governing land in particular. Some forms of fragmentation are only made possible by legal doctrine. For instance, different legal persons can have property rights in the one piece of land – rights such as ownership, lease, easement, or mortgage. Fragmented property interests such as these are reasonably well defined in law but can become distorted by market forces: in the subprime mortgage crisis, for instance, mortgages were bundled up, sold on, and disguised in various ways.[80] Private property therefore is fragmentary

---

75. Jane Holder and Tatiana Flessas, 'Emerging Commons' (2008) 17 Social and Legal Studies 299–310; Alison Young, 'Cities in the City: Street Art, Enchantment, and the Urban Commons' (2014) 26(2) Law and Literature 145–61; Matthew Turner, 'Political Ecology III: The Commons and Commoning' (2017) 41(6) Progress in Human Geography 791–802.
76. Antonia Layard, for instance, has written about the 'swathes' of property privatizations in England, and argued that they are 'a clear example of accumulation by dispossession', as analysed by David Harvey. See Layard, 'Public Space: Property, Lines, Interruptions' (2016) 2 Journal of Law, Property, and Society 1–47, 15; see also David Harvey *The New Imperialism* (Oxford University Press, Oxford 2001); Saskia Sassen, 'A Savage Sorting of Winners and Losers: Contemporary Versions of Primitive Accumulation' (2010) 7(1) Globalizations 23–50.
77. Robert Costanza et al., 'Twenty Years of Ecosystem Services: How Far Have We Come and How Far Do We Still Need to Go?' (2017) 28 Ecosystem Services 1–16.
78. Morgan Robertson, 'Measurement and Alienation: Making a World of Ecosystem Services' (2012) 37 Transactions of the Institute of British Geographers NS 386–401; Matthias Schröter et al., 'Ecosystem Services as a Contested Concept: A Synthesis of Critique and Counter-Arguments' (2014) 7(6) Conservation Letters 514–23.
79. Nicole Graham, *Lawscape: Property, Environment, Law* (Routledge, Abingdon 2011); 'Dephysicalized Property and Shadow Lands' in Robyn Bartel and Jennifer Carter (eds), *Handbook on Space, Place, and Law* (Edward Elgar, Cheltenham UK 2021).
80. Adam Ashcraft and Til Schuermann, *Understanding the Securitization of Subprime Mortgage Credit* (Now Publishers, Boston 2008); Amiyatosh Purdanandam, 'Originate-to-Distribute Model and the Subprime Mortgage Crisis' (2011) 24 Journal of Financial Studies 1881–915.

in form but is also obviously responsible for producing eco-social fragmentation of the types I have already spoken of.[81] Ecosystem destruction and fragmentation are the results of land clearances made in the name of improvement and economic advancement, and the many forms of human social fragmentation can at least partly be attributed to multifaceted inequality caused by unlimited accumulation and by successive removals of resources from public and common ownership.

Private property carves up conceptual and physical space and creates eco-social vulnerability because it consists of a right to exclude the world at large. Because private property is a right to exclude, it is a form of private power exercised by an owner over the rest of humanity and over nature. As Van der Walt pointed out '… property law is not exclusively or even primarily about owners and holders of rights, but about … those who are required to respect property and who are owned as or through property'.[82] Property law creates a system that necessarily gives private owners power over non-owners and in fact that is its main point, which is operationalized through property's legal form. And because the objects of property, whether land, artworks, or plastic buckets, are reducible to monetary value, there is no limit to what a single person can own. The accumulation of property is never just an accumulation of money in the bank or a portfolio of shares and investments – such property amounts to an accumulation of power over others. This is a very old point,[83] but one that is often still unrecognized in neoliberal thinking, which insists on formal notions of equality even while promoting aggressive individualism. Private property may have emerged out of feudalism, but the inequalities it generates amount to a neo-feudalism based on intense concentrations of power and the ability of those who wield that power to extract service from people in endlessly creative ways.[84]

Commodification and fungibility are offset to some degree, however, by the interest that the public or community has in certain resources: not all property is privately owned and not every aspect of privately owned property is exclusively under the power of its owner. The opportunities for unlimited accumulation and the transfer of the costs of accumulation can be reined in by effective government regulation. In many instances, externalities produced by an unregulated market are in fact controlled in this way. Employment laws protect workers from the worst exploitation, building regulation prevents the most dangerous construction, while the role of environmental law is to put a brake on the worst forms of environmental destruction. However, government regulation has many weaknesses, partly because of its instrumental focus[85] – it often represents a compromise, is ineffectively applied, can be watered down or abandoned, is frequently under-resourced, and often prioritizes short-term goals. Moreover, just as significantly, governments are now more susceptible than

---

81. See, eg, Peter Burdon 'What is Good Land Use? From Rights to Relationship' (2010) 34 Melbourne University Law Review 708–55.
82. AJ Van der Walt, 'Property and Marginality' 81–105 in Gregory Alexander and Eduardo Penalver, *Property and Community* (Oxford University Press, Oxford 2010).
83. See Morris Cohen, 'Property and Sovereignty' (1928) 13 Cornell Law Review 8–30; Roger Cotterrell, 'Power, Property and the Law of Trusts: A Partial Agenda for Critical Legal Scholarship' in Peter Fitzpatrick and Alan Hunt (eds), *Critical Legal Studies* (Blackwell, Oxford 1987).
84. See, eg, Peter Drahos and John Braithwaite, *Information Feudalism* (Earthscan, London 2002).
85. See, eg, Christine Parker and Fiona Haines, 'An Ecological Approach to Regulatory Studies?' (2018) 45(1) Journal of Law and Society 136–55.

ever to corporate power. The neoliberal state is hardly a reliable guarantor of adequate regulatory protection.

In sum, private property in its modern Western and imperial form is constituted by a rift between individualized human subjects and their objectified world and by the fragmentation, or potential fragmentation, of interests in this objectifiable world. Private property underpins and facilitates high-flow capitalism, which relies on the massive circulation of fungible commodities and on the 'accumulation by dispossession'[86] of insufficiently protected resources, including the ecosystems, broadly understood, that support human and nonhuman life. Private property promotes, but is also is driven to its extremes by, such dynamics. Transforming property rests on a number of strategies across the continuum of promoting alternative practices and imaginings of private property itself, through to efforts to strengthen the commons and the public domain.[87] Such possibilities are forged around reconnecting the relationships broken by private property. In the next section, I turn to one narrative that can help guide these strategies.

5 HABITAT[88]

At its simplest, the remedy for all forms of fragmentation and rift is relational and integrated thinking of the type that feminism and ecological philosophy have been promoting for some decades and that Indigenous philosophies have understood for millennia. Such thinking does not mean a return to pre-industrial or to communal forms of life, even though extractive industrial capitalism has so widely been identified as the critical driver of a disintegrating world. History is cumulative and there can never be any return, even where such a thing might at first glance appear desirable. Rather, the imperative is for new eco-social formations that are balanced, fair, and sustainable in the long term.

Relational thinking proceeds on the understanding that people and things do not pre-exist their relationships but are formed in adaptive connections with their surroundings.[89] Any 'fixed' properties that a person, a class of people, or a thing

---

86. David Harvey, *The New Imperialism* (Oxford University Press, Oxford 2001); Saskia Sassen, 'A Savage Sorting of Winners and Losers: Contemporary Versions of Primitive Accumulation' (2010) 7(1) Globalizations 23–50.
87. Davina Cooper, 'Opening Up Ownership: Community, Belonging, Belongings, and the Productive Life of Property' (2007) 32(3) Law and Social Inquiry 625–64; Nicholas Blomley 'Performing Property: Making the World' 26(1) Canadian Journal of Law and Jurisprudence 23–48; Sarah Keenan, *Subversive Property: Law and the Production of Spaces of Belonging* (Routledge, Abingdon 2015); Antonia Layard, 'Public Space: Property, Lines, Interruptions' (2016) 2 Journal of Law, Property, and Society 1–47; Cristy Clark and John Page, 'Of Protest, the Commons, and Customary Public Rights: An Ancient Tale of the Lawful Forest' (2019) 42(1) UNSW Law Journal 26–59.
88. See, further, Margaret Davies, Lee Godden and Nicole Graham, 'Situating Property Within Habitat: Reintegrating Place, People, and the Law' (2021) 6 Journal of Law, Property, and Society, article 1 (online).
89. Jennifer Nedelsky, 'Law, Boundaries, and the Bounded Self' (1990) 30 Representations 162–89; Jennifer Nedelsky, *Law's Relations: A Relational Theory of Self, Autonomy, and Law* (Oxford University Press, Oxford 2011); Karen Barad, *Meeting the Universe Halfway: Quantum Physics and the Entanglement of Matter and Meaning* (Duke University Press, Durham 2007); Ian Hodder, *Entangled: An Archaeology of the Relationships Between Humans and Things* (Wiley-Blackwell, Chichester 2012); Will Adams, 'The Primacy of Interrelating: Practicing Ecological Psychology with Buber, Levinas, and Merleau-Ponty'

appears to have are in reality the product of complex and dynamic relationships that emerge and are sedimented over different time scales – from eons to moments.

Feminist thought addresses the politics of being human and, for it, relationality has mainly been theorized as concerning the relations that constitute an intra-human sphere and the ways in which such relationalities are disrupted and fractured by a male-centred consciousness. Ecofeminism combines this political consciousness with ecological thinking,[90] which is relational in that it perceives that in biology 'everything in the environment is connected to everything else'.[91] Indigenous peoples across the globe have understood these connections for far longer: Mary Graham is an Aboriginal philosopher of the Kombu-merri people. She says: 'The two most important kinds of relationship in life are, firstly, those between land and people and, secondly, those among people themselves, the second always being contingent upon the first. The land, and how we treat it, is what determines our human-ness'.[92] The attachment of people to place has received some legislative recognition and support in Aotearoa New Zealand, where the personhood and rights of several natural entities have been recognized – a national park (Te Urewera); a river (Whanganui); and a mountain (Mount Taranaki).[93] These reforms are specifically located, and do not necessarily suggest that nature as a whole possesses rights or personality. Nevertheless, such legal reforms do illustrate the possibilities for a more holistic and relational view of eco-society and an approach that brings human and nonhuman into a single frame of reference.[94] They therefore represent one method of addressing historical and eco-social fragmentation and rift for particular human-nonhuman communities.

There have been many efforts to reimagine private property in a more relational way. Many property thinkers have emphasized that because it is socially constituted, property therefore requires obligations as well as rights.[95] After all, the only reason anybody owns property is because the law creates and protects it. This fact in itself

---

(2007) 38 Journal of Phenomenological Psychology 24–61; Anna Grear, 'The Vulnerable Living Order: Human Rights and the Environment in a Critical and Philosophical Perspective' (2011) 2(1) Journal of Human Rights and the Environment 23–44.

90. See, eg, Val Plumwood, *Feminism and the Mastery of Nature* (Routledge, London 1993); see also Karen Warren, 'The Power and the Promise of Ecological Feminism' (1990) 12(2) Environmental Ethics 121–46; Vandana Shiva, *Staying Alive: Women, Ecology and Feminism* (Zed Books, London 1989).

91. Barry Commoner, *The Closing Circle: Nature, Man, and Technology* (Bantam Books, New York 1972) 11. See also Arne Naess, 'The Shallow and the Deep, Long-Range Ecology Movement: A Summary' (1973) 16 Inquiry 95–100; Simone Bignall, Steve Hemming, and Daryl Rigney, 'Three Ecosophies for the Anthropocene: Environmental Governance, Continental Posthumanism, and Indigenous Expressivism' (2016) 10(4) Deleuze Studies 455–78.

92. Mary Graham, 'Some Thoughts About the Philosophical Underpinnings of Aboriginal Worldviews' (2008) 45 Australian Humanities Review 181–94, 181.

93. Andrew Geddis and Jacinta Ruru, 'Places as Persons: Creating a New Framework for Maori-Crown Relations' in Jason Varuhas (ed), *The Frontiers of Public Law* (Hart Publishing, Oxford 2020); Katherine Sanders, '"Beyond Human Ownership": Property, Power, and Legal Personality for Nature in Aotearoa New Zealand' (2018) 30 Journal of Environmental Law 207–34.

94. See, generally, Cristy Clark, Nia Emmanouil, John Page, and Alessandro Pelizzon, 'Can You Hear the Rivers Sing? Legal Personhood, Ontology, and the Nitty-Gritty of Governance' (2018) 45 Ecology Law Quarterly 787–844.

95. Eric Freyfogle, 'Context and Accommodation in Modern Property Law' (1989) 41 Stanford Law Review 1529–56; Gregory Alexander, 'Ownership and Obligations: The Human Flourishing Theory of Property' (2013) 43(2) Hong Kong Law Journal 451–62; Joseph William Singer, *Entitlement: The Paradoxes of Property* (Yale University Press, New Haven 2000).

should be sufficient to generate extensive reciprocal obligations to society and to the public at large. Many have also argued that land ownership ought to bring with it the obligation to act as a steward or custodian so that it is passed to the next owner in an ecologically improved state.[96] The challenge for law is to integrate these ideas of responsibility into legal ownership and in particular into legal ownership of land. Is it possible to connect and to deepen the legal obligations of owners so that property is regarded as bringing a commitment to both human and nonhuman life? How can property be thought ecologically to encompass intersecting planes of human and nonhuman sociality?[97] Is it possible to recreate real property so that it is co-extensive with the conditions for life, that is, with human and nonhuman habitat?

Such a recreation would necessarily involve recalibrating what it means to be a person under the law: rather than a bounded individual with specific rights, we would need to be legally visible as ecologically connected beings who subsist in constitutive connection with place, land, and nonhuman beings. In ongoing research, Lee Godden, Nicole Graham, and I have been working on the notion of 'habitat' as a critical point of material connection between the human and the nonhuman, and a conceptual bridge across the legal divide that presently separates life forms.[98] As Samantha Frost says:

> [W]hen an organism develops and lives its life, it not only assimilates, appropriates, and engages with its habitat but also is modified through that assimilation, appropriation, and engagement. … We could say then, that a developing and growing organism constitutes and reconstitutes itself, composes and recomposes itself, through its responses to features of its habitat.[99]

In the scientific register, the idea of habitat primarily speaks to the biological needs of organisms.[100] Habitat is thus ordinarily associated with the unique characteristics of particular places and the biodiversity that brings resilience and adaptability to life. Given organism adaptability, habitat is not necessarily provided only by undamaged natural areas, but can refer to any place where life is possible. However, not only are organisms responsive to habitat, they alter it – adaptation is not

---

96. James Karp, 'A Private Property Duty of Stewardship: Changing Our Land Ethic' (1993) 23 Environmental Law 735–62; William Lucy and Catherine Mitchell, 'Replacing Private Property: The Case for Stewardship' (1996) 55 Cambridge Law Journal 566–600; see, generally, Emily Barritt, 'Conceptualising Stewardship in Environmental Law' (2014) 26 Environmental Law Journal 1–26.

97. This is not a new question at all: see Margherita Pieraccini, 'Property Pluralism and the Partial Reflexivity of Conservation Law: The Case of Upland Commons in England and Wales' (2012) 3(2) Journal of Human Rights and the Environment 273–87; Anna Grear, 'Human Rights, Property, and the Search for "Worlds Other"' (2012) 3(2) Journal of Human Rights and the Environment 173–95.

98. The literature on habitat is vast. For a discussion of the use of the term see Peter Alagona, 'What is Habitat?' (2011) 16 Environmental History 433–8; see also Linnea Hall, Paul Krausman, and Michael Morrison, 'The Habitat Concept and a Plea for Standard Terminology' (1997) 25(1) Wildlife Society Bulletin 173–82. For a more extensive discussion of habitat and property see Margaret Davies, Lee Godden and Nicole Graham, 'Situating Property Within Habitat: Reintegrating Place, People, and the Law' (2021) 6 Journal of Law, Property, and Society, article 1 (online).

99. Samantha Frost, *Biocultural Creatures: Toward a New Theory of the Human* (Duke University Press, Durham 2016) 122.

100. A scientific discussion is found in Peter Alagona, 'What is Habitat?' (2011) 16 Environmental History 433–8, 438.

unidirectional, but rather multifaceted and distributed. Clearly, habitat can be evaluated according to both quantitative and qualitative factors. In social-ecological thought the idea of habitat extends across the multiple intersecting ecologies of physical and social well-being. As Deleuze and Guattari put it, '[e]very territory, every habitat, joins up not only its spatiotemporal but its qualitative planes or sections'.[101] If eco-social habitat were to function as a guiding material practice of property, therefore, it has the potential to promote a more inclusive, more relational, more situated, and less hierarchical view of property, which would, by definition, make the externalization of costs in the process of aggregating property impossible. I will explain these points in more detail shortly, after a brief detour via a previous attempt to conceptualize property as habitat.

5.1 Habitat as a metaphor for property: Reich's view

The connection of property with habitat was made nearly thirty years ago by the well-known US property theorist, Charles Reich. Reich was famous in property circles for his argument that all forms of valuable government distributions – jobs, welfare, licences, and contracts – should be recognized as private property.[102] In a highly individualistic society, his concern was to bolster individual resilience against wealthy interests and against political intrusions into people's economic well-being. Reich also argued that property is like animal habitat:

> Like an animal's habitat, property represents the individual's means of survival. It is attached to the individual by a biological bond. Indeed, it is part of the definition of the individual. We would not define a fish in such a way as to exclude the water in which it swims, nor would we define a bird without its nesting site, nor an otter without its food supply. Life does not exist in artificial isolation.[103]

Animals, in other words, need habitat to survive and humans need property. Habitat is the condition of survival for all life – without habitat, there is no life:[104] if you take the fish out of water, in a short while you just get a dead fish.[105] Ultimately, if you remove or fragment too much human habitat, we will also die. But Reich switches too quickly from animal habitat to human property without considering how property might need to change in order to be habitat. Property in its current form is not the same for humans as habitat is for animals (including humans): in fact, the idea of property

---

101. Gilles Deleuze and Felix Guattari, *What is Philosophy?* (Verso, London 1994)185, as discussed by Lorraine Code, *Ecological Thinking: The Politics of Epistemic Location* (Oxford University Press, Oxford 2006) 25–7.
102. Charles Reich, 'The New Property' (1964) 73 Yale Law Journal 733–87. Reich's analysis is discussed further in Margaret Davies, Lee Godden and Nicole Graham, 'Situating Property Within Habitat: Reintegrating Place, People, and the Law' (2021) 6 Journal of Law, Property, and Society, article 1 (online).
103. Charles Reich, 'Beyond the New Property: An Ecological View of Due Process' (1990) 56 Brooklyn Law Review 731–45, 737.
104. The habitat-organism relation is examined in minute detail by Samantha Frost in *Biocultural Creatures: Toward a New Theory of the Human* (Duke University Press, Durham 2016).
105. You also get dead fish if you allow the oxygen to be removed from the water, as Australia found a few years ago, with millions of native fish dying in one of our river systems. See *Investigation of the Causes of Mass Fish Kills in the Menindee Region NSW Over the Summer of 2018–2019* (Australian Academy of Science, February 2019).

that allows unlimited accumulation and the externalization of harms, as I have already argued, is the source of enormous problems and has resulted in the degradation of both human and nonhuman habitat. The *liberal* solution to inequality among humans as promoted by Reich is to improve individual security by widening the definition of property but not changing its form.[106] In a highly commercialized world, private property does supply habitat in the short term for many, and the very wealthy may be able to buy their means of survival for quite a long time – but this approach will not help eco-society at large.

5.2 Towards property as habitat

Reich's solution was limited by his liberalism. But property needs to be aligned with, or secondary to, human *and* nonhuman habitat – in more imaginative and relevant ways. Several particular directions for further development are worth mentioning.[107]

It is vital that the distinctive characteristics of particular places should be understood in order to maximize the chances of protecting biodiversity and ecosystems. As Robyn Bartel and Nicole Graham have suggested, developing consciousness of person-place attachment, and finding ways to strengthen its protection in law, will allow a more localized understanding of property to emerge.[108] Habitat is local but it is also connected to global eco-social systems. An idea of property that is embedded in localities and tied to protecting the ecological integrity of places also needs to be practised ecologically, which means looking beyond immediate locations and ensuring that costs are not externalized to distant 'shadow places'.[109] Geographical inequalities in the existence of habitat also need to be identified and eliminated by pairing rights to draw on the resources of a particular location with responsibilities to sustain it.[110]

A relational understanding of property would therefore also involve flattening the hierarchies between owner and owned and those between owner and non-owner, as well as comprehending all as components of a networked agency. A more equal

---

106. See, generally, Charles Reich, 'The New Property' (1964) 73 Yale Law Journal 733–87; Charles Reich, 'Beyond the New Property: An Ecological View of Due Process' (1990) 56 Brooklyn Law Review 731–45, 735.
107. Some of these are reflected in the UN-Habitat Agenda: <https://open.unhabitat.org/>.
108. See generally Robyn Bartel and Nicole Graham, 'Property and Place Attachment: A Legal Geographical Analysis of Biodiversity Law Reform in New South Wales' (2016) 54(3) Geographical Research 267–84. See also Sarah Keenan, *Subversive Property: Law and the Productive Spaces of Belonging* (Routledge, Abingdon 2015). The *Yarra River Protection (Wilip-gin Birrarung murron) Act 2017* (Victoria, Australia) defines particular areas as Yarra River land that are exclusive of private property. It is possible, however, to imagine such a regime that did extend to private property, as it provides a framework for conceptualizing the whole river; similarly the *Te Awa Tupua (Whanganui River Claims Settlement) Act 2017* (New Zealand) is a co-management agreement and involves collective ownership, but could potentially be combined with private property.
109. Val Plumwood, 'Shadow Places and the Politics of Dwelling' (2008) 44 Australian Humanities Review 139–50; see also Nicole Graham, 'Dephysicalized Property and Shadow Lands' in Robyn Bartel and Jennifer Carter (eds), *Handbook on Space, Place, and Law* (Edward Elgar, Cheltenham UK 2021).
110. Val Plumwood, 'Shadow Places and the Politics of Dwelling' (2008) 44 Australian Humanities Review 139–50; see also Nicole Graham 'Dephysicalized Property and Shadow Lands' in Robyn Bartel and Jennifer Carter (eds), *Handbook on Space, Place, and Law* (Edward Elgar, Cheltenham UK 2021).

relationship between owner and owned involves recognition that the subject-object positions in any relationship are mobile and emergent, rather than fixed.[111] The 'owner' is addressed or interpellated by the object of property, which also expresses itself as an agent,[112] even as the owner has certain interests in relation to it. The human legal subject who is truly understood as emergent from relationships is one where belonging is understood as the relationship of a part to a whole, as Davina Cooper has argued.[113] An owner who belongs in this way can never rise above their plural ecological connections, though some differentiation, some 'relational autonomy' is essential and desirable. The idea that human beings care for resources that they 'own' is not at all foreign to even the most individualistic thinking, whether that thing is a pet, an heirloom, a home, a garden, or a farm. The step away from individualism however can only occur when such care is understood as owed across all of the different registers of social-ecological becoming. A more equal relationship between owners and non-owners can be promoted in many ways: finding ways to limit destructive forms of accumulation, improving distributions of property, and rigorously protecting and strengthening the commons and public space. Where the community or public has an interest in a resource, the positions of subject and object are necessarily more fluid, even interchangeable: each person in a group with common rights over a thing is answerable both to the resource and to the others who use it. More radical change is also warranted that would acknowledge that property is a gift from the commons to the individual, not an entitlement of those who have happened to secure whatever 'object' of property is in question.

Thinking of property within the framework of habitat is therefore about making property more inclusive, rather than defining it primarily through exclusive rights.[114] Habitat is biodiverse, not monocultural. Engaging habitat as a conceptual benchmark for property might mean promoting multiple uses (including nonhuman uses) that can co-exist with individual human rights: there are examples of this already outside urban areas with the rights of way that exist in Britain, the co-existence of native title with pastoral leases in Australia, and communal forest rights in Sweden. From the perspective of the private owner, the co-existence of public and private rights is often experienced as a loss of their own amenity and property. A more integrated narrative of place, ecology, and human-nonhuman communities would in time render this idea of a 'loss' less coherent. Where non-private elements are regarded as inherent to property, and where real property is securely attached to place and the continuance of nonhuman life, the power associated with the property is necessarily less concentrated and less hierarchical.

---

111. Margaret Davies, 'Material Subjects and Vital Objects: Prefiguring Property and Rights for an Entangled World' (2016) 22(2) Australian Journal of Human Rights 37–60.
112. On agency of the object of property see Margherita Pieraccini, 'Property Pluralism and the Partial Reflexivity of Conservation Law: The Case of Upland Commons in England and Wales' (2012) 3(2) Journal of Human Rights and the Environment 273–87; Margaret Davies, 'Can Property be Justified in an Entangled World?' (2020) 17(7) Globalizations 1104–17.
113. Davina Cooper, 'Opening Up Ownership: Community, Belonging, Belongings, and the Productive Life of Property' (2007) 32(3) Law and Social Inquiry 625–64; see also Sarah Keenan, *Subversive Property: Law and the Productive Spaces of Belonging* (Routledge, Abingdon 2015), especially ch 4.
114. Anna Grear, 'Human Rights, Property, and the Search for "Worlds Other"' (2012) 3(2) Journal of Human Rights and the Environment 173–95.

6 CONCLUSION

Calls to reform property have existed for decades and have intensified in recent years. Urgency about the issue arises from several ongoing processes: environmental destruction, continuing colonialism and imperialism, and increasing inequality. Calls for radical reform are undoubtedly also a reaction to the extremes of neoliberalism that have characterized the last few decades of economic policy and the consequential intensification of property-led destruction. A long historical view illustrates that property as a practice and an idea does change, very substantially, despite its apparent resistance to change in the present legal system. Changes to the form of property coincide with and are co-implicated in changes to landscapes, to political systems, to geopolitical and personal distributions of power, and to the status of human individuals.

The problem posed by ecocide is that change to conceptions of property is needed more or less immediately, not over the next few centuries, and is needed on several fronts simultaneously. In this article, I have endeavoured to re-frame certain theoretical aspects of the debate about property reform, so that both the negative impacts and the constructive reform of property are seen as eco-social interventions.

'For the trees have no tongues': eco-feedback, speech, and the silencing of nature

Matt Harvey*
PhD Candidate, Department of Political Science, The University of Colorado at Boulder

Steve Vanderheiden**
Departments of Political Science and Environmental Studies, The University of Colorado at Boulder

When Christopher Stone argued for the extension of legal standing to natural objects, he proposed a guardianship model for representing the rights or interests of nonhuman nature. This approach requires that natural objects or systems be able to intelligibly communicate information regarding needs associated with their continued sustainable flourishing. Drawing upon both 'law beyond the human' approaches to legal theory and New Materialist theories about nonhuman subjectivity, we conceive of this mode of communication as a political speech act, albeit one that must be interpreted through eco-feedback collected in the study of natural systems rather than directly transmitted from speaker to listener. We then apply this conception of communication to human rights contexts in which efforts to distort or to otherwise manipulate this eco-feedback could be construed as an anti-democratic interference in speech rights, arguing for the extension of such rights to protect against such interference.

Keywords: *guardianship, New Materialism, nature, communication, representation, environment, human rights*

1 INTRODUCTION

Can nonhuman nature 'speak' to humans, in order that humans may in turn speak on its behalf? In his defense of extending legal standing to natural objects such as trees, Christopher Stone claims that nature can and does communicate. Stone insists that 'natural objects *can* communicate their wants (needs) to us, and in ways that are not terribly ambiguous'.[1] To illustrate, he suggests that his lawn communicates its need for water 'by a certain dryness of the blades and soil—immediately obvious to the touch—the appearance of bald spots, yellowing, and a lack of springiness after being walked on'.[2] By using the term 'objects' in this context, Stone means

---

* matthew.t.harvey@colorado.edu
** vanders@colorado.edu. The authors would like to thank the editorial staff at the Journal of Human Rights and the Environment – Anna Grear, Joshua Sterlin, and Emille Boulot, as well as the anonymous reviewers for their thoughtful and incisive comments.
1. CD Stone, 'Should Trees Have Standing? – Toward Legal Rights for Natural Objects' (1972) 45 Southern California Law Review 450, 471.
2. ibid.

to denote nonhuman things that are not presently protected by rights (he notes that some nonhuman animals 'already have rights in some senses') such as 'forests, oceans, rivers' as well as 'the natural environment as a whole', to which he proposes extending rights.[3] We use the term 'object' here to indicate the conventional denial of subjectivity to such things. Stone implies that through a kind of metaphorical speech, other such objects may also communicate with humans, through the generation of what we call *eco-feedback* – observational data concerning nonhuman entities or systems that allow humans to make assessments about unmet needs or unwelcome disturbances that adversely affect the health of the object or objects in question. We conceptualize eco-feedback as a communicative mechanism through which legal and political ontologies can situate humanity within (rather than as teleologically separated from) what Fritjof Capra refers to as the 'web of life' – a complex system of interrelated and codependent forms of life.[4] Many Indigenous ontologies also situate humans within nature rather than outside of it, and avoid the Lorax problem[5] through guardianship models that accord legal recognition to nonhuman agents as cooperative partners in sustaining the web of life. Such a legal ontology is what Aaron Mills describes as a 'lifeworld' legal system, which centers freedom on the interdependence of living beings (or earthways) rather than on liberal notions of individual sovereignty.[6] Rather than re-invent such an ontology we seek to broaden the ontological reach of existing liberal legal theories that cannot otherwise capture the communicative and agentic capacity of nonhuman nature – and that have historically contributed to the silencing and exploitation of nonhuman nature. With this theoretical framing, we suggest, comes the obligation to foster greater sensitivities to nonhuman forms of communication in an era of ecological crisis.

From the provision of eco-feedback, humans can make some reliable inferences about the needs or interests of some kinds of natural objects. Our lawn needs watering; the forest in the midst of another prolonged drought also needs water, as evidenced by the proliferation of dead trees or the ubiquity of wildfire smoke throughout an increasingly severe, long-lasting, and ecologically unsustainable fire season. It does not require any special expertise for humans to apprehend the meaning of the eco-feedback that we receive in such cases; it is 'immediately obvious' to human senses when these objects are disturbed or neglected in a harmful way – and, assuming that citizens of the polis, and the measurements and discourses produced by science, are able to cultivate a greater receptivity to nonhuman nature in an exclusionary and hierarchical liberal paradigm, such sensitivity can expand beyond immediate sensory encounter. Faced by the quotidian example of the lawn, we could simply respond to this expression of needs ourselves by watering it (obviously, the irrigation of entire forests is another matter). However, if we require the cooperation or assistance of others in meeting such needs on a broader scale and averting future harms, we can *represent* those natural objects by speaking for them and for other

---

3. ibid 456.
4. F Capra, *The Web of Life: A New Scientific Understanding of Living Systems* (Anchor Books, New York NY 1996).
5. We expand further on our treatment of the Lorax problem, drawn from the classic Dr Seuss tale, further in this paper. In brief, the Lorax problem calls into question whether human agents are capable of 'hearing' the feedback of non-human nature, either due to an internal lack of receptivity or externally imposed deafness.
6. A Mills, 'The Lifeworlds of Law: On Revitalizing Indigenous Legal Orders Today' (2016) 61/4 McGill Law Journal 847, 864.

nonhuman collectives, and serve as their guardians in political and legal institutions which would otherwise be deaf to the nonhuman world. Protection of natural objects through 'rights beyond the human' requires such representation as part of a response to eco-feedback, where advocates might speak for nonhuman interdependent collectives in court, identifying their interests as well as any offending human actions that harm the flourishing of ecosystems and thus violate their rights. Stone's argument for extending legal standing to natural objects such as trees proposes a species of such a guardianship model, by which advocates such as the Sierra Club, whose challenge to a proposed ski resort in Sequoia National forest prompted Stone's paper, are authorized to speak for the trees.[7]

Extension of legal standing to natural objects such as trees or forests would thus allow guardians to speak *for* them, should some proposed action threaten those objects with harm. As former US Supreme Court Justice Douglas put it in his famous dissent in *Sierra Club v Morton* (1972), such an approach would grant legal recognition to natural objects or systems as plaintiffs (a status that connotes the applicability of protections from legal rights[8]). *Sierra Club v Morton* (1972), Justice Douglas suggested in his dissent, could instead be *Mineral King v Morton*, with the land itself challenging the Interior Secretary's actions (assisted by its legal guardian, of course, but on behalf of its own interests rather than those of the guardian). In doing so, the law would view the forest as having interests of its own, protected by legal rights, with courts available to remedy threats of injury to those interests, rather than conceiving of the injury as being one to humans exclusively: 'Those inarticulate members of the ecological group cannot speak', Justice Douglas writes, 'But those people who have so frequented the place as to know its values and wonders will be able to speak for the entire ecological community'.[9]

This kind of guardian role had been popularized by the publication of Dr Seuss' book *The Lorax* in June 1971, six months prior to the oral arguments of *Sierra Club v Morton*. In the popular children's story, the eponymous character pops up out of the stump of a fallen Truffula tree and demands that the antagonist (the Once-ler) stop cutting the trees down. The Lorax 'speaks for the trees, for the trees have no tongues', establishing himself as the guardian not just of the trees but of the entire Truffula forest ecosystem including Bar-ba-loots, Swamee-swans, and Humming-fish, all of which depend on the trees for their well-being. This focus on a keystone species, and/or an encompassing natural system, is also echoed in Douglas' dissent, where the river is 'the living symbol of all the life it sustains or nourishes' and 'as plaintiff speaks for the ecological unit of life that is part of it'.[10] Speaking for all of these things at once by speaking for trees, the Lorax acts as guardian of this complex natural system, listening to it and serving as its representative on the basis of his ability to discern the forest's interests, an ability not possessed by the Once-ler until after the damage from his ecological exploitation has become overwhelmingly apparent. We borrow the title of this article from this story, along with a name for the family of objections it raises, in order to emphasize the mix of listening to and speaking for nonhuman nature that guardianship involves.

The guardianship role that Stone proposes offers one model for 'law beyond the human' approaches to challenging anthropocentric conceptions and applications of

---

7. Stone (n 1) 468–9.
8. *Sierra Club v Morton* 405 U.S. 727 (1972).
9. ibid 752.
10. ibid 743.

rights, approaches which inquire into 'our moral relations to other beings, natural and man-made' and ultimately 'challenge ... the central role that the human/nonhuman boundary currently plays in rights law'.[11] By extending legal standing to natural objects, attaching legal personhood to nonhuman things such as rivers or mountains, or otherwise seeking to protect nonhumans through legal or constitutional rights, the guardianship model promises to enlist law on behalf of the more-than-human world, allowing guardians to speak for the interests of nonhuman others in court. In so doing, the approach establishes and/or strengthens legal rights against harm for other beings as well as for places and systems, and generates an enhanced moral status by connoting that such objects are worthy of protection so long as we can establish a link between their interests and the human actions that impair them.

Stone's extension of legal paradigms to the nonhuman simultaneously relies on the cultivation of human sensibilities in order to recognize and respond to eco-feedback, as well as on the capacity of natural objects to communicate their interests to human guardians. Whether in the readily observable forms of eco-feedback of the kind that Stone suggests or through more complex forms of feedback discernible only to scientific experts through data collection using sensitive instruments over long time scales,[12] these legal guardianship models have attracted criticism for a related set of objections that we term the *Lorax problem*. The Lorax problem, which we examine below, is founded upon a skepticism concerning either the capacity of nature to speak or the human ability to hear and understand its message. Others go further, denying that such objects have interests at all, but we leave these objections aside to focus on communicative difficulties. At its core, the Lorax problem doubts that any human guardian really can 'speak for the trees' and validly or legitimately represent the natural principals for which such guardians act as agent and advocate. With its focus on the legal protection of nonhumans through rights (or on political advocacy through other forms of representation), the guardianship model is vulnerable to charges that it anthropomorphizes the nonhuman world by extending a liberal legal paradigm that emphasizes stewardship over nature rather than harmonization with it, such that it can neither legitimately represent nor effectively protect the natural world.[13] In so doing, it is further argued, this approach also reinforces human/nonhuman binaries rather than undermining them, drawing as it does on notions of agency and responsibility rooted in human exceptionalism.[14]

As many contemporary environmental philosophers and legal scholars have noted, the Western philosophical tradition has often relegated nature to a wholly separate ontological domain from that of the human, with corresponding differences of moral and legal status that are implied in the subject/object distinction.[15] Both the liberal and the Marxist traditions (to varying degrees) frame nature as being a source of property and resources, to be appropriated and instrumentalized for human use. This framework is deeply exclusionary, reifying the human/nonhuman binary, sanctioning

---

11. A Huneeus, 'Beyond the "Human" in Human Rights: The Universal Declaration at 70', *Scientific American*, 10 December 2018, online at <https://blogs.scientificamerican.com/voices/beyond-the-human-in-human-rights-the-universal-declaration-at-70/>.
12. M Hulme, *Why We Disagree about Climate Change* (Cambridge University Press, New York NY 2009) ch. 1.
13. S Jasanoff, 'A New Climate for Society' (2010) 27/2–3 Theory, Culture, & Society 233.
14. R Eckersley, *Environmentalism and Political Theory: Toward an Ecocentric Approach* (SUNY Press, Albany NY 1992).
15. V Plumwood, *Feminism and the Mastery of Nature* (Routledge, New York NY 1993).

human exceptionalism, and limiting the reach and efficacy of legal institutions to recognize nature as anything but an instrumental or exotic 'other' to humanity.[16] In this article, we draw on New Materialist scholarship that seeks to transcend this binary by conceptualizing vibrant materiality in order to illustrate the potential for nonhuman forms of agency, to conceptualize the signaling of vital materiality as a form of communication, and so to challenge this exclusionary human/nature binary. Following Dipesh Chakrabarty's characterization, we view nonhuman agency as subsuming humanity in the ecological web of life, even while humanity uniquely acts within and upon nature as a geological force.[17] Drawing on an ontology that conceptualizes humans as residing within a communicative environment constituted by interdependent and interacting material things and systems, we develop an alternative to the guardianship model (where humans reside beyond the encompassing and dynamic world of nonhuman nature while trying to be sensitive to its needs and protective of its interests).[18] We make this ontological move precisely in order to conceptualize a kind of speech as being central to an embedded form of stewardship and to establish legal protection as being integral to the proper functioning of such stewardship.

2 THE LORAX PROBLEM

Whether conceived of in terms of legal guardianship or of political representation, advocates for nonhuman nature rely upon the claim that they speak for, and on behalf of, natural objects or systems, which are presumed to have interests of their own. Such approaches attempt to reach beyond speaking for the merely human interests whereby nature is reduced to its instrumental value in serving those interests. Stone's proposal for extending legal standing would allow environmental groups to challenge actions that would degrade ecosystems by claiming that trees would be harmed by such actions, rather than having to show harm to human group members. Lawyers for groups such as the Sierra Club would speak for the trees, expressing the wants or needs of affected nonhumans and showing how human activities impair those. Such guardians for nature would translate the (metaphorical) speech of nature itself, rendering it intelligible to courts of law, but not altering or co-opting it. By granting legal standing in cases involving harm to nonhumans without requiring mediating claims about harm to human interests, the law would recognize the intrinsic value of nonhumans and generate the legal power to protect or to promote that value, as articulated by its guardians.

Stone anticipates an important objection to this Lorax function that later critics would seize upon and develop. According to this objection, legal guardians could be appointed to advocate for natural objects or for systems such as rivers or forests, but might not be able to accurately assess the needs of such objects and/or systems. 'Indeed', Stone writes, 'the very concept of "needs," it might be said, could be used here only in the most metaphorical way', at least insofar as they are to be understood in terms of goals or intentions (as human needs are), goals and intentions that natural

---

16. A Grear, 'Human Rights, Property, and the Search for "Worlds Other"' (2012) 3/2 JHRE 173.
17. D Chakrabarty, 'Humanities in the Anthropocene: The Crisis of an Enduring Kantian Fable' (2016) 47/2–3 New Literary History 377.
18. C Gianolla, 'Human Rights and Nature: Intercultural Perspectives and Intentional Aspirations' (2013) 4/1 JHRE 58.

objects like trees or forests putatively lack.[19] As Stone admits, in discerning and articulating the needs of such an object, its guardian would inevitably conflate such needs with their own, anthropomorphizing the object in order to render it familiar enough for the empathetic transfer of neediness and/or the projection of human needs or narratives upon it.[20] Unless prepared to criminalize *arborcide*[21] as an offense against *any* tree, the claim that some grove of trees needs to remain standing in the part of Mineral King slated for development but not in an adjacent parcel slated for a timber sale, would likely owe its justification to the aesthetic or recreational preferences of human users rather than to the needs of the trees themselves. In this case, suspicion that guardians were less interested in advocating for the needs of trees than in protecting specific parcels of forested land with high commercial or aesthetic value would be well founded. Likewise, critics could then claim that guardians were selecting natural objects for protection based on their perceived worth to humanity, rather than on the basis of the objects' need.

This dimension of the Lorax problem could therefore be considered to be a matter of inauthentic translation by legal guardians, which Steve Vogel casts in terms of the distinction between a translator and a ventriloquist. Translators, he writes, 'are those who speak for another speaker, saying the words that [the] speaker is for whatever reason unable to speak herself', and providing an accurate translation of the original speech, while the ventriloquist 'is someone who speaks for something that is not a speaker, projecting her own words onto a mute object and then pretending that it is that object [which] is speaking and not herself'.[22] As we discuss later, Vogel's distinction between the translator and ventriloquist does not consider the difficulty in translating nonhuman communication in a wholly objective manner that retains the veracity and intent of the speaker. However, this initial interrogation still raises significant concerns for Stone's guardianship model. Insofar as the guardian projects her own interests onto those of a tree or a forest, identifying only those trees valued by the guardian as being in need of protection, the guardian acts as a ventriloquist, or as an inauthentic guardian. Her claims to 'speak for the trees' would be disingenuous, since human rather than arboreal interests would motivate and delimit the protective advocacy, at least insofar as the guardian was conscious of this ventriloquism. Such advocacy could be more accurately understood in terms of speaking for a group of humans that prefers the area to remain undeveloped (a perfectly respectable objective, if attributed to the needs of trees rather than humans), but vesting this preference in a forest, or a particular group of trees or a tree, in order to avoid this appearance.

Vogel does not dispute that trees have needs of their own or that these are important and in need of protection from human actions, but he doubts that trees can speak to humans in the way claimed by those advocating for the guardianship model. He argues that humans cannot represent the interests of nonhuman nature unless those interests can be communicated directly, or at the very least, authentically translated. As he writes, 'something can only be represented if it is in principle possible for it not to be represented but rather to speak for itself', and since nonhuman nature cannot speak for itself in the relevant sense there can be no valid translation and thus no

19. Stone (n 1) 471.
20. ibid 498.
21. J Mooney, 'Arborcide, He Wrote', *The New York Times*, 4 April 2008, online at <https://cityroom.blogs.nytimes.com/2008/04/04/arborcide-he-wrote/>.
22. S Vogel, 'The Silence of Nature' (2006) 15/2 Environmental Values 145.

legitimate representation of its interests.[23] Vogel's view of representation as requiring dialogue between principal and agent would rule out other proposed forms of representation of absent or mute others, including that of future generations of humans, given its positivist reliance upon in-principle verification of fidelity. Those claiming to be translators speaking for nature are nothing but ventriloquists, Vogel suggests, feigning their ability to hear metaphorical voices from beyond their own consciousness and interests. Nonetheless, such speakers vest such anthropogenic speech in nonhuman others in order to conceal and/or amplify human interests: nature as plaintiff becomes the ventriloquist's dummy through which guardians such as the Sierra Club project their voices through sleight of hand.[24] Whether or not would-be guardians are aware of this projection of their own understandings and interests onto nonhuman others (as real ventriloquists certainly are), representation through the model of translation requires at least the possibility of original speech (not metaphorical speech) and Vogel doubts that nature has or exercises this capacity for original speech. Like Nagel's bat, nature might have interests that defy translation of empathetic transfer to human listeners,[25] and if political subjects were to accept the deceit of the ventriloquist as being a genuine translation, Vogel argues, the ventriloquist would tacitly be granted a potentially dangerous power that other representatives lack: 'the power to make truth-claims without the responsibility to provide first-person justifications for them'.[26]

Stone underestimates the objection upon raising it: he compares the 'guardian-attorney for a smog-endangered stand of pines' with the legal representative for a corporate board (also a nonhuman object that has been granted legal standing).[27] Stone claims that the wants or needs of the corporation are 'far less verifiable' and 'far more metaphysical'[28] than those of the pine forest, and yet the legal guardians of corporations make claims about such wants and needs every day without throwing the law into chaos. Denying legal guardians the ability to speak for one kind of nonhuman entity while allowing them to speak for another would be arbitrary, Stone suggests, especially if the wants and needs of nonhuman nature are more verifiable and less metaphysical than those of a corporation (a contention that Vogel would surely reject).[29] After all, Stone claims that his lawn speaks with less ambiguity than do other objects vested with legal guardianship and accorded legal standing: as long as corporations are granted legal standing (along with other rights associated with legal personhood) and their guardians are allowed to speak for the wants or needs of such entities, why not allow the same kind of guardianship to be applied to trees? Stone's reply to the Lorax problem of inauthentic translation is unpersuasive, however: ships and corporations are fundamentally different from forests and rivers. As human contrivances designed to advance specific kinds of human interests alone, the value of ships and corporations is wholly reducible to the human interests they serve. Guardians can speak for ships and/or for corporations without the pretense that either speaks for itself. This kind of guardianship involves a principal-agent relationship in which the corporation or ship (apart from its owners) is neither principal nor agent except by an expedient legal fiction that vests it with some human interests

---

23. ibid 165.
24. ibid 162–4.
25. T Nagel, 'What Is It Like to Be a Bat?' (1974) 83/4 The Philosophical Review 435.
26. Vogel (n 22) 164.
27. Stone (n 1) 471.
28. ibid.
29. ibid.

but not others.[30] Legal guardians for corporations and ships speak for the interests of a group of human persons that can express its interests if needed to (and occasionally does so), creating a check upon any tendency of guardians to misinterpret or misrepresent the needs of the nonhuman entity. Contrary to Stone's claim, the largely economic imperatives of the ship or corporation are certainly more verifiable, and perhaps also less metaphysical, than those of the river or forest. It is possible to know their 'wants' because these entities have been constructed specifically in order to advance those wants, which ultimately belong to human beings.

The corporation is a useful fiction for its owners (if often a pernicious one for society) because it feigns the existence of an autonomous entity that can allow assets to pass through to owners while shielding them from liability. The fiction of authentic translation of nature's voice aims in the opposite direction: attempting to attach greater liability to human actions (or those of their inhuman fictions), in the process potentially stemming the flow of profits from the extraction of natural resources such as trees.

Founding the fiction of such translation on the metaphysical status of the corporation (as Stone seems to do) would rest the legitimacy of guardianship advocacy upon the prior legal recognition of perhaps its greatest social and political adversary – the corporation. In the United States, the corporation now derives its excessive legal power to engage in protected acts of speech by the Supreme Court decision of *Citizens United v FEC* (2010). Indeed, the corporation's legal status and that of its spokespersons might be more accurately compared to a megaphone for amplifying calls for the exploitation of nature than to a ventriloquist's dummy.

Is Stone, then, also mistaken about his ability to discern his lawn's desire for water? While humans can and do attribute flourishing interests to plants such as grass, the reaction of which to drought conditions can express its failure to thrive, this is not the same as the blades of grass *wanting* to be green and springy (much less communicating this to their guardian when he neglects to water them) rather than to be dry and yellow or brown. For Stone's account, grass can only 'in the most metaphorical way' have an interest in remaining in a flush, well-irrigated condition, a presumed interest that looks suspiciously like a projection of human aesthetic preferences.[31] The popular preference for bright green lawns all year round requires extensive chemical treatment along with regular irrigation, which could hardly be described as being rooted in a desire for nature to flourish on its own. There is no coherent sense in which Stone's grass 'wants' to be maintained in this (or any other) condition, a point that makes his lawn a poor surrogate for the natural systems to which he proposes extending rights. Perhaps by wilting the grass is expressing its disdain for having been planted in an arid region such as southern California, where non-native plants such as bluegrass require extensive human intervention in order to survive, and the irrigation of which would be an affront to its more natural preference to wither and die rather than to persist in this most unnatural environment for it.[32]

Even where nonhuman interests are more readily ascertainable, as in the case of extensions of personhood to individual nonhuman animals that can express

---

30. D Ciepley, 'Beyond Public and Private: Toward a Political Theory of the Corporation' (2013) 107/1 Am Pol Sci Rev 139.
31. Stone (n 1) 471.
32. For example, see M Simmons and others, 'The Performance of Native and Non-Native Turfgrass Monocultures and Native Turfgrass Polycultures: An Ecological Approach to Sustainable Lawns' (2011) 37/8 Ecological Engineering 1095.

emotions and communicate desires, the well-being interests of collectives or whole systems remain opaque. Understandings of such collectives or systems also unhelpfully draw upon extensions of legal instruments designed for far more discrete, individual entities. The parched lawn might inhibit the interests of some nonhuman creatures that enjoy its more lush condition, but the 'interest theory' of individual rights upon which such analyses are premised cannot account for the forest as a bearer of rights or as a subject warranting moral considerability without importing individualistic reductivism.[33]

A related aspect of the Lorax problem arises in proposals for guardians to provide political rather than legal representation for nonhuman nature, advocating for nonhuman interests in democratic fora rather than in court. Mark Brown (drawing on Michael Saward's account of representation[34]) casts Vogel's translator in terms of a 'correspondence view of representation' through which the role of the representative is conceived in terms of 'the unidirectional transmission of information from nonhuman nature to its representatives'.[35] Such a role, he argues, 'involves first discerning and then promoting nature's interests in a manner that is either morally authentic or scientifically objective', requirements implicit in claims that guardians can speak for the trees.[36] But representations of nonhuman nature 'are always partly constituted by cultural values, social interests, and political decisions' rather than adhering to the correspondence view, Brown argues, casting doubt upon the authenticity or objectivity of such representations. Moreover, he cautions, when guardians or representatives of nonhuman nature adopt this correspondence view 'they are likely to become either moral or scientific technocrats who attempt to shut down democratic debate with claims to speak for nature's objective interests'.[37] As such, the guardian of nonhuman nature lacks democratic legitimacy (an analogue to Vogel's concerns about moral legitimacy described above) when 'speaking for the trees' in a political rather than a legal context, at least while posing as a delegate rather than as a trustee of the more-than-human world.[38]

All this combines to make the guardianship model a perilous foundation for the extension of rights to nonhuman nature. Rights against harm require legal guardianship to access relevant legal powers, but the tendency toward ventriloquism rather than authentic translation of nature's voice invites skepticism about how robust a determination of nonhuman nature's wants or needs (as opposed to the wants and needs of guardians) such guardianship can provide. Insofar as 'law beyond the human' objectives include the challenge to human/nonhuman binaries, the solicitation of nonhuman plaintiffs to be used for the purpose of advancing one set of human preferences against another set again risks relegating the nonhuman to an instrumental status, this time in terms of being used for legal convenience. Since liberal frameworks of legal rights apply to all members of a kind, their selective use to protect some but not other trees or forests smacks of further instrumentalism, reflecting differentiation according to human rather than nonhuman priorities. The extension of such rights to trees but not to edible plants (an approach which parallels the extension of rights to wild animals

---

33. JP Manalich R, 'Animalhood, Interests, and Rights' (2020) 11/2 JHRE 156.
34. M Saward, 'Representation' in A Dobson and R Eckersley (eds), *Political Theory and the Ecological Challenge* (Cambridge University Press, Cambridge 2006) 183–99.
35. MB Brown, 'Speaking for Nature: Hobbes, Latour, and the Democratic Representation of Nonhumans' (2018) 31/1 Science & Technology Studies 31, 33.
36. ibid.
37. ibid.
38. ibid 35.

but not to those used in agriculture) reflects human regard for, or use of, the nonhuman entity rather than reflecting its status as an intrinsically valuable entity in its own right.

Some of the objections raised by the Lorax problem might be attenuated by the extension of legal rights to whole systems rather than to individual entities of a single species within a limited space. Insofar as rights are grounded in protecting dignity rather than prioritizing the individual over the group (as is also suggested by collective rights such as those to culture or to territory), the extension of rights to natural systems could help to dislodge the ontological attachment of dignity to discrete individual entities, and allow for its recognition in certain kinds of collectives.[39] Christine Winter, for example, defends the extension of legal personhood of New Zealand's Mt. Taranaki in terms of a conception of 'Relational Functioning Dignity' through which living things as well as inanimate objects are 'interlinked in ecosystems' that 'strive to function and fulfil their (type-specific) potential' and so possess a dignity that can be advanced or frustrated by human actions.[40] As US Supreme Court Justice Douglas asserts in *Sierra Club v Morton*, the river is 'the living symbol of all the life it sustains or nourishes' and 'as plaintiff speaks for the ecological unit of life that is part of it'.[41] Granting legal rights or legal personhood to whole systems rather than to their constituent parts may help to reduce concern about arbitrariness in application, even if it does not ameliorate concerns about objectivity, translation or legitimacy of representation. Nevertheless, this kind of ontological shift away from framing humanity as a loose collective of sovereign individuals who act as stewards of nature, toward humanity as being embedded within an interdependent nature with distributed agency of the kind implied by Winter's approach invites consideration of New Materialist foundations for, rather than the guardianship model for, rights beyond the human. And, as we shall also argue, the shift in focus from rights to flourishing or against harm, to rights of speech for nonhuman nature, might help to identify constructive pathways toward enlisting legal rights in the service of more harmonious human-nonhuman relationships without encountering the objections associated with the Lorax problem.

We now turn to consider some key limitations of the guardianship model as well as to an exploration of such an alternative foundation.

3 SOME LIMITATIONS OF THE GUARDIANSHIP MODEL

We begin with a few cursory observations about the limitations of the guardianship approach before turning to its alternative.

Stone's guardianship model requires legal representation of nonhumans, but we note a critical omission in his work: it does not consider the possible need for nonhumans' political representation. Those calling for the political enfranchisement of nonhumans, their inclusion into the *demos* or their representation in governance institutions,[42] draw

---

39. I Watson, 'Aboriginal Relationships to the Natural World: Colonial "Protection" of Human Rights and the Environment' (2018) 9/2 JHRE 119.
40. CJ Winter, 'Decolonising Dignity for Inclusive Democracy' (2019) 28 Environmental Values 9, 17.
41. 405 U.S. 727 (1972), 743.
42. For example, see A Domoso, 'New Politics: Sovereignty, Representation, and the Nonhuman' in L Valera and J Castilla (eds), *Global Changes: Ethics, Politics and Environment in the Contemporary Technological World (46 Ethics of Science and Technology Assessment* (Springer, New York NY 2020) <https://doi.org/10.1007/978-3-030-29443-4_5>.

upon similar concepts, but typically eschew the rights-based approach that the 'rights beyond the human' project embraces. Under the liberal iterations of guardianship model, nonhuman nature is granted a new legal status, but not necessarily a new moral one, insofar as the entities vested with rights are still treated as objects rather than as subjects. In the model of guardianship that Stone developed to broaden the standing rule for the purpose of enabling the Sierra Club to meet justiciability requirements in its legal challenge, the objective can be recast as seeking to elevate one kind of human interest or use of nature (its preservation in a minimally transformed condition) against another (its extractive use). This is essentially an extensionist approach, residing within legal reformism, rather than presenting a more radical challenge to what many see as the roots of the ongoing domination of nature. Thus, while extensionism is not insignificant in its potential for increasing legal protections against the exploitation of nonhuman nature, the law's treatment of nature as inert matter subject to regimes of property rights (and as possessing no value other than that reflected in human willingness to pay for it) remains firmly locked within human exceptionalism. Extensionist arguments[43] (such as that offered by Stone and reflected in Justice Douglas' dissent), which break the human/nonhuman binary (with respect to ships and corporations), nevertheless underestimate the importance to law of a different binary. Ships and corporations cannot have inherent worth, but only instrumental and largely economic value. Ships convey cargo, with the law vesting property rights in the means of conveyance that enables economic globalization. To the extent that ships speak to us (eg with their mechanical and navigation systems), they only communicate about how humans and corporations can more efficiently move persons and goods around, an aim that reflects the interests of humans rather than those of the ship. Ships exercise no independent agency – where inattentive pilots collide with icebergs or rupture oil tanks this is usually viewed as being pilot error rather than the result of another agent with conflicting wants or needs – and we do not ordinarily conceive of ships as having goals or intentions that do not mirror those of their owners. The case for extending rights to nonhuman nature is thus more compelling when building upon the extension of human rights, rather than the assumed personhood/rights of human-crafted objects.

Ships – like corporations – have been granted legal standing because they represent human property interests, with this status enhancing the property rights of some humans while also allowing them to more effectively engage in capitalist accumulation. Laws that protect things as property are not necessarily ennobling: slaves were also protected as the property of their masters while being denied the moral status or legal rights of persons. That the law had already transcended the human/nonhuman divide entails neither that such boundary crossing would challenge that binary, nor that the new legally recognized entity would be invested with some new moral status befitting any rejection of differences between humans and nonhumans as being morally arbitrary. While the vesting of corporations with legal personhood allows for the metaphorical extension to them of speech rights and kinds of autonomy implying independent agency, that speech has mainly been used to amplify the voices of capital, while that autonomy has been deployed to shield the corporation's shareholders from financial and legal liability. Insofar as the guardianship model invites law to treat nonhuman nature as it treats ships or corporations, the emancipatory or transformative potential of guardianship is likely to be limited.

---

43. See also GL Comstock, 'An Extensionist Environmental Ethic' (1995) 4 Biodiversity & Conservation 827.

Stone's proposal might, however, be more radical than he claims, but in a different way. He seeks to limit property rights and to challenge administrative procedures that privilege them by asserting a more capacious value for the environment, and by demanding that the law should recognize and protect non-consumptive uses of nature over extractive ones. His proposal gives meaning and substance to the idea of public lands, where management practices had systematically favored some uses and users over others rather than practicing stewardship of the kind necessary to (as directed by the Wilderness Act of 1964) 'secure for the American people of present and future generations the benefits of an enduring resource of wilderness'.[44] However, this approach falls short in that it does not require a new ontology of the human, and nor does it challenge prevailing conceptions of agency or responsibility. It does not attempt to challenge the binary of the human vs. the nonhuman (despite law's existing crossing of that boundary), but rather endorses a greater ecological sensitivity while maintaining a human orientation toward maintaining stewardship over nonhuman nature. In this sense, Stone's model owes more to John Muir's preservationist reply to utilitarian resource managers like Gifford Pinchot than it does to Aldo Leopold's rejection of human exceptionalism and of instrumental regard for nonhuman nature in *A Sand County Almanac*.[45]

Stone's guardianship model also relies on a limited and tendentious form of metaphorical speech. As noted above, guardians speak for nature because nature speaks first to the guardian, communicating its wants or needs in a direct and readily comprehensible manner: his grass tells him that it needs water by changing color and texture, and the trees tell the Sierra Club that they would prefer to remain as living organisms rather than be transformed into lumber and wood products to make way for a ski resort. This speech is communicative but is not conceived as a kind of action. The approach relies entirely upon the guardian's agency in intervening to assist nature to realize its aims. The message, moreover, which requires no expertise to receive or to interpret, is perceived through the senses in a manner that requires no instruments or models to understand it, and usually amounts to one of two related imperatives: *protect me against other humans* or *leave me alone*. Accordingly, the medium and the message are both characterized as being straightforward and accessible, yet worry persists concerning how guardians might misinterpret it themselves (eg by anthropomorphizing) and/or misrepresent it to others.

This model of listening to nature works better for some problems than others. Impacts that can be apprehended by the senses (such as dying grass) or that can be straightforwardly grasped as injurious (eg plans to fell trees and to build roads into wilderness areas) fit it, because the harm is direct and straightforward and the party responsible for it readily identifiable. However, other kinds of threats are not so easily detectable, nor so easy to assign. Others might also have noticed the strange silence where birds formerly sang, but only Rachel Carson connected this 'silent spring' to the proliferation of toxic chemicals.[46] The kind of speech that Stone's guardianship model relies upon might be attuned to the death of a single bird but would not necessarily be able to apprehend the collapse of an entire species. Humans have little trouble hearing how weather events may 'speak', but cannot necessarily 'hear' when the

---

44. 16 U.S.C. 1131–6, 78 Statute 890, Public Law 88-577, Section 2(a).
45. A Leopold, *A Sand County Almanac: And Sketches Here and There* (Oxford University Press, New York NY 1949).
46. R Carson, *Silent Spring* (Houghton Mifflin Harcourt, Boston MA 1962).

climate changes. The kinds of metaphorical speech that are now predicting massive biodiversity loss or dangerous climatic changes speak to us only through experts that need models and instruments to properly hear it. Inability to hear such communication, and a related tendency to allow its willful suppression or distortion, inhibits the original presentation of nonhuman interests and so frustrates the human ability to understand and to respond to eco-feedback about the health of the planet and its systems. Models of representation for nonhuman nature must be able to grasp this more complex and urgent communication by the complex systems in which humans are embedded if humans are to live sustainably in them.

Whether the speech of more complex systems such as the global climate or biotic pyramid is more or less subject to the objections of the Lorax problem than that of the simple speech of the guardian model is another matter. Worries about the conservation biologist or climate scientist accurately translating the speech that their unique expertise allows them to hear (rather than performing ventriloquism in their communication of scientific findings) persist. This raises concerns about empowering a democratically illegitimate form of technocracy whereby guardians of the climate or of biodiversity are vested with coercive rather than merely discursive powers. The specialized knowledge of experts to hear and understand the speech of complex ecosystems adds another challenge for the guardianship model insofar as the roles of scientific expert and policy advocate are combined in a single guardian (raising fears about the politicization of science) in the case of politically engaged scientists, but also in cases that involve a division of labor between scientist and advocate, producing another communicative gap where translation failure and ventriloquism can potentially arise. Even so, while expert knowledge is not meant to be the sole authoritative source for conceptualizing alternative human/nature relations, when such knowledge is incorporated into diverse ontological approaches to environmental politics, it can illuminate the scale of the climate crisis and its temporal effects on various ecosystems that current legal paradigms fail to take into account.

Those who are skeptical about trees having wants or needs are likely to be even more unconvinced in consideration of complex systems such as the global climate system, which resists the sort of teleological classification of the kind that Aristotle attached to acorns and oak trees.[47] Human flourishing very much depends on whether and how the climate system stabilizes, as it has in the past and will again in the post-human future. However, the climate system does not itself have wants or needs that can be defined by its flourishing. On the other hand, whole ecosystems might manifest a compelling flourishing-based interest in maintaining a complex biotic pyramid that makes such systems more resilient against disturbances. This possibility is well captured by Leopold's imperative in his land ethic to maintain an ecosystem's stability, integrity, and beauty.[48] As Dipesh Chakrabarty notes, the history of the natural world and the history of humanity have long been treated as separate by Western teleology, and this separation is reflected in the colonial political and economic

---

47. Aristotle, *Metaphysics, Books Gamma, Delta and Epsilon*, translated with notes by Christopher Kirwan (Oxford University Press, New York NY 1971), 1049b14–19. While Aristotle acknowledges the interconnectivity between the acorn and the oak in that the former has the potential to become the latter, his concern is with the oak as a self-sustained final cause. The connectivity between the oak and the ecosystem that sustains it is not recognized in Aristotle's teleology.
48. Leopold (n 45).

institutions that have exacerbated the climate crisis.[49] If the legal institutions Stone entrusts as guardians are built on this teleological separation, they may serve to exacerbate the exploitation of nonhuman nature rather than preserve its sustainable flourishing.

These limitations, in combination with objections raised against the guardianship model by the Lorax problem, prompt our consideration of an alternative framework for theorizing law beyond the human.

4 NEW MATERIALIST APPROACHES

Articulated most clearly in 'New Materialist' ontologies[50] and here drawn primarily from Jane Bennett's recent work on vital materialism, this alternative framework challenges the guardianship model's restriction of subjectivity to the human.[51] It does so by extending agency from atomistic human individuals to 'swarms' or conglomerates of human and nonhuman actants, and dismisses the reductive narratives of efficient causality through which single human agents are viewed as linked to environmental harm in direct and discrete chains of cause and effect, action and outcome. In essence, the New Materialist perspective supplements Stone's call for more vigilant stewardship of nonhuman nature with a view that attributes a kind of agency and imputes a form of subjectivity to collectivities that include nonhuman (and even non-living) elements. Given the New Materialist focus on complex causation, we also consider here the kinds of eco-feedback generated by complex systems – the metaphorical speech of which, to be 'heard', often requires expertise, specialized instruments and complex models rather than raw perception.[52]

Our inquiry concerns a search for alternative foundations, for 'law beyond the human', in order to support efforts to extend legal rights to nonhuman nature and to create space for the legal and/or political representation of nature's interests. A turn toward New Materialist ontology and toward accounts of 'distributed agency'[53] leads us, as we will argue, to view nature's speech as a form of action that connotes a kind of agency for its utterers. Whereas conventional accounts of agency relegate nonhuman nature to inert matter, vesting humans with the sole power to direct action and to shape ends, New Materialists view this human-centered account of action as being another artifact of human exceptionalism and the hubris that it encourages. This orientation, from a New Materialist perspective, overestimates

---

49. D Chakrabarty, 'Postcolonial Studies and the Challenge of Climate Change' (2012) 43/1 New Literary History 1, 10–11.
50. For a more explicitly political development of New Materialist ontology, see D Schlosberg and R Coles, 'The New Environmentalism of Everyday Life: Sustainability, Material Flows and Movements' (2016) 15/2 Contemporary Political Theory 160, or R Coles, *Visionary Pragmatism: Radical and Ecological Democracy in Neoliberal Times* (Duke University Press, Durham NC 2016).
51. J Bennett, *Vibrant Matter: A Political Ecology of Things* (Duke University Press, Durham NC 2006).
52. One example of such eco-feedback might be the 'Arctic blasts' that devastated the critical infrastructure of the American south in February 2021, and the complex relationship between the rapid ecological collapse of the Arctic zones and the resulting impacts on ocean currents that exacerbate such phenomena. Such metaphorical 'speech acts' require the vantage point of specialized measurement to assess, versus simply gazing at the ocean shore.
53. Bennett (n 51) x–ix.

the formative power of the human will upon the world and underestimates the generative powers of things and forces around us.

Bennett argues in the preface to her book *Vibrant Matter* that 'the philosophical project of naming where subjectivity begins and ends' has defined the human/nonhuman boundary and 'is too often bound up with fantasies of a human uniqueness in the eyes of God, of escape from materiality, or of mastery of nature'.[54] Insofar as agency is understood in terms of efficient causality or as the causal efficacy of the human will in directing action and/or producing outcomes, its account of how human actions shape the world is too narrow. Some discrete human actions may be able to be understood in this way, but 'if one extends the time frame of the action beyond that of even an instant, billiard-ball causality falters'[55] and so fails adequately to account for either the full origins of 'our' actions or the full determinants of their effects. Humans can be prompted to act by events external to our bodies or by the material within them: for example, Bennett notes on the first page of the preface that 'omega-3 fatty acids can alter human moods',[56] and human agency may be directed, constrained, or otherwise affected by entities beyond the human. Similarly, Samantha Frost casts humans as inherently 'biocultural creatures' that construct the political fiction of individual autonomy and exclusive subjectivity by denying the fluidity and porous reality of human embodiment.[57] Rejecting human-centered theories of action as ontologically impoverished, Bennett and Frost both defend an alternative conception of agency as a 'counter to human exceptionalism, to, that is, the human tendency to understate the degree to which people, animals, artifacts, technologies, and elemental forces share powers and operate in dissonant conjunction with each other'.[58]

Bennett and other New Materialists defend a conception of agency that is 'distributed across an ontologically heterogeneous field, rather than being a capacity localized in a human body or in a collective produced (only) by human efforts'.[59] Bennett casts nonhuman nature, and even inanimate human artifacts such as power lines or economic systems, as being a 'swarm of vitalities'[60] in which the agency of humans and nonhumans merge as generative sources of effects, and where the 'relationship between tendencies and outcomes' is 'imagined as more porous, tenuous, and thus indirect' than agency is conceived in the Kantian autonomy of the will that informs dominant conceptions of agency and responsibility.[61] Rather than denying subjectivity to nonhuman nature by virtue of its lack of human capacities for language, reason, or moral reflection, New Materialism allows for agency and subjectivity to be shared with nonhumans by attaching agency and subjectivity to the generative capacities of assemblages in which 'all forces and flows (materialities) are or can become lively, affective, and signaling'.[62]

Insofar as vital materialities signal and act as they interact within the swarm (climate change, for example, signals anthropogenic interference in the climate system

---

54. ibid.
55. ibid 33.
56. ibid vii, 41.
57. S Frost, *Biocultural Creatures: Toward a New Theory of the Human* (Duke University Press, Durham NC 2016).
58. Bennett (n 51) 34.
59. ibid 23.
60. ibid 32.
61. ibid 36.
62. ibid 117.

and also acts on human systems that depend on climatic stability), their metaphorical speech is best regarded as being a form of action with consequences for all rather than as the unidirectional transmission of the needs or wants of an Other that humans can choose to ignore with impunity. Eco-feedback originates in interactions with non-human others where combined actions yield a kind of metaphorical speech that in turn presages further actions and interactions. The climate system provides feedback through the droughts, storms, floods, and wildfires that humans cannot help but notice. Nevertheless, climate scientists do not 'speak for the trees' in the sense of articulating a set of interests of nonhuman nature that conflicts with human interests or are harmed by human actions: the climate system does not have desires or intentions and is not in need of an effective guardian to represent any such desires/intentions. In the same way, entomologists warning about the collapse of pollinator colonies do not, in our view, 'speak for the bees' in advocating for a species with interests foreign to human interests but rather remind humans of our vital dependence upon pollinators in maintaining a livable world for all. Moving away from the guardianship model's suppositions and conceiving of nonhuman agency and the role of eco-feedback in this way focuses attention upon listening more than upon speaking.

This listening is a form of active listening in which 'hearing' does not necessarily follow, and in relation to which properly reacting is another matter still.[63] This approach treats unimpeded human receptivity to eco-feedback as being a democratic imperative. It thus treats the silencing of such eco-feedback as an offense against ecological democracy. This ontological perspective does not frame listening as a task that positions humans as exogenous stewards over nature – as is the case in Stone's liberal conception of the guardianship model – but recognizes humanity's connectivity to and dependency upon the web of life. Within this framework of beautifully diverse forms of life, eco-feedback operates as a mode of communication, connecting nodes within this web in a manner similar to that of the network of mycorrhizal fungi that connect trees within the 'wood wide web'.[64]

Bennett suggests that the 'ethical task' for the vital materialist is to 'cultivate the ability to discern nonhuman vitality, to become perceptually open to it'.[65] Listening to nonhuman nature rather than speaking for it thus becomes the more critically important role, even if skilled listeners are needed to translate those signals for non-specialists when receiving the eco-feedback of complex systems. Viewing the human relationship between humans and nonhuman nature in a more horizontal rather than vertical or hierarchical way – or as Leopold put it, viewing ourselves as plain citizens rather than as external to or as conquerors of the biotic community – likewise prioritizes listening over speaking. As Bennett writes, to recognize that humans share worlds and exchange properties with nonhumans 'is to begin to see the relationship between persons and other materialities more horizontally' and thus 'to take a step toward a more ecological sensibility'.[66]

The ongoing COVID-19 pandemic further illustrates this interdependence of human and nonhuman in a shared world of distributed agency and vital materiality.

---

63. S Choat, 'Science, Agency and Ontology: A Historical-Materialist Response to New Materialism' (2018) 66/4 Political Studies 1027–42.
64. R Macfarlane, 'The Secrets of the Wood Wide Web', *The New Yorker*, 7 September 2016, online at <https://www.newyorker.com/tech/annals-of-technology/the-secrets-of-the-wood-wide-web>.
65. Bennett (n 51) 14.
66. ibid 10.

While it is not clear, as yet, what the origins of the COVID-19 pandemic are, it is probable that as human incursions into natural, wild spaces become more common, the rate of zoological to human transmission of diseases will likely increase as viruses adapt to and interact with the cellular structure of humans.[67] There is also likely to be an increase in new (or rather, old) infectious bacterial outbreaks in humans as sheet ice and permafrost continue to melt, releasing ancient lifeforms, such melting being the response of the ice to human activities that release greenhouse gasses into the atmosphere.[68] While these are overwhelmingly anthropogenic problems, they should not be regarded anthropocentrically, as if involving only humans in their causes and/or impacts. Insofar as pandemics or climate change actively resist human attempts to constrain outcomes, they act with a kind of agency or generative force. Here, viral and bacterial actants 'speak' for nature in (non-intentional) response to harmful human intervention, as floods and wildfires 'speak' about and for anthropogenic climate change. While these forces do not require guardians to represent their interests, as the current pandemic demonstrates there can be high costs for failing to heed these warning signals.

5 CONCLUSION – SPEECH RIGHTS AND THE SILENCING OF NATURE

If the alternative ontology of New Materialism offers a unique foundation for rights of nature, it cannot be, we suggest, in the form of an argument for the extension of rights to legal recognition or against harm to new kinds of things. Stone's guardianship approach already adopts this kind of mere extensionism, and faces the challenges of the Lorax problem. A 'New Materialist' extensionism would face some related challenges. While Stone's approach extends agency beyond the human, it does not do so in a way that would be pertinent to the application of conventional negative rights, such as those against harm or interference. And nor would nonhuman subjectivity bring new subjects under legal jurisdictions as bearers of correlative duties – responsibility for violations of the rights of nature would still be confined to human agents (individual or collective), at least insofar as courts could be used as instruments of environmental protection.

If anything, the New Materialist view of distributed agency could diminish human responsibility for environmental harm by sharing human causal agency with a host of other things that the law is powerless to sanction or to direct.[69] Neither does distributed agency evade the critique from the Lorax problem about the potential for erroneous or otherwise inauthentic translation by those tasked with speaking for nature, which someone must do if nature is to be represented as a plaintiff in court. Additionally, New Materialism's more complex view of causality would seem to heighten worries about the legitimacy or accountability of guardians too, with fewer listeners able to discern and translate the signals from the eco-feedback of complex systems.

---

67. United Nations Environment Programme and International Livestock Research Institute, *Preventing the Next Pandemic: Zoonotic Diseases and How to Break the Chain of Transmission* (UNEP, Nairobi 2020).
68. AJ Parkinson and B Evengard, 'Climate Change, its Impact on Human Health in the Arctic and the Public Health Response to Threats of Emerging Infectious Diseases' (2009) 2/1 Global Health Action 2075.
69. SR Krause, 'Bodies in Action: Corporeal Agency and Democratic Politics' (2011) 29/3 Political Theory 299.

However, the New Materialist framework supplies something that Stone's guardianship model does not – a case for the protection of speech rights for nature. Moreover, it does so through a conception of speech as being vital to a more inclusive and egalitarian democracy attuned to the embeddedness of the *polis* within the interdependent ecological web of life that the planet's limited capacity simultaneously sustains and constrains. As Robyn Eckersley notes of the affinities between New Materialist ontology and a revitalized '2.0' version of ecological democracy, New Materialism's 'relational ontology and inclusive ethics' are reminiscent of the first wave of ecocentric critiques of liberal democracy, and so continue to challenge the human/nature binary intrinsic to existing guardianship conceptions and to 'underscore human embodiment and embeddedness in ecological relations'. However, the New Materialist variant has 'brought technology into the human-nonhuman ontological entanglement'. And, according to Eckersley, shares an affinity for deliberative forms of democracy while seeking to 'tilt deliberative democracy away from institutions or larger deliberative systems and towards the building of local publics in civil society'.[70] We seek to emphasize the role of communication between humans and nonhumans as being vital to the inclusion of materiality within such a democracy, and thus we cast interference in processes of communication through eco-feedback as undermining its reflexive potential.

In Stone's model, nature could only be silenced by silencing all the users of (or participants in) some natural system, but eco-feedback is not dependent on the presence of human listeners, even though the representation of such eco-feedback is. Silencing all human users of systems such as the global climate is not possible, but nature can be silenced by reducing eco-feedback sensing by defunding the instruments and monitoring programs that collect the data or the modelling programs deployed. Such a silencing is indeed possible. Where scientific agencies are prevented from releasing their data to other scientists or to the public, or have their reports (which are prepared for policymakers according to the division of Lorax labor noted above) censored or manipulated in order to distort their findings or their policy implications, the ability to silence nature can be pernicious. Insofar as the intentional silencing of nature now stands among the leading contributors to the misrepresentation of nature's health and interests, we might consider the protection of legal speech rights (again, for metaphorical speech) as being a procedural guarantee that could help to give substance to other rights of nature, just as procedural rights of informed consent, disclosure and transparency, and participation in decision making do for human interests and thus give force to substantive human rights to subsistence and security.[71]

The task of distinguishing the ventriloquist from the translator remains fraught even without the threat of silencing nature. We suspect that even the most honest translators might aim in good faith to accurately represent nature, but slide into a degree of ventriloquism in the ways in which they note and articulate its interests. However, such anthropocentric moments of projection do not undermine the validity of the New Materialist ontological approach to nature's 'speech'. Against critics of guardianship who worry about humans projecting their own interests onto nature, some New Materialists endorse the anthropomorphizing of nonhuman nature as a strategy, precisely in order to challenge human exceptionalism and the human/nonhuman binary. Bennett casts anthropomorphism as being among 'everyday tactics for cultivating

---

70. R Eckersley, 'Ecological Democracy and the Rise and Decline of Liberal Democracy: Looking Back, Looking Forward' (2020) 29/2 Environmental Politics 214–34.
71. E Massimino, 'The Power of Human Rights Law' (2015) 41/2 Human Rights 2.

an ability to discern the vitality of matter' and commends it for countering a tendency toward anthropocentrism. As she writes, when people project human qualities or aspirations onto nonhuman others, 'a chord is struck between person and thing and I am no longer above or outside a nonhuman "environment"'.[72] Vesting such others with human characteristics and aspirations would at any rate be relatively unobjectionable from a New Materialist ontological standpoint, since neither the subjectivity nor the anticipated outcomes would be exclusively human or nonhuman.

Nonhuman nature need not be regarded as purposive to be conceived as engaging in metaphorical speech, and nor must nature engage in dialogue with humans in order to affirm its value. Neither of these positions entails that nonhuman nature cannot engage in metaphorical speech to which human others should listen, nor that such speech can rightfully be silenced by those seeking to stifle or distort the communicative acts that nonhuman nature issues through eco-feedback. To conceive of the more-than-human world as having a speech right does not entail that it should be objectively represented by a guardian in court (or in democratic politics). It does not entail representation of nature as either aggrieved plaintiff or as interested constituent. As the political marginalization of human groups has illustrated over the course of history, the silencing of the oppressed or downtrodden affects not only those made unable to effectively advocate for themselves but also the receptivity of the community to some of its constituent members. In such dynamics, all are deprived of the silenced voice whose feedback from excluded periphery to empowered center makes reflexivity possible.[73] Recognizing such a speech right for nonhuman nature would thus also entail a companion right on the part of the larger community to have the opportunity to listen and to consider the feedback without the distorting influence of those seeking to prevent both. Since the right would place focus on actions or actors that had sought to interfere with its process rather than on the content of the speech or on the accuracy of its translation, many of the objections against the guardianship model noted in relation to the Lorax problem would be diminished.

Conceived of as an actant with a kind of agency or generative capacity to affect the shared human-nonhuman lifeworld, nature 'speaks' through actions and reactions, often presaging more serious actions or reactions such as mass extinctions or runaway climate change. Nature should not be silenced. And nature, like others with inauthentic representatives, can be silenced when its appointed representatives make claims on its behalf without listening to it first (as noted by critics through the Lorax problem). Misrepresentation thus involves a kind of silencing. This kind of silencing is a more excusable one than deliberate silencing, and is more a feature, perhaps, of the extent to which 'mute' nature can be misinterpreted by a well-meaning guardian that fails to disentangle the human from the nonhuman in the way in which guardianship requires that binary to be asserted. Of more pernicious effect is the deliberate silencing on the part of the climate science denier who fears that a more expansive legal recognition of nonhuman nature might lead to carbon pricing, multilateralism, or to some other feared shift in the sensibilities of a listening public. Closing down global climate monitoring stations, inserting climate science deniers into the national climate assessment office, censoring science advisory bodies and/or the scientific reports issued by government agencies – all these strategies amount to a more pernicious silencing of nature than is even conceivable under the guardianship model. Our proposed alternative

---

72. Bennett (n 51) 110.
73. R Eckersley, 'Geopolitan Democracy in the Anthropocene' (2017) 65/4 Political Studies 983.

framework thus offers the advantage of allowing us to theorize these ongoing forms of intentional silencing as being an offense against nonhuman nature as well as against those humans (that is to say, nearly all of us humans) that stand to be harmed by the silencing of these voices. From this perspective, the notion of a speech right for the nonhuman world becomes more comprehensible and compelling. It also becomes less objectionable, since the guardians that seek to represent this voice are not viewed as representing an incomprehensibly foreign Other alone, as when such a guardian speaks only 'for the trees' but not for the humans that dwell in the forest or depend upon its vital ecosystem services, yet are appropriately viewed as representing the shared environment and can be authorized as such.

Threats to human speech rights are different from the above examples of silencing nature in some respects but continuous with them in other ways. Governments seek to limit dissent in order to consolidate their power and to maintain an ideological superstructure against opposition, whether that opposition is based on inconvenient facts, competing interests, or opposing values.[74] Governments occasionally impose limits on the content of speech in order to prevent the challenge to their authority that dissent entails, but face resistance for offending against speech rights when they do. Where this oppositional speech is political, its need for protection is greatest, as this kind of speech comprises the disagreements most fundamental to democracy. Democratic polities sometimes allow restrictions on time, manner and place, but less often on the content of political speech in order to maintain the freedom to dissent, with the feedback that dissent provides and the self-correcting responses that it enables. Countervailing security values in a healthy democracy allow for restrictions on incitement, but do not permit the complete silencing of speech merely because it is disturbing. Political speech is that which is related to the maintenance of the social and political order, and the political speech most in need of protection is precisely that which most directly and potentially persuasively challenges those orders. The human right to self-determination requires this corollary right of speech through which the various components of the polity gathers and processes feedback of various kinds from the full range of its constituent members, whether directly or through representatives.[75]

Extending such rights beyond the human merely recognizes nonhuman nature as an integral component of the polity. The climate system might, in this respect, engage in political speech, or at least attempt to do so – through the eco-feedback that reactions to the human disturbance of that system have generated. This is not to attribute consciousness or intentions to the climate system, nor is it to conflate human interests in maintaining climatic stability with the wants or needs of the climate system. This kind of speech is tailored to no particular audience. It forms no determinate judgements. It makes no discernible claims. This remains the case, even if such judgements or claims can be drawn from the content of such speech in conjunction with value premises of various kinds. Indeed, much such speech is not discernible to the lay observer at all, manifesting as weather events that are only probabilistically related to the underlying systemic changes reported: increasing concentrations of some gases in the atmosphere, the slow acidification of oceans, or shifting disease vectors. Unlike the dramatic expressions of political speech familiar to its most ardent defenders, as Rob Nixon describes: processes of environmental change that elude direct

---

74. TM Scanlon, 'Why Not Base Free Speech on Autonomy or Democracy?' (2011) 97 Va. L. Rev. 541.
75. A Dobson, 'Democracy and Nature: Speaking and Listening' (2010) 58/4 Political Studies 752–68.

human perception but which can be captured in disturbances such as climate change – the slow violence of terrestrial responses to anthropogenic processes – nonetheless call out in a way that allow humans to hear if they are inclined to listen, and not prevented from doing so.[76] This possibility is precisely why some try to block the transmission of such 'speech' and/or attempt to distort its reception.

Without the elaborate monitoring programs and sophisticated climate models that comprise climate science, there would be a speaking planet but no ability to discern its message or likely even an awareness of its utterances. Having developed the capacity to hear this kind of speech and to translate it into a language accessible to lay persons in politics and society, the perceived threat that such science poses to established power structures has led to its systematic suppression and distortion. To the extent that the climate system possesses a critical voice in dissent against troubled ongoing human relationships with the planet and its assemblages of human and nonhuman constituents, it exhibits the key elements of political speech.

Corporations, as is well known, already have speech rights, which they use for openly political purposes – most of which involve maintaining the existing socioeconomic order against those that would dissent from it. To paraphrase Stone (and Douglas paraphrasing him): so long as the law has already (problematically) granted speech rights to a distinctly 'human' nonhuman entity in the corporation, why not grant the climate system a speech right of its own, which preserves its prerogative to challenge that order in its preservation of the sustainable flourishing of life? Given the financial resources that corporations have to amplify their speech, political subjects should not worry about a dissenting nature silencing the corporation, which at any rate it would lack the capacity to do. Given ongoing campaigns of climate science denial, among the numerous other attacks against environmental defenders, however, we should be very concerned about corporations (along with their allies) silencing nature. Speech rights offer a legal mechanism for countering the marked imbalance between these two kinds of nonhuman speakers, potentially allowing political and legal institutions to better hear the quieter one before its whispers turn into a roar and its agency undermines our human ability to maintain 'ours'.

---

76. R Nixon, *Slow Violence and the Environmentalism of the Poor* (Harvard University Press, Cambridge MA 2013).

Climate change, environmental justice and the unusual capacities of posthumans

Nick J Fox
University of Huddersfield, UK

Pam Alldred
Nottingham Trent University, UK

In this article, we theorize and develop a posthumanist and new materialist approach to sustainable development policy. We trace a humanist and anthropocentric emphasis in policy discussions of 'sustainable' development that reaches back almost 50 years, and still underpins recent United Nations (UN) statements. This UN approach has tied policies to counter environmental challenges such as anthropogenic climate change firmly to sustaining and extending future human prosperity. By contrast, we chart a path beyond humanism and anthropocentrism, to establish a posthumanist environmentalism. This acknowledges human matter as an integral (rather than opposed) element within an all-encompassing 'environment'. Posthumanism simultaneously rejects the homogeneity implied by terms such as 'humanity' or 'human species', as based on a stereotypical 'human' that turns out to be white, male and from the global North. Instead, 'posthumans' are heterogeneous, gaining a diverse range of context-specific capacities with other matter. Some of these capacities (such as empathy, altruism, conceptual thinking and modelling futures) are highly unusual and – paradoxically – may be key to addressing the current crises of environmental degradation and anthropogenic climate change.

Keywords: *climate change, environmental justice, new materialism, posthumanism*

1 INTRODUCTION

One of the ontological opportunities supplied by the new materialisms derives from their acknowledgement that all matter, both 'human' and 'non-human', 'animate' and 'inanimate' possesses capacities to materially affect[1] – an attribute that in modernist social science and some humanities has conventionally been restricted to human agents.[2] This recognition has enabled new materialist ontology to step beyond a culture/nature dualism that has been a feature of much social science,[3] thereby enabling a more thorough engagement with a range of phenomena that are both 'natural' and 'cultural'. Not least among these are environmental sustainability and the challenge of anthropogenic climate change.[4]

---

1. G Deleuze, *Spinoza: Practical Philosophy* (City Lights, San Francisco 1988) 11.
2. DH Coole and S Frost, 'Introducing the New Materialisms', in DH Coole and S Frost (eds), *New Materialisms: Ontology, Agency, and Politics* (Duke University Press, Durham MA 2010) 1–43, 8.
3. NJ Fox and P Alldred, *Sociology and the New Materialism* (Sage, London 2017) 25.
4. NJ Fox and P Alldred, 'Re-Assembling Climate Change Policy: Materialism, Posthumanism, and the Policy Assemblage' (2020) 71(2) British Journal of Sociology 269–83.

Cutting across a nature/cultural opposition[5] should not, however, be taken to imply that the new materialisms collapse disparate kinds of matter (an apple, a tiger, a human body, a stone, the wind) into a singular amorphous mass – as some critics of the perspectives have suggested.[6] Rather, this ontological move has the effect of replacing dualism with multiplicity.[7] Among other things, this problematizes aggregative and unitary categories such as 'human', 'humanity' and 'inanimate'.

In this article we use these insights as a starting point to theorize and develop a post-anthropocentric perspective that draws together issues of sustainable development, environmental justice and social inequalities within a new materialist framing. We follow a trajectory that leads beyond both humanism (an overarching concern with human well-being and social justice) and its antithesis – anti-humanism – to posthumanism (terminology fully defined below). We draw upon feminist materialist and posthuman scholars, who argue for the affectivity or vitality of all matter[8] – and upon non-Western and indigenous ontologies in which 'a multiplicity of beings cast as human and non-human – people, plants, animals, energies, technological objects – participate in the coproduction of socio-political collectives'.[9] Such approaches offer the possibility of achieving what Rosiek et al. have called a 'sense of responsibility to something more than human'.[10] Such approaches establish a posthuman ecological perspective that sees humans as fully integral to the environment. In turn, this de-stabilizes conventional notions of 'sustainable development' set out in successive policy statements, which we shall argue have retained an anthropocentric focus (a perspective that places humans and their concerns centre-stage) on human well-being. Instead, we promote an understanding of sustainability as ecological potential.

At the same time, a posthuman perspective is critical of terms such as 'humanity' and 'human species'. Such terminology aggregates and homogenizes bodies with disparate capacities, often asserting a narrow and privileged model of the 'human'.[11] These aggregating tendencies have been revealed by scholarship on 'environmental justice'/'climate justice'[12] that acknowledges the vast divergences between humans in terms of (a) the contributions they make to anthropogenic climate change; (b) how climate change will impact on their lives; and (c) their capacities to alter their behaviour in order to reduce the negative impact of climate change on the environment or to positively counter its effects.

---

5. I van der Tuin and R Dolphijn, 'The Transversality of New Materialism' (2010) 21(2) *Women: A Cultural Review* 153–71.
6. See for example, B Braun, 'The 2013 Antipode RGS-IBG Lecture on New Materialisms and Neoliberal Natures' (2015) 47/1 Antipode 1–14; S Lettow, 'Turning the Turn: New Materialism, Historical Materialism and Critical Theory' (2017) 140/1 Thesis Eleven 106–21, 107.
7. G Deleuze, and F Guattari, *A Thousand Plateaus* (Athlone, London 1988) 20.
8. J Bennett, *Vibrant Matter* (Duke University Press, London 2010); R Braidotti, *The Posthuman* (Polity, Cambridge 2013); D Haraway, *Cyborgs, Simians and Women* (Free Association Books, Cambridge 1991).
9. J Sundberg, 'Decolonizing Posthumanist Geographies' (2014) 21(1) Cultural Geographies 33–47, 33.
10. JL Rosiek, J Snyder and SL Pratt, 'The New Materialisms and Indigenous Theories of Non-Human Agency: Making the Case for Respectful Anti-Colonial Engagement' (2020) 26(3) Qualitative Inquiry, 331–46, 342.
11. R Braidotti, *Nomadic Theory* (Columbia University Press, New York NY 2011) 82.
12. D Schlosberg and LB Collins, 'From Environmental to Climate Justice: Climate Change and the Discourse of Environmental Justice' (2014) 5(3) Wiley Interdisciplinary Reviews: Climate Change 359–74.

To move beyond such aggregations, we adopt Rosi Braidotti's alternative terminology of 'posthumans' and 'post-humanity', which acknowledges the diversity of individual bodies in terms of capacities to act and interact.[13] We shall argue that any policy to address threats to environmental sustainability such as anthropogenic climate change and environmental degradation must recognize the diversity of posthumans, and the complex interactions of race, gender, material prosperity and geography that produce these differences. Recognizing posthuman diversity overcomes both the narrow focus of humanism on social justice *and* anti-humanist inclinations to regard 'humanity' as the enemy of all other matter.[14]

The posthumanist perspective instead considers posthumans as an integral part of 'the environment' – not separate from it – and as possessing rights to achieve their potential, as should be accorded to all matter. This shift requires that we acknowledge fully the capacities of posthumans, some of which are highly unusual and rarely seen elsewhere in the known universe. These include the capacity to attribute meaning to – or otherwise conceptualize – events; to act altruistically towards unknown others; to imagine the future and create technologies to deliver it; and to use reason to theorize, predict or anticipate future or unseen events. In the concluding section of this article we shall argue that, paradoxically (given the part that some posthumans have played in producing anthropogenic climate change), these unusual capacities will be essential to address the imminent crisis of global climate change. We also set out some ways in which these capacities might be harnessed.

2 SUSTAINABLE DEVELOPMENT: ANTHROPOCENTRISM, HUMANISM, AGGREGATION

For the past 30 years, 'sustainable development' has become an explicit objective within policy initiatives on topics including housing, food, transport, employment and energy production/consumption. Typically, it has been predicated upon the needs and desires of current and future human generations. Thus, in 1987, the *Report of the World Commission on Environment and Development* (commonly known as the Brundtland Report) defined sustainable development as 'development that meets the needs of the present without compromising the ability of future [human] generations to meet their own needs'.[15] Two decades on, the United Nations *Millennium Ecosystem Assessment* (established at the behest of UN Secretary-General Kofi Annan in 2001) confirmed its aim as: 'to assess the consequences of ecosystem change upon human well-being and to establish the scientific basis for actions needed to enhance the conservation and sustainability of those ecosystems, so that they can 'continue to supply the services that underpin all aspects of human life'.[16]

Whitehead has traced this anthropocentric focus in sustainable development discourse back to 1972, and to a speech on 'the pollution of poverty' by Indian premier Indira Gandhi at the first United Nations conference on the Human Environment

---

13. Braidotti, *The Posthuman* (n 8); R Braidotti, *Posthuman Knowledge* (Polity, Cambridge 2019).
14. M Kowalik, 'The Rise of Anti-Humanism' (2018) 62(5) Quadrant 60–61.
15. G Brundtland, M Khalid, S Agnelli et al., *Our Common Future* (*The Brundtland Report*) (Oxford University Press, Oxford 1987).
16. World Health Organization, *Ecosystems and Human Well-Being – A Report of the Millennium Ecosystem Assessment* (WHO, Geneva 2005) ii.

(UNCHE).[17] Ghandi's intervention established a thread in North/South global environmental politics in which environmental protection and economic development are treated as 'mutually supportive',[18] and conversely establishing that poverty and environmental degradation go hand in hand (such as the illegal logging of the rain forest by indigent farmers).[19] This theme has echoed down through subsequent UN statements on sustainable development, even though the claimed positive relationship between economic development and environmental protection is highly questionable[20] and, in many cases, antagonistic.[21] So, for example, the United Nations *Agenda for Sustainable Development 2030* argues that social justice and environmental protection are 'integrated and indivisible' goals.[22]

This anthropocentrism within sustainable development policy is further manifested in suggestions that humans are exceptional or a special case. Thus, the *5th Assessment Report of the Intergovernmental Panel on Climate Change* argued for a comprehensive approach based on the assertion that (unlike other living entities) human well-being depends on economic, social and environmental sustainability:

> Sustainability in the economy refers to the preservation of standards of living and the convergence of developing economies towards the level of developed countries. Sustainability in the social sphere refers to fostering the quality of social relations and reducing causes of conflicts and instability, such as excessive levels of inequality and poverty, lack of access to basic resources and facilities, and forms of discrimination. Sustainability in the environmental sphere refers to the conservation of biodiversity, habitat, natural resources and to the minimisation of impacts upon ecosystems generally.[23]

The 17 objectives agreed by world leaders in 2015 at the UN Sustainable Development Summit[24] further illustrates this anthropocentric and exceptionalist focus. Later released as the United Nations' *2030 Agenda for Sustainable Development*, the Summit's overarching anthropocentric commitment was set out explicitly in its opening paragraph as

> a plan of action for people, planet and prosperity. It also seeks to strengthen universal peace in larger freedom. We recognize that eradicating poverty in all its forms and dimensions, including extreme poverty, is the greatest global challenge and an indispensable requirement for sustainable development.[25]

---

17. M Whitehead, 'Sustainability' in C Death (ed), *Critical Environmental Politics* (Routledge, London 2014) 257–66.
18. M Whitehead, 'Sustainability', in P Cloke, P Crang and M Goodwin (eds), *Introducing Human Geography* (Routledge, London 2014) 448–60, 452.
19. Whitehead (n 17) 259.
20. WE Rees, 'Economic Development and Environmental Protection: An Ecological Economics Perspective' (2003) 86(1) Environmental Monitoring and Assessment 29–45.
21. V Wallis, 'Beyond "Green Capitalism"' (2010) 61(9) Monthly Review 32.
22. United Nations, *Transforming our World: The 2030 Agenda for Sustainable Development. UN General Assembly Resolution 70/1* (United Nations, Geneva 2015) <https://sustainabledevelopment.un.org/post2015/transformingourworld/publication> 1.
23. M Fleurbaey, S Kartha and S Bolwig et al., 'Sustainable Development and Equity' in O Edenhofer, R Pichs-Madruga and Sokona et al. (eds), *Climate Change 2014: Mitigation of Climate Change. Contribution of Working Group III to the Fifth Assessment Report of the Intergovernmental Panel on Climate Change* (Cambridge University Press, Cambridge 2014) 322.
24. United Nations (n 22).
25. ibid 1.

Moreover, of its 17 objectives, 13 address aspects of human well-being, such as ending poverty, achieving gender equality, access to clean water and affordable energy. Only three (on climate action, and conserving marine and terrestrial wildlife) focus on the non-human environment, while one concerns both human and non-human.[26]

In terms of applied sustainability policy (for instance, policies addressing environmental degradation and more recently anthropogenic climate change), such anthropocentrism and humanism have supplied a foundation for 'liberal environmentalism',[27] a position that aims to 'nudge' humans towards actions enhancing environmental sustainability (for instance, reducing waste and meat consumption) without a critical assessment of the wider impacts of human population and economic growth on environmental degradation.[28] This policy approach is given a further neoliberal twist in 'green capitalist' assertions that economic development, free markets and entrepreneurialism can save Earth from climate change through competition and the development of technologies.[29]

These policies, and the actions they spawn, perpetuate the anthropocentrism that sets humans apart from (perhaps even 'above') the environment, both in terms of 'needs' and 'rights'. We would argue (from a new materialist and posthumanist perspective) that there are two foundational flaws in this perspective: each of which we shall explore and critique in this article. The first is founded on the dualist premise that human matter is in some ways essentially and qualitatively distinct from other matter. The second – which is in some ways a consequence, and in other ways a precondition, of the first – derives from the aggregations implied by terms such as 'human', 'humanity' and 'human rights'. Such terminology glosses over the sheer diversity and multiplicity of capacities of individual bodies and downplays the inequalities between posthumans in contemporary capitalist and neoliberal societies.

To supply an ontological framing within which to unpack these two critiques fully, the following two sections explore how a posthumanist perspective opens up new understandings of environmental sustainability and of the diversity of posthuman capacities.

3 NEW MATERIALISM: FROM HUMANISM TO POSTHUMANISM

The dualism constructed between culture and nature supplied post-Enlightenment philosophers, scientists and social scientists with a neat way to set limits on the respective concerns of the social and natural sciences.[30] This dichotomy is seductive. At first sight, it seems fair to ascribe phenomena such as patterns of atmospheric pressure or the operation of living cells and organs to the 'natural' world and others such as

---

26. ibid 14.
27. S Bernstein, 'Ideas, Social Structure and the Compromise of Liberal Environmentalism' (2000) 6(4) European Journal of International Relations 464–512, 471.
28. S Bernstein, *The Compromise of Liberal Environmentalism* (Columbia University Press, New York NY 2001) 3; G Talshir, 'The Role of Environmentalism' in Y Levy and M Wissenburg (eds), *Liberal Democracy and Environmentalism: The End of Environmentalism?* (Routledge, London 2012) 22–43; Whitehead (n 17).
29. S Prudham, 'Pimping Climate Change: Richard Branson, Global Warming, and the Performance of Green Capitalism' (2009) 41(7) Environment and Planning A 1594–613, 1596.
30. K Barad, 'Meeting the Universe Halfway: Realism and Social Constructivism without Contradiction' in LH Nelson and J Nelson (eds), *Feminism, Science and the Philosophy of Science* (Kluwer, Dordrecht 1996) 161–94, 181; Braidotti (n 8) 3; NJ Fox and P Alldred, 'Sustainability, Feminist Posthumanism and the Unusual Capacities of (Post)Humans' (2020) 6(2)

industrialization or sexuality to an alternative realm: the 'social' world. However, when the social sciences and humanities begin to explore embodiment, anthropogenic climate change, or the effects of the built environment on human well-being such a distinction is more problematic. It swiftly becomes clear that the natural and cultural are intertwined, and that the culture/nature dualism imposes a false division in the understanding of these complex processes.[31] Social and natural scientists in fields as disparate as epigenetics, macroeconomics and environmental science are recognizing a need to cut across these artificial distinctions and to work across disciplinary boundaries to formulate new questions and solutions.[32]

Nature/culture dualism in Western philosophy and social theory has also sidelined rival non-Western ontologies that treat humans as fully part of the 'environment',[33] instead imposing Eurocentric and colonialist knowledge and ideological perspectives that have considered 'nature' to be an inferior domain to be exploited for human benefit.[34] Though the new materialisms are plural and disparate, with nuanced and sometimes major divergences between their advocates, they offer a contemporary means to acknowledge the insights to be drawn from these alternative ontologies by challenging essentialism (the assertion that an entity such as a table or a human has inherent attributes that define its identity and function) and anthropocentrism. Here, we shall explore these insights via the work of feminist materialist and posthumanist scholars Donna Haraway, Rosi Braidotti and Jane Bennett.[35]

Biologist and feminist theorist Donna Haraway has suggested that 'culture' has carved out its identity in opposition to 'the natural'.[36] Such nature/culture dualism – she has argued – is unfortunate and both theoretically and politically enfeebling, given the increasing and inevitable convergence of the organic and the inorganic in contemporary technological society.[37] Furthermore, the nature/culture dualism is

Environmental Sociology 121–31; M Meloni, 'From Boundary Work to Boundary Object: How Biology Left and Re-Entered the Social Sciences' (2016) 64(1) Sociological Review Monograph 61–78.
31. B Latour, *We Have Never Been Modern* (Harvard University Press, Cambridge MA 1993).
32. H Landecker and A Panofsky, 'From Social Structure to Gene Regulation, and Back: A Critical Introduction to Environmental Epigenetics for Sociology' (2013) 39 Annual Review of Sociology 333–57; M Meloni, 'How Biology Became Social, and What it Means for Social Theory' (2014) 62(3) The Sociological Review 593–614; J Niewöhner, 'Epigenetics: Embedded Bodies and the Molecularisation of Biography and Milieu' (2011) 6(3) BioSocieties 279–98, 281.
33. Z Todd, 'An Indigenous Feminist's Take on the Ontological Turn: "Ontology" is Just Another Word for Colonialism' (2016) 29(1) Journal of Historical Sociology 4–22.
34. BW Braun, 'Buried Epistemologies: The Politics of Nature in (Post)Colonial British Columbia' (1997) 87(1) Annals of the Association of American Geographers 3–31; J Sundberg, 'Decolonizing Posthumanist Geographies' (2014) 21(1) Cultural Geographies 33–47, 33.
35. Apart from these authors, the following analysis of new materialist ontology also draws its inspiration from other materialist scholarship, including M DeLanda, *A New Philosophy of Society* (Continuum, London 2006); G Deleuze and F Guattari, *Anti-Oedipus: Capitalism and Schizophrenia* (Athlone, London 1984); B Latour, *Reassembling the Social: An Introduction to Actor Network Theory* (Oxford University Press, Oxford 2005); N Thrift, *Non-Representational Theory: Space, Politics, Affect* (Routledge, London 2008).
36. D Haraway, 'Otherworldly Conversations; Terran Topics; Local Terms' (1992) 3(1) Science as Culture 64–98, 65.
37. Haraway (n 8); D Haraway, *Modest_Witness@Second_Millennium. Femaleman_Meets_Oncomouse* (Routledge, London 1997).

expressed and intensified in colonialism and racism, patriarchy and sexism, and in the capitalist appropriation of nature for human benefit.[38]

Haraway's feminist and materialist project has explored the proliferation of technologies and associated scientific perspectives that increasingly impinge upon human bodies, with the cultural trope of the 'cyborg' as her locating hook. Though cyborgs (a meld of flesh and technology) feature in *Terminator*-style science fiction, they are commonplace in the contemporary world – products of scientific and medical innovations that draw bodies into intimate proximity with inorganic matter: from joint replacements to genetically modified organisms and biotech.[39]

But, just as cyborgs challenge the nature/culture dualism, Haraway argues that entities labelled as 'apes' and 'women' also unsettle the 'evolutionary, technological and biological narratives' that have fostered distinctions between 'the natural' and 'the human'. As such, these transgressive entities provide opportunities to reveal the continuities between humans and the rest of the material universe.[40] Such transgressions, she suggests, have the potential to demolish the conventional distinction between nature and culture.[41]

Haraway's work is among the influences cited in Rosi Braidotti's development of a materialist, feminist and posthuman philosophy and ethics of environment,[42] in which she argues that the interests of humans cannot be divorced from the interests of other living things and of the Earth. Braidotti's work navigates a path between and beyond both humanism and anti-humanism within social theory and the humanities towards an emergent posthumanism.[43]

Humanism provided a post-Enlightenment anthropocentric challenge to religious authority by elevating secular human reason over all else, including God[44] its secularism supplying the foundations for social and political changes including the French Revolution, first-wave feminism and the anti-slavery movement.[45] While Braidotti acknowledges that humanism has promoted issues of solidarity, community-building and principles of social justice and equality,[46] she also notes that the 'human' who was the measure of all things in humanist doctrine turned out to be white, male, able-bodied and exploitative of all other life-forms.[47]

Anti-humanism rejected this anthropocentric focus, and – most recently in the shape of post-structuralist theory – presented an alternative to humanism that proclaimed the death of 'Man' as an intrinsically progressive agent.[48] Though sympathetic to this critique, Braidotti has argued that anti-humanism risks throwing out

---

38. Haraway (n 8) 150.
39. CM Klugman, 'From Cyborg Fiction to Medical Reality' (2001) 20(1) Literature and Medicine 39–54.
40. Haraway (n 8) 154.
41. Haraway, *Modest_Witness@Second_Millennium. Femaleman_Meets_Oncomouse* (n 37) 270.
42. R Braidotti, *Transpositions: On Nomadic Ethics* (Polity, Cambridge 2006); Braidotti, *Nomadic Theory* (n 11); Braidotti, *The Posthuman* (n 30); Braidotti, *Posthuman Knowledge* (n 13).
43. Braidotti (n 8) 26.
44. J Carroll, *Humanism: The Wreck of Modern Culture* (Fontana, London 1993) 117.
45. Braidotti (n 8) 32.
46. ibid 29.
47. R Braidotti, 'Posthuman, All Too Human: Towards a New Process Ontology' (2006) 23(7–8) Theory Culture & Society 197–208, 200; Braidotti, *Nomadic Theory* (n 11) 82, 88–9.
48. Braidotti (n 8) 23.

the progressive achievements of humanism concerning solidarity, social justice and equality,[49] while it would be an ironic act of humanist hubris for humans to assert the end of humanism.[50]

For Braidotti, the justification for overturning the nature/culture dualism lies in the recognition, cognate with Haraway's, that the interests of humans are not divorced from the interests of other living things and of the physical environment. Moving beyond this humanism/anti-humanism duality, she instead establishes a 'posthuman' project in which matter and culture are not dialectically opposed. This understanding of the posthuman supplies Braidotti with the basis for an 'eco-philosophy' that establishes a continuum between human and non-human matter[51] and between human subjectivity and planetary ecology.[52] This eco-philosophy in turn constitutes a posthuman ethics based on a new sense of inter-connectedness between human and non-human; 'an affirmative bond that locates the subject in the flow of relations with multiple others'.[53]

The relational and materialist posthumanism in the work of Braidotti, Haraway and other new materialist scholars reflects the two features of a new materialist ontology noted earlier: anti-essentialism and post-anthropocentrism. On the first of these, new materialisms reject essentialist notions of entities such as bodies, animals and inanimate things as possessing pre-existing and fixed attributes.[54] Rather, these myriad materialities are relational, gaining form and continuity through their engagements with the other material relations with which they assemble, and through the emergent capacities or 'becomings' that these interactions co-generate.[55] Events and interactions are to be understood as *assemblages*:[56] arrangements or orderings[57] of relations (bodies, things, social institutions and constructs) that are inherently fluid and continually in flux.[58]

A new materialist perspective is post-anthropocentric in its displacement of humans as privileged elements within the global environment and of human agency as the prime mover of social production. The new materialisms treat all the disparate materialities in an assemblage as possessing capacities to *affect*, or to be affected by,

---

49. ibid 29.
50. ibid 30.
51. ibid 104.
52. Braidotti, *Transpositions: On Nomadic Ethics* (n 42) 41.
53. Braidotti (n 8) 50, see also AF Conty, 'The Politics of Nature: New Materialist Responses to the Anthropocene' (2018) 35(7–8) Theory, Culture & Society 73–96, 91; E Cudworth and S Hobden, 'Liberation for Straw Dogs? Old Materialism, New Materialism, and the Challenge of an Emancipatory Posthumanism' (2015) 12(1) Globalizations 134–48; A Franklin, 'Burning Cities: A Posthumanist Account of Australians and Eucalypts' (2006) 24(4) Environment and Planning D: Society and Space 555–76; A Pickering, 'Asian Eels and Global Warming: A Posthumanist Perspective on Society and the Environment' (2005) 10(2) Ethics and the Environment 29–43, 33–5.
54. Braidotti (n 11) 3.
55. G Deleuze, *Spinoza: Practical Philosophy* (City Lights, San Francisco 1988) 125; M DeLanda, *A New Philosophy of Society* (Continuum, London 2006) 3.
56. J Bennett, 'The Agency of Assemblages and the North American Blackout' (2005) 17(3) Public Culture 445–65, 445; Pickering (n 53) 34.
57. I Buchanan, 'Assemblage Theory, or, the Future of an Illusion' (2017) 11(3) Deleuze Studies 457–74, 465.
58. Deleuze (n 55) 128; T Lemke, 'New Materialisms: Foucault and the "Government of Things"' (2015) 32(4) Theory, Culture & Society 3–25.

other assembled relations.[59] New materialists such as Jane Bennett proclaim the liveliness and affectivity of all matter: a 'thing-power'[60] – that is, a capacity to affect or be affected – associated with all materiality. In Bennett's view, human agency is consequently no more than a particular variety of thing-power: the product of a body's component materialities (bone, muscle, blood and so forth) rather than any unique motivation such as an active mind or soul.[61] In this posthuman eco-philosophy, non-human materialities are 'bona fide participants' rather than 'recalcitrant objects, social constructs, or instrumentalities' within events and interactions.[62]

Furthermore, from this perspective, 'the environment' is no longer simply the context for human agency, but the arena for the production of the entirety of both 'natural' and 'social' worlds. 'Human' bodies (and other 'human' stuff such as thoughts, ideas, memories, aspirations and so forth which have capacities to materially affect), 'social' stuff such as organizations and social formations, and all the 'natural' stuff that comprises the physical environment are drawn together into a single assemblage.[63] The entirety of the natural and social world *is* the environment, with nothing beyond it, and nothing (for instance, humans and their diverse cultures) excluded from it.

Together, these aspects of new materialist ontology supply the starting-point for new ways of thinking about nature and culture, and – as we shall show later – for a new perspective upon sustainable development and responses to crises such as anthropogenic climate change. In place of an 'environmentalism' in which humans are stewards or protectors of 'the environment', posthuman bodies are intricately entangled within environment-assemblages. However, to complete this analysis of a posthuman perspective, we must first address the aggregations of bodies that terms such as 'human' and 'humanity' establish.

4 POSTHUMANS, ENVIRONMENT AND ENVIRONMENTAL JUSTICE

The work of the materialist feminists that we have reviewed establishes a new posthuman eco-philosophy and ethics that affirms the commonalities and connectedness of all matter.[64] However, this posthuman position also challenges the sexualization, racialization and naturalization of the West's Others[65] that has led to both the despoliation of the environment (including the current environmental crisis of climate change) *and* the inequalities between global North and South.[66] The category of 'human' and the concept of 'humanity' are revealed as part of a darker side to humanism, which obscures both the diversity and the inequalities between genders, races, incomes, abilities, nationalities and other stratifications.[67]

59. Deleuze (n 55) 101.
60. Bennett (n 8) 2.
61. ibid 10.
62. ibid 62, see also Conty (n 53); NJ Fox and P Alldred, 'Social Structures, Power and Resistance in Monist Sociology: (New) Materialist Insights' (2018) 54/3 Journal of Sociology 315–30.
63. I van der Tuin and R Dolphijn, 'The Transversality of New Materialism' (2010) 21(3) Women: A Cultural Review 153–71.
64. Braidotti (n 8) 50.
65. Haraway (n 8) 50.
66. H Baer, 'Global Warming as a By-product of the Capitalist Treadmill of Production and Consumption – the Need for an Alternative Global System' (2008) 19(1) *The Australian Journal of Anthropology* 58.
67. Braidotti, *Posthuman Knowledge* (n 13) 159.

A posthuman ontology and ethics consequently incorporates a concern with social justice to challenge these inequities, while policies to address climate change must also address 'climate justice'.[68] To mark out this critical recognition of diversity and inequalities, from here on we refer to 'posthumans', in place of the aggregating terms 'humans' and 'humanity'.[69] Rather than focusing upon humans as 'individuals' (literally: 'indivisible'), what we term a 'posthuman' is an assemblage of biological, sociocultural and environmental elements, whose capacities to affect and be affected are contingent upon its setting and emergent in its relations with other matter.[70]

This new materialist recognition that matter's capacities are always context-dependent requires acknowledgement of the unevenness of how posthumans' capacities manifest. Diverse capacities mean that some posthumans (predominantly those who are white, male, comparatively rich and from the global North) play a much greater part in using energy and resources and generating pollution than others[71] and have access to a range of resources not available to those from other contexts. This unevenness has consequences when it comes to assessing the impacts of environmental degradations on posthuman bodies. Two-thirds of greenhouse emissions has been produced by rich white posthumans in the EU, US and Japan,[72] while much of the impact (such as flooding, drought, loss of biodiversity, land quality degradation) has been experienced – and will increasingly be felt – by poor posthumans in the global South.[73] Furthermore, environmental policies to counter the effects of anthropogenic climate change (such as switches to renewable energy sources and controls on rain forest clearances for agriculture, etc.) might disproportionately affect the poorest posthumans and be far more onerous for them, increasing inequalities between rich and poor.[74]

The need to link social justice to environmental sustainability has been recognized in the 'environmental justice' and 'climate justice' movements.[75] A posthuman analysis of sustainable development weaves these two threads of justice and sustainability by emphasizing the connectedness of human and non-human materialities, while acknowledging the diversity and multiplicity of posthumans. A 'posthuman politics'[76]

---

68. D Schlosberg and LB Collins, 'From Environmental to Climate Justice: Climate Change and the Discourse of Environmental Justice' (2014) 5(3) Wiley Interdisciplinary Reviews: Climate Change 359–74.
69. NJ Fox and P Alldred, 'Sustainability, Feminist Posthumanism and the Unusual Capacities of (Post)Humans' (2020) 6(2) Environmental Sociology 121–31, 124.
70. K Barad, '(Re)configuring Space, Time and Matter', in M Dekoven (ed), *Feminist Locations* (Rutgers University Press, New Brunswick, NJ 2001) 75–109, 96; M DeLanda, *A New Philosophy of Society* (Continuum, London 2006) 10–11; Fox and Alldred (n 69) 124.
71. J Agyeman and B Evans, '"Just Sustainability": The Emerging Discourse of Environmental Justice in Britain?' (2004) 170(2) Geographical Journal 155–64; S Klinsky, T Roberts, S Huq, C Okereke, P Newell, P Dauvergne et al., 'Why Equity is Fundamental in Climate Change Policy Research' (2017) 44 Global Environmental Change 170–73.
72. P Baer, S Kartha, T Athanasiou and E Kemp-Benedict, 'The Greenhouse Development Rights Framework: Drawing Attention to Inequality within Nations in the Global Climate Policy Debate' (2009) 40(6) Development and Change 1121–38, 1127.
73. Schlosberg and Collins (n 68) 360; United Nations (UN), *The Sustainable Development Goals Report* (United Nations, Geneva 2019) 3.
74. N Taconet, A Méjean and C Guivarch, 'Influence of Climate Change Impacts and Mitigation Costs on Inequality between Countries' (2020) 160 Climatic Change 15–34, 17.
75. Schlosberg and Collins (n 68) 360–61.
76. S Hobden, 'Posthumanism', in C Death (ed), *Critical Environmental Politics* (Routledge, London 2014) 175–83, 182.

addresses the mutual dependency of posthuman and non-human capacities. It evaluates any event (that is: a specific assemblage of human and non-human materialities) in terms of the breadth of possibilities it produces in its constituent relations.[77] Environmental policy, in this posthuman perspective, will aim to enhance the capacities of both non-human and posthuman. It will neither privilege the latter over the former (humanism) or the former over the latter (anti-humanism) (perspectives both represented in contemporary environmental politics), nor privilege the capacities of rich, white, global North posthumans over others.

In the next section, we draw out the novel implications of this dual commitment to the diversity of matter and to posthuman multiplicity, focusing upon the harnessing of material capacities in policies to address climate change.

5 SUSTAINABILITY, POSTHUMANISM AND THE UNUSUAL CAPACITIES OF POSTHUMANS

The posthumanist and new materialist ontology of environment that we have set out in the previous two sections undermines the anthropocentric perspective on environmental sustainability and sustainable development that has developed in high-level policy fora over the past 40 years. Indeed, a new materialist ontology of flux and emergence must step back from any conception of sustainability as continuity. Most assemblages are not sustainable, and have within them contradictory forces that will lead them to fall apart or to transmogrify into something else in a day or an hour or a minute.[78] Indeed the universe, we are told, is not sustainable: at some time in the future it will either expand to infinity and slowly chill to near absolute zero, or collapse into a singularity; one day the Earth will fall into the sun and all its matter be utterly transformed.

Instead, this ontology establishes the foundations for an alternative understanding of sustainability as 'ecological potential', challenging a narrow model of sustainability tied to human lives and future human generations. This alternative view focuses not upon stable attributes and continuities of human or non-human matter, but upon the capacities and potentials of posthumans that emerge when assembled with other matter.[79] New materialist ontology moves beyond the usual narrow focus on human potential to acknowledge the capacity of all matter (non-human as well as human) to 'become other'.[80] Sustainable development in this perspective should seek ways to enhance the capacities and 'becomings' of all elements of the planetary assemblage. These becomings include interactions between earth, air and water, and the nitrogen and water cycles of the physical environment; the productive life-courses of the diverse multiplicity of plants and wild animals; and opportunities for all posthumans to work, play and interact productively. Sustainability further requires that such becomings are enabled in ways that do not oppose human capacities to those of other materialities.

---

77. Braidotti (n 8) 60. For a discussion of Deleuze's Spinozist and Nietzschean ethics of becoming, see Buchanan (n 57).
78. Deleuze and Guattari (n 35) 5.
79. Braidotti (n 11) 312–13; A Parr, *Hijacking Sustainability* (MIT Press, Cambridge MA 2009) 161.
80. F Guattari, *The Three Ecologies* (Athlone, London 2000) 20.

Such a posthuman perspective rejects the inherent humanism of liberal environmentalism,[81] the UN's anthropocentric position on environmental sustainability, *and* the anti-humanism of some 'radical environmentalism' that regards opportunities to enhance human potential as foundationally inimical to 'the environment'.[82] With humans no longer ontologically separate from the environment, but instead fully integral alongside other animate and inanimate elements, then an ethics of becoming[83] must apply to posthuman capacities and desires as much as to the becoming of the non-human. What counterposes such a recognition to an anthropocentric focus is that, within a sustainability grounded in ecological potential, possibilities for becoming are located within the broader concern with ecological possibility and biodiversity. What sustains 'the environment' can also be 'emancipatory' for posthumans.[84]

A posthuman perspective on sustainability as potential subtly shifts how we should consider the 17 goals for sustainable development agreed by world leaders at the United Nations summit in 2015, discussed above.[85] These objectives were articulated within a discourse that ties environmental sustainability to economic and human social development – indeed, that considers the latter to be a necessary precondition for the achievement of the former. While not rejecting the valid aspirations of the UN and other bodies to emancipate humans economically and socially, once humans are regarded as integral to the environment, this distinction dissolves. The posthuman commitment must be instead to promote those actions that can enhance the environment's (and hence human) potentialities, and to moderate actions that would limit that potential – be that by exhausting natural resources, filling the atmosphere with greenhouse gases, or by limiting human possibilities through poverty, economic inequities or threats to health.

To further unpack this posthuman perspective on sustainability as ecological potential, we turn once again to the feminist materialist scholars discussed earlier. The affectivity and emergent capacities of all matter[86] undermine both the humanist hubris that has led to exploitation of 'the environment' for human interests, and the anti-humanism of 'hard' environmentalism that considers human life to be inimical to Earth's ecology. Humans are not in charge of the 'irrepressible flows of encounters, interactions, affectivity and desire' that produce the world and everything in it.[87] These flows *are* the 'becoming' of the planet: the engine by which the global environment continually assembles, dis-assembles, transforms and becomes other. Posthumans may be an integral part of that becoming, but they are not its prime mover.

Bennett's analysis offers a means to operationalize a posthuman sustainable development policy. All matter possesses capacities that produce the becomings of the planet, be they geological, meteorological, biological, economic, cultural, emotional or psychological. An ethics of environmental sustainability can be founded on assessments of how actions enable or constrain environmental becoming. Enabling actions include reducing greenhouse gas emissions and plastic waste, or providing clean water to enhance human health. Constraining actions include exploiting natural resources such as heavy metals for economic gain, clearing forest for agriculture,

---

81. Bernstein (n 28); Talshir (n 28).
82. Kowalik (n 14).
83. Braidotti (n 8) 100.
84. Cudworth and Hobden (n 53) 144.
85. United Nations (n 22).
86. Bennett (n 8) 11.
87. Braidotti (n 8) 100.

or undercutting local food production with cheap imports that increase social and economic inequalities and injustices.

While this ethics may redress the ecological balance between human and non-human, the capacities of posthumans – as part of 'the environment' – must not, however, be sidelined or trampled upon. Bennett suggests that while posthumans should reduce their environmental impact, sometimes environmental becoming may need 'grander, more dramatic and violent expenditures of human energy'. Building on this assessment, our next proposition is radical, perhaps even counter-intuitive. We would suggest that posthumans possess some unusual capacities. As noted earlier, these include the capacity to attribute meaning to events; to act altruistically towards unknown others; to imagine the future and create technologies to deliver it; and to use reason to theorize, predict or anticipate future or unseen events.[88]

We would further suggest that these unusual capacities are now significant for addressing current environmental challenges. These capacities must not be denied or rejected simply to assert some kind of anti-humanist purism, but must be added to the mix, along with the material capacities of non-human elements of the environment.[89] The present climate change crisis will not only affect human existence but that of many millions of living organisms, many of which face extinction – with unknown consequences for a biosphere that has evolved over millions of years.[90] Anthropogenic de-stabilizations of ecologies can lead to catastrophic changes such as desertification or out-of-control greenhouse gas emissions,[91] which in a worst-case scenario could render Earth uninhabitable.

Evolutionary and geological time-scales are too slow to address the causes of anthropogenic climate change, such as conflicts between economic and environmental interests concerning continued fossil fuel extraction. In these circumstances, the physical capacities of non-human matter must be augmented with these unusual human capacities to predict, model and enact possible environmental, political and economic futures; to develop technologies that can reverse the effects of greenhouse gases; and to act altruistically to protect the non-human elements of the environment.

This acknowledgement does not mark a return to a humanist re-privileging of human agency or reason, however. A posthuman environmental ethos displaces posthumans from any kind of privileged status that elevates their aspirations or priorities over non-human elements of the environment. Instead, it fully recognizes an environment that is endlessly emerging, changing, fragmenting and fracturing, opening up both human and non-human possibilities rather than closing them down. Together, these posthuman and non-human capacities can supply the means to enable the becomings of a vital, self-organizing and emergent environment-assemblage.

---

88. Fox and Alldred (n 69) 126, see also J Schmidt, 'The Empirical Falsity of the Human Subject: New Materialism, Climate Change and the Shared Critique of Artifice' (2013) 1(3) Resilience 174–92, 189–90.
89. J Lorimer, *Wildlife in the Anthropocene: Conservation after Nature* (University of Minnesota Press, Minneapolis MN 2015) 4.
90. CD Thomas, A Cameron, RE Green, M Bakkenes, LJ Beaumont, YC Collingham et al., 'Extinction Risk from Climate Change' (2004) 427(6970) Nature 145–8; MC Urban, 'Accelerating Extinction Risk from Climate Change' (2015) 348(6234) Science 571–3.
91. M Scheffer, C Carpenter, JA Foley, C Folke and B Walker, 'Catastrophic Shifts in Ecosystems' (2001) 413(6856) Nature 591–6.

We develop this suggestion further in the concluding section, as we consider posthumans and climate change policy.

6 CLOSING REFLECTIONS: CLIMATE CHANGE POLICY AND POSTHUMANS' CAPACITIES

In this article we have applied new materialist ontology and feminist posthumanist theories to establish a post-essentialist and post-anthropocentric perspective on sustainability and sustainable development. We critiqued the UN policy statements on sustainable development for their implicit anthropocentrism, which treats the Earth simply as a resource to be enjoyed by future generations of humans. In particular, we questioned the approach to sustainability that links environmental protection firmly to the social and economic development of human beings, while ignoring the detrimental effects that the latter has upon the former. In its place, we asserted a posthumanist understanding of sustainability as ecological potential, based on two propositions: the post-anthropocentric recognition of the relational vitality of all matter; and an ethics of environment that fosters matter's potential for becoming.

When considered in relation to policy on anthropogenic climate change, these two features of a posthumanist perspective can overcome shortcomings in current approaches.[92] On one hand, these two propositions broaden the conception of sustainable development beyond the humanist prioritization of the well-being of current and future generations of humans,[93] instead acknowledging a need to assure the future potential of all matter, both 'animate' and 'inanimate'. On the other hand, this approach rejects anti-humanist arguments that to protect the environment, the human footprint on the Earth must be radically reduced,[94] regardless of the dire consequences of this policy for particular groups of posthumans such as the poor and those in the global South.[95] By treating humans as part of, rather than separate from 'the environment', and by establishing an ethics based on fostering all matter's potential for becoming, this posthumanist approach ties justice for both posthuman and non-human matter inextricably to environmental sustainability. At the same time, it focuses attention on the opportunities afforded by matter's capacities, including the unusual capacities of posthumans highlighted in the previous section. Amongst those unusual posthuman capacities are those to devise and implement policy.

Conventionally, environmental policymaking weighs human economic interests against concerns for protecting the natural environment and mitigating climate change.[96] Such clashes might be played out at the level of global climate change meetings attended by the world's Heads of States, but they are also more locally contested. For example, the UK is exploring shale gas extraction as a way to lower prices and provide energy security, while Australia mines and exports large quantities of coal to China in order to benefit the Australian trade balance, even though continued use of fossil

---

92. Fox and Alldred (n 4).
93. Cudworth and Hobden (n 53) 144–5.
94. Bennett (n 8) 121.
95. M Bosquet, *Capitalism in Crisis and Everyday Life* (Harvester Press, Hassocks 1977) 185–6.
96. Fox and Alldred (n 3) 39.

fuels runs counter to the global climate policy that these countries support. The affective interactions in this complex assemblage include the physical, biological and chemical processes that produced coal or gas deposits in the first place and subsequently allow it to be used as a fuel to generate electricity and carbon dioxide. Affects between fossil fuel, money, mining, machinery and miners turn a subterranean mineral millions of years old into a product to be sold commercially, and at the same time provide work and wages to local people. Planners and elected representatives, planning laws and procedures, the public, political parties and governments interact to produce planning decisions. Public opinion for and against industrial developments fuels protests and counter-protests. Together these affects interact, conflict, antagonize and coalesce in ever-changing ways.

A posthuman approach cuts across the opposition of human/environment that informs the poles of this debate. Instead, issues of sustainable development require analysis of a simultaneously geological, geographical, cultural, social and affective assemblage, in which minerals, wind, air, trees, wildlife, humans and their technologies are among the many constitutive relations. Within an environment in which posthuman and non-human are inextricably linked, sustainable development cannot be considered as a balancing act between 'environmental' and 'human' concerns. Understanding the environment as *incorporating* posthumans as an integral component means that posthuman and non-human matters are inextricably entangled in a complex affective flow. 'Sustainable development' requires fostering processes of becoming that open up both posthuman and non-human possibilities, rather than closing down one to benefit the other. A materialist framework based on an ontology of relations, assemblages and economies of affect requires attention to the complexities and contradictions that emerge whenever application of such policies and initiatives is sought, from the level of global policy down to the local planning committee adjudicating on the proposals for the natural and built environment.

Elsewhere, we have assessed four contemporary approaches within climate change policy: liberal environmentalism; the UN approach (outlined earlier); 'green capitalism' and no-growth economics.[97] We found that all four approaches fail to fully engage with the complex interactions between non-human and (post)human matter that produce anthropogenic climate change, in part because of their foundational humanist or anti-humanist commitments. We would argue here that the posthumanist perspective on sustainable development that we have set out supplies a way beyond these policy shortcomings.

In contrast to humanist privileging of human socioeconomic well-being, policies need to enact radical and comprehensive action to address the depredations of humanity: from

---

97. Fox and Alldred (n 4). 'Green capitalism' asserts that competition and the market economy can be the means to replace human practices that have led to climate change with technologies that can limit greenhouse gas emissions or sequester atmospheric carbon dioxide. See S Prudham, 'Pimping Climate Change: Richard Branson, Global Warming, and the Performance of Green Capitalism' (2009) 41(7) Environment and Planning A 1594–613; J Zysman and M Huberty, *Can Green Sustain Growth? From the Religion to the Reality of Sustainable Prosperity* (Stanford University Press, Stanford CA 2014). No-growth approaches recognize the environmental harm that capitalism's endless search for growth and profit brings, and aim to replace this with a 'steady-state' economy, possibly also signalling a move from capitalism to eco-socialism. See HA Baer, *Democratic Eco-Socialism as a Real Utopia: Transitioning to an Alternative World System* (Berghahn Books, New York NY 2018).

the industrialization of production, the consequent consumption of resources, and the damage caused by waste products. This addressal must include acknowledgement that a market economy – with its primary objective of profit and its secondary objective of growth – is the driver of the industrialization that has led to climate change and environmental destruction.[98] This view challenges a discourse that simplistically links environmental protection with economic development, replacing it with a much more nuanced recognition of the diversity of posthumans and the need to overcome inequalities between posthumans produced by a range of class, gender, race and geographic intersectionalities. Furthermore, this new materialist, posthumanist approach entails a new ethics of environment in which *all* matter is recognized as relationally vital, and is assured opportunities for becoming. This includes extending the opportunities currently enjoyed by rich, white, global North posthumans both to other posthumans and to other 'animate' and 'inanimate' matter.

At the same time, the posthumanist perspective acknowledges the contributions that posthuman ingenuity and other unusual capacities make to the material environment as resources for countering anthropogenic climate change. These capacities (for instance, the ability to model climate change futures, to develop green technologies, and to act altruistically towards non-human matter) provide the basis upon which to manage down growth and competition; to implement the social and political transformations to enable this economic shift; to redistribute wealth among posthumans; and to end the human exploitation of non-human matter as resources.

Together, these interventions can provide the foundation for a policy of incremental actions – some very local, others national or global in scale – that address the breadth of natural, biological, social, economic and political affects within the climate change assemblage. These interventions are not a 'pick and mix' selection of policy initiatives, but a mutually interdependent skein of actions that together can articulate successfully with the complexity of climate change. Furthermore, this is a long-term and global programme that depends for its success on political will, incisive leadership and collaboration across stakeholder groups.

To conclude: a posthumanist and new materialist ontology of an environment that fully incorporates posthumans can establish a research and action agenda to counter anthropogenic climate change. Practically speaking, this means designing and undertaking research that is capable of exploring the constellations of relations and socio-material interactions that comprise 'the environment'. In terms of active engagement, it entails translating research findings into a posthuman ecology of becoming. This latter must address both policy development and (inter)governmental negotiations on sustainable development, and the affects and interactions of daily life that can foster ecological capacities and potentialities and thereby succour a posthuman ethics of planetary becoming. Local action can remain local, or it can be scaled: to a city, a nation and a planet.

A posthumanist perspective on sustainable development does not mean stepping back from 'the environment' but integrating fully within it. It is founded on the post-anthropocentric replacement of human privileging with a recognition of the relational vitality of all matter; and an ethics of environment that focuses on matter's potential for

---

98. NJ Fox and P Alldred, 'Climate Change, Economics and the Policy-Assemblage: Four Policies and a Materialist Synthesis' (2020) Globalizations DOI: 10.1080/14747731.2020.1807857.

becoming, including fully utilizing the unusual capacities of all posthumans. Given where we are now (a planet already substantively degraded by anthropogenic pollution and the effects of burning carbon fuels), action is urgent and must be radical. Though it may seem paradoxical – given the state to which anthropogenic climate change has brought us – a substantive investment in posthumans' unusual capacities is now required to overcome this global crisis.

Posthuman international law and the rights of nature

Emily Jones*
School of Law and Human Rights Centre, University of Essex

Both posthuman theory and the rights of nature (RoN) movement have the potential to challenge the anthropocentrism of international environmental law (IEL). Scholars have begun to document the transformative shifts that could occur through the application of posthuman legal theory to IEL, but these theories have yet to be applied to law in practice. On the other hand, RoN have been applied in domestic law but hardly in international law, while the question of what RoN includes and excludes remains contested.

This article brings posthuman theory and RoN together, reflecting on how posthuman legal theory can contribute to the framing of RoN, with a focus on challenging the anthropocentrism of IEL. The article argues, first, that the next step for posthuman legal theory will be its application to existing law. Noting convergences between posthuman legal theory and the rights of nature (RoN), the article contends that those seeking to apply posthuman legal theory might find some interesting alliances by turning to RoN. Second, it is argued that using posthuman theory to frame RoN could help to ensure that RoN live up to their transformative potential.

Keywords: *posthuman theory, rights of nature, international law, environmental law*

1 INTRODUCTION

International environmental law (IEL) has developed greatly over the past few decades, seeking in part to address some of the challenges posed by environmental degradation.[1] However, IEL is anthropocentric, situating human needs, and particularly their

---

*   I would like to thank Eliana Cusato, Alice Finden, Craig Kauffman, Birsha Ohdedar and Stephen Turner for their invaluable comments on drafts of this article. A version of this article was presented at the Global Law at Reading (GLAR) Ghandi Research Seminar Series at the University of Reading in November 2020. With thanks to those in attendance for their insightful feedback. Special thanks to Marie Aronsson-Storrier at GLAR for her enthusiasm about my work and for inviting me to speak. I also presented this paper at the University of Essex Law and Theory discussion group in 2021. With thanks to all those who attended and provided feedback on the paper. Thank you to Rosi Braidotti for helping me think through the some of the theoretical tensions in this article. The origins of this article ultimately come from earlier work I undertook as part of my doctoral degree. I therefore give thanks to Gina Heathcote, Vanja Hamzić and Yoriko Otomo for their comments and support at those initial stages. I would also like to thank the three anonymous reviewers of this article whose thoughtful insights greatly helped me develop my argument and the article overall and the journal and special issue editors for their detailed and thoughtful feedback.
1.   For an overview of the development of IEL and the multiple ways in which it seeks to protect the environment, see: P Sands and J Peel, *Principles of Environmental Law* (4th edn, Cambridge University Press, Cambridge 2018).

has also been applied to environmental law.[9] While scholarship on posthuman theory and law has been successful in challenging the humanist and anthropocentric underpinnings of legal frames, as legal theorist Margaret Davies notes, the application of these theories to the law itself – to legal practice – is the next step that needs to be taken.[10]

In response to this challenge, this article draws on the work of critical environmental law scholars who use posthuman theory to challenge the current onto-epistemic basis of IEL,[11] while taking up Davies' call for applied posthuman legal theory. The article focuses on the rights of nature (RoN) movement, noting the links between some of the understandings of the environment that underpin RoN and posthuman theory. While nature has been recognized as having rights in some domestic contexts,[12] RoN have yet to be adopted within international law.[13] However, there is increasing international interest in doing so, and this article argues that those seeking to apply posthuman legal theory to IEL might find some useful alliances with RoN approaches. At the same time, it is also argued that posthuman theory can provide some insights for RoN. Seeking to think the law through the posthuman, this article outlines the potentials in RoN from a posthuman perspective, while addressing the limitations and highlighting the barriers faced when working within, albeit seeking to change, the liberal humanist and anthropocentric frame of IEL.

It should be noted that Indigenous peoples have played a central role in ensuring the recognition of RoN in many domestic jurisdictions.[14] While some posthuman theories and some strands of Indigenous thought have commonalities,[15] there are also divergences, with Indigenous theories and practices being multiple and differing. It should be noted that not all Indigenous peoples support a RoN approach. Some

---

9. Eg A Grear, '"Anthropocene, Capitalocene, Chthulucene": Re-encountering Environmental Law and its "Subject"' with Haraway and New Materialism' in LJ Kotzé (ed), *Environmental Law and Governance for the Anthropocene* (Hart, Oxford and Portland, Oregon 2017).
10. Davies supra (n 7) 72.
11. Grear supra (n 9); A Philippopoulos-Mihalopoulos, 'Towards a Critical Environmental Law' in A Philippopoulos-Mihalopoulos (ed), *Law and Ecology: New Environmental Foundations* (Routledge, Abingdon 2011); D Otto and E Jones, 'Thinking Through Anthropocentrism in International Law: Queer Theory, Posthuman Feminism and the Postcolonial' (2020) LSE Centre for Women, Peace and Security blog <https://www.lse.ac.uk/women-peace-security/assets/documents/2020/Final-Jones-and-Otto-Anthropocentrism-Posthuman-Feminism-Postcol-and-IL-LSE-WPS-Blog-2019-002.pdf> last accessed 23 November 2020; A Grear and D Otto, 'International Law, Social Change and Resistance: A Conversation between Professor Anna Grear (Cardiff) and Professorial Fellow Dianne Otto (Melbourne)' (2018) 26 Feminist Legal Studies 351.
12. I discuss some of these contexts in more detail below. However, for an overview of the multiple contexts where RoN have been recognized, see: Global Alliance for the Rights of Nature's (GARN), 'RoN Map' <https://www.therightsofnature.org/map-of-rights-of-nature/> last accessed 8 April 2021.
13. See: H Harden-Davies et al., 'Rights of Nature: Perspectives for Global Ocean Stewardship' (2020) 122 Marine Policy 1. There are multiple international documents which have called for the recognition of RoN – see Section 4.
14. E O'Donnell et al., 'Stop Burying the Lede: The Essential Role of Indigenous Law(s) in Creating Rights of Nature' (2020) 9(3) Transnational Environmental Law 403. On the links between Indigenous thought and Earth jurisprudence, see: K Anker, 'Ecological Jurisprudence and Indigenous Relational Ontologies' in K Anker et al. (eds), *From Environmental to Ecological Law* (Routledge, Oxford and New York 2021).
15. See: S Bignall and D Rigney, 'Indigeneity, Posthumanism and Nomad Thought: Transforming Colonial Ecologies' in R Braidotti and S Bignall (eds), *Posthuman Ecologies*

economic interests,[2] above other values and considerations while separating the governance of humans, non-humans, and their environments into different areas of law.[3] This fragmentation operates to ensure that different entities and systems are protected in different ways, and IEL's understanding of 'the environment' has produced a legal system that does not reflect the reality of how ecosystems work. Legal understandings of the environment, therefore, not only uphold problematic value hierarchies but also deny the reality that environments, humans, and non-humans are interconnected and interdependent.[4]

This article argues that posthuman theories (which seek to dismantle hierarchies between humans (such as gender, race, and class) as well as the idea that the human sits in hierarchical superiority over all other entities, including matter and non-humans[5]) can be used to destabilize the problematic anthropocentrism of the law and to re-think the onto-epistemological basis of IEL.

Posthuman legal theory has expanded as an area of research over the past few years. Scholarship has focused on various key issues in law, from posthuman data to military technologies.[6] Scholarship has also emerged addressing questions concerning how the law can better account for matter,[7] with research beginning to emerge on how international law, specifically, can better account for matter.[8] Posthuman theory

---

2. The prioritization of economic interests is also a problem within international law generally. See: G Baars, *The Corporation, Law and Capitalism: A Radical Perspective on the Role of Law in the Global Political Economy* (Haymarket Books, Chicago 2020); N Tzouvala, *Capitalism as Civilisation: A History of International Law* (Cambridge University Press, Cambridge 2020). On IEL's neoliberal anthropocentrism, see: L Kotzé et al., 'Friend or Foe? International Environmental Law and its Structural Complicity in the Anthropocene's Climate Injustices' (2021) 11(1) Oñati Socio-Legal Series 180.

3. For example, the governance of human interests in environmental issues tends to be covered, at the international level, primarily through human rights law. However, the sea is governed under the Law of the Sea, whereas issues relating to biodiversity are covered in different Conventions again. While these instruments are sometimes brought together to bear on one another, too often they are treated as distinct, resulting in conflicts. See: UN General Assembly, Convention on the Law of the Sea, 10 December 1982; United Nations, Convention on Biological Diversity, 5 June 1992 (1760 U.N.T.S. 69).

4. While the term 'the environment' is sometimes used within environmental governance to denote flora and fauna only, I have taken this term to mean the wider material world.

5. R Braidotti, *Posthuman Knowledge* (Polity Press, Cambridge 2019).

6. On conflict and military technologies, see: M Arvidsson, 'Targeting, Gender, and International *Posthuman*itarian Law and Practice: Framing the Question of the Human in International Humanitarian Law' (2018) 44.1 Australian Feminist Law Journal 9; G Heathcote, 'War's Perpetuity: Disabled Bodies of War and the Exoskeleton of Equality' (2018) 44.1 Australian Feminist Law Journal 71; E Jones, 'A Posthuman-Xenofeminist Analysis of the Discourse on Autonomous Weapons Systems and Other Killing Machines' (2018) 44.1 Australian Feminist Law Journal 93; L Wilcox, 'Embodying Algorithmic War: Gender, Race and the Posthuman in Drone Warfare' (2016) Security Dialogue 1; L Wilcox, 'Drones, Swarms and Becoming-Insect: Feminist Utopias and Posthuman Politics' (2017) 116 Feminist Review 25. On posthuman data, see: J Käll, 'The Materiality of Data as Property' (2020) 61 Harvard International Law Journal Frontiers 1; J Käll, 'A Posthuman Data Subject? The Right to be Forgotten and Beyond' (2017) 18(5) German Law Journal 1145.

7. See: M Davies, *Law Unlimited* (Routledge, Oxford and New York 2017); A Philippopoulos-Mihalopoulos, *Spatial Justice: Body, Lawscape, Atmosphere* (Routledge, Oxford and New York 2015).

8. J Hohmann, 'Diffuse Subjects and Dispersed Power: New Materialist Insights and Cautionary Lessons for International Law' (2021) Leiden Journal of International Law 1.

Australian Nations have, for example, rejected the approach, calling instead for stronger Indigenous environmental governance through 'Caring for Country'.[16]

While much work needs to be done to bring Indigenous and posthuman thought together, noting cross-overs and differences, such a project lies outside the scope of the present article, which focuses on why posthuman legal theorists should engage with and support the RoN movement and what its advocates might also learn from such engagements.[17]

2 THE ANTHROPOCENTRIC AND FRAGMENTED 'ENVIRONMENT' OF INTERNATIONAL ENVIRONMENTAL LAW

IEL is made up of a series of focused instruments that govern different parts of the environment, with different principles and approaches emerging accordingly. Examples include treaties that focus on conservation and the sustainable use of natural resources and biodiversity,[18] the obligation to preserve the marine environment,[19] and instruments to decrease pollution,[20] and so forth. Positive obligations focus on specific areas, and there is no general obligation in international law to protect the environment.[21] While the UN General Assembly has taken up the task of environmental protection, most notably through the work of the UN Environment Programme

---

(Rowman & Littlefield, London 2019); S Bignall, S Hemming and D Rigney, 'Three Ecosophies for the Anthropocene: Environmental Governance, Continental Posthumanism and Indigenous Expressivism' (2016) 10.4 Deleuze Studies 455.

16. V Marshall, 'Removing the Veil from the "Rights of Nature": The Dichotomy between First Nations Customary Rights and Environmental Legal Personhood' (2020) Australian Feminist Law Journal <https://www.tandfonline.com/doi/abs/10.1080/13200968.2019.1802154> accessed 23 November 2020. It is also important to note that Caring for Country is a rich and complex concept. Deborah Bird Rose's work on the many meanings of Country exemplifies this well. See: DB Rose, 'Country' in DB Rose, *Nourishing Terrains: Australian Aboriginal Views of Landscape and Wilderness* (Australian Heritage Commission, 1996) 6. Pelizzon and Kennedy also discuss the many meanings of Country. See: A Pelizzon and J Kennedy, 'Welcome to Country: Legal Meanings and Cultural Implications' (2012) 16 Australian Indigenous Law Review 58, 65–66.

17. For more on indigenous perspectives on RoN, see: J Ruru, 'Listening to Papatūānuku: A Call to Reform Water Law' (208) 48 Journal of the Royal Society of New Zealand 215; TA Eisenstadt and K Jones West, *Who Speaks for Nature? Indigenous Movements, Public Opinion and the Petro-State in Ecuador* (Oxford University Press, Oxford 2019); I Vargas-Roncancio, 'Conjuring Sentient Beings and Relations in Law' in K Anker et al. (eds), *From Environmental to Ecological Law* (Routledge, Oxford and New York 2021). On Indigenous legal theory and the environment (though not necessarily from a RoN perspective), see: A Mills, 'Aki, Anishinaabek, kaye tahsh Crown' (2010) 9(1) Indigenous Law Journal 107 (here, on concepts of relation to land and natural resources); and S Hemming et al., 'Indigenous Nation Building for Environmental Futures: Murrundi Flows Through Ngarrindjeri Country' (2019) 26(3) Australasian Journal of Environmental Management 216 (here, on Indigenous Nation (re)building and water management).

18. United Nations, Convention on Biological Diversity supra (n 3).

19. UN General Assembly, Convention on the Law of the Sea, supra (n 3) Article 192.

20. Conference of the Parties, Adoption of the Paris Agreement, 12 December 2015, U.N. Doc. FCCC/CP/2015/L.9/Rev/1.

21. For example, looking at the Stockholm Declaration, it seems Principle 2 comes closest to seeking to protect the environment overall. However, environmental protection is named as

(UNEP), there is also no single organization that has the competence over all environmental matters.[22] The issue of fragmentation within public international law generally[23] is thus a key challenge within IEL too,[24] and while certain areas of IEL are moving towards a more integrated approach, changes are occurring only within specific areas.[25] While some efforts to unite IEL are being made through the ongoing negotiations to create a Global Pact for the Environment,[26] the aim of the Pact is to consolidate existing principles, with new principles being created only as required for consolidation purposes.[27] Simultaneously, environmental protection regimes[28] – and thereby the principles that Pact negotiations are seeking to consolidate – remain anthropocentric. Overall, and despite integrative developments, IEL remains highly fragmented. Different parts of the environment remain subject to different legal regimes and obligations.[29] In addition, as a specialized area of general international law, IEL is formed by laws arising from the sovereign will of states – a framework for international law-making that ensures that state interests, and thereby economic interests, must be balanced against environmental damage and may even be protected over environmental interests.[30] These structural formations work to ensure that the central subject of IEL remains stubbornly anthropocentric.[31]

---

needed for the sake of 'future generations', retaining an anthropocentric stance. See: Stockholm Declaration, UN General Assembly, United Nations Conference on the Human Environment, 15 December 1972, A/RES/2994.

22. The UN Environment Assembly (UNEA) does do some important work here, however. See: <https://environmentassembly.unenvironment.org/> last accessed 23 November 2020.

23. M Koskenniemi, 'Fragmentation of International Law: Difficulties Arising from the Diversification and Expansion of International Law' International Law Commission 2006 A/CN.4/l.682.

24. This has been noted by the UN Secretary General as well as the Ecological Law and Governance Association in the Oslo Manifesto. See: UN General Assembly, Report of UN Secretary General, 'Gaps in International Environmental Law and environment-related instruments: towards a global pact for the environment' 30 November 2018, A/73/419; Ecological Law and Governance Association, 'Oslo Manifesto', <https://elgaworld.org/oslo-manifesto> last accessed 4 March 2021.

25. Redgwell argues that ongoing developments within the remit of the UN Convention on Biological Diversity 1992 are possibly the strongest example of attempts at integration. C Redgwell, 'International Environmental Law' in Malcolm D Evans (ed), *International Law* (5th edn, Oxford University Press, Oxford 2018) 677.

26. UN General Assembly, 'Resolution Adopted by the General Assembly on 10 May 2018: Towards a Global Pact for the Environment' 10 May 2018, A/Res/72/277. See also: Global Pact for the Environment, 'Where Are We Now?' <https://globalpactenvironment.org/en/the-pact/where-are-we-now/> last accessed 8 April 2021. For a good overview of ongoing negotiations on the Pact, see: Y Aguila and JE Viñuales, 'A Global Pact for the Environment: Conceptual Foundations' (2019) 28(1) Review of European, Comparative and International Environmental Law 3.

27. On the balance in the negotiations between consolidation and innovation and the ability of the Pact to put forward provisions which may go beyond those found in existing Treaty regimes, see: Aguila and Viñuales, supra (n 26) 8.

28. See: the Stockholm Declaration supra (n 21).

29. See: U Natarajan and J Dehm, 'Where is the Environment? Locating Nature in International Law' (2019) TWAILR <https://twailr.com/where-is-the-environment-locating-nature-in-international-law/> last accessed 23 November 2020.

30. See, eg the Principle of Sustainable Development.

31. While the central subject of international law has never been the human per se, in that the state is the primary subject of international law, this point remains. For example, Grear and

One key attempt at bringing a more integrated/holistic approach to environmental protection invokes international human rights law standards. The intersections between human rights and the environment are wide ranging, from the issue of environmental refugees to the environmental impacts of conflict.[32] One of the most promising and rapidly developing convergences between human rights and the environment is to be found in the right to a healthy environment. While there is no global treaty that recognizes the right, the right has emerged in recent decades in the form of multiple hard and soft law sources, including treaties and international instruments;[33] the statutes and jurisprudence of regional human rights systems;[34] and the jurisprudence of UN human rights bodies and mechanisms.[35] The right to a

---

Blanco exemplify the central role transnational corporations play in the global order. See: E Blanco and A Grear, 'Personhood, Jurisdiction and Injustice: Law Colonialities and the Global Order' (2019) 10(1) Journal of Human Rights and the Environment 86. Similar points have also been made by Baars and Tzouvala. See: Baars supra (n 2); Tzouvala supra (n 2). While indeed, the corporation, the state, international organizations (ie non-human legal subjects) play a central role in international law, alongside, of course, individuals within specific areas of the law (eg human rights), my conjecture is that the law remains anthropocentric despite this. This is because the law serves human needs primarily. In fact, as the work cited above exemplifies, the central role of the corporation upholds global inequalities between humans and the privileging of some human interests over others, despite the façade of the corporation itself. As Blanco and Grear argue (99–102), this has occurred in part due to the liberal, individual framing of legal personhood which has allowed some subjects which fit this problematic, racialized and masculinist model well, such as the corporation, to foster power. See also here, on the latter point: R Sydney Parfitt, 'Theorizing Recognition and International Personality' in A Orford and F Hoffman (eds), *The Oxford Handbook of the Theory of International Law* (Oxford University Press, Oxford 2016) 583.

On a similar note, Usha Natarajan and Kishan Khoday argue that IEL is set up in a way that re-enforces ecological harm. See: U Natarajan and K Khoday, 'Locating Nature: Making and Unmaking International Law' (2014) 27(3) Leiden Journal of International Law 573.

32. The relationship between the enjoyment of rights and the quality of the human environment was first recognized in 1968. See, UN General Assembly, 1968, UNGA Res 2398 (XXII). On environmental refugees see: UNHCR, 'Climate Change and Disaster Displacement' <https://www.unhcr.org/uk/climate-change-and-disasters.html> last accessed 23 November 2020. On the environmental impacts of conflict, see: E Cusato, 'International Law, the Paradox of Plenty and the Making of Resource-Driven Conflict' (2020) 33(3) Leiden Journal of International Law 649; K Hulme, *War Torn Environment: Interpreting the Legal Threshold* (Brill, Leiden 2004).

33. See, eg: the 1972 Stockholm Declaration supra (n 21), Principle 1; UN General Assembly, UNGA Res 45/94 (1990). Many instruments that invoke ideas around the right to live in a quality environment are also linked to the rights of future generations, eg Declaration of the Hague on the Environment, 11 March 1989, 28 ILM 1308 (1989), or the rights of the child, eg Convention on the Rights of the Child, 28 November 1989, in force 2 September 1990, 29 ILM 1340 (1990), Article 29(e).

34. Eg African Charter on Human and Peoples' Rights, 1982, CAB/LEG/67/3 rev. 5, 21 I.L.M. 58, Article 24 Organization of American States (OAS), Additional Protocol to the American Convention on Human Rights in the Area of Economic, Social and Cultural Rights ('Protocol of San Salvador'), 16 November 1999, Article 11; Inter-American Court of Human Rights Advisory Opinion OC-23, 15 November 2018.

35. Much here has been developed specifically in relation to human rights and the movement and dumping of toxic and dangerous products and wastes. See, eg: Sub-Commission on Prevention of Discrimination and Protection of Minorities (1998), Res 1998/26; UN Human Rights Council, (2007) Res 5/1, UN Doc. A/HRC/RES/5/1, Appendix I; UN Human Rights Council,

healthy environment encompasses many elements, including 'the right to breathe clean air, [and to have] access to clean water and adequate sanitation, healthy and sustainable food, a safe climate, and healthy biodiversity and ecosystems'.[36] The right has developed extensively in recent years, but is not universally accepted, yet '[i]n total, 124 States are parties to legally binding international treaties that explicitly include the right to a healthy environment'.[37] The UN Special Rapporteur on Human Rights and the Environment has argued that there is 'a compelling basis for the United Nations to move expeditiously to provide global recognition of the right to a healthy and sustainable environment'.[38] Despite this, the human right to a healthy environment still has some way to go to be universally recognized, and what the right includes and how it is enforced differs greatly across regions and states. While the right to a healthy environment thus comprises many possible elements, potentially providing a more integrated means by which a locality and its overall 'health' can be protected, the right remains limited, not only in terms of its enforcement but also in the way in which it is framed. Anthropocentrism, after all, is central to human rights. Since the right to a healthy environment is a human right and therefore protects human interests primarily, the right is enforced to ensure that humans live within a healthy environment. Naturally, this means that environmental damage that does not (at first glance) impact humans and/or their immediate environments but nevertheless impacts other species – and/or habitats without human occupants (such as the high seas) – is not addressed by the right in its current framing.[39] Accordingly, while the human right to a healthy environment is indeed one of the most promising areas of global environmental protection, it, like IEL generally, continues primarily to promote human interests and is marked by the deep anthropocentrism that pervades the fragmented way in which interests are protected in IEL.

As Stephen Turner argues on the basis of related concerns, 'the very design of the law itself is fundamentally predisposed to environmental degradation and forms part of a dysfunctional global legal architecture which cannot achieve environmental sustainability'.[40] IEL reproduces a problematic subject/object binary for which humans are the central subject of the law and 'the environment' is a mere object. This remains the case both when the environment is being protected (where it is still seen as an object) as well as when it is being exploited, that is, as an economic resource. Non-humans and the environment thus range along what Anna Grear calls a 'spectrum of objectifications'.[41]

Such critiques have led Grear to ask whether 'environmental law [can] respond to alternative modes of knowing and coordination? Can environmental law respect multiple forms of sharing the world?'[42] It is clear from the brief overview of IEL just

---

(2008), Res 9/1, UN Doc A/HRC/RES/9/1. See also: Report of the Special Rapporteur on Human Rights and the Environment, 'Issue of human rights obligations relating to the enjoyment of a safe, clean, healthy and sustainable environment', Human Rights Council, 2019, A/HRC/40/55, pp. 2–4.

36. Special Rapporteur on Human Rights and the Environment supra (n 35) para 17.
37. ibid para 11.
38. ibid para 16.
39. This is a point Neimanis has raised, albeit in relation to the right to water. See: A Neimanis, 'Bodies of Water, Human Rights and the Hydrocommons' (2009) 21 TOPIA: Canadian Journal of Cultural Studies 161, 173.
40. SJ Turner, *A Global Environmental Right* (Routledge, Oxford 2014) 32.
41. Grear supra (n 9) 87.
42. ibid 90.

offered that IEL has a long way to go to address these questions in the positive. Grear draws on posthuman and new materialist theory to seek to answer the questions she poses.[43] It is to such theories that this article now also turns its attention.

3 POSTHUMAN THEORY

To understand whether posthuman theory can help re-imagine IEL, there is a need to outline what posthuman theory is and what strands of posthuman theory I will draw on here. Posthuman theories broadly call for an account of subjectivity that includes non-human entities, including a better understanding of the agency of matter and/or 'the environment'.[44] Critical posthuman theory sits at the convergence between post-humanism and post-anthropocentrism, and explicitly seeks to dismantle hierarchies between humans, such as gender, race and class, as well as to dismantle the idea that the human sits in hierarchical supremacy over other subjects – including the environment and non-humans.[45] Posthuman theory therefore brings critiques of humanism as found, for example, in critical race studies, gender theory and critical disability studies together and alongside critical animal and environmental studies, and sites itself at the conjunction between these areas of study to provide a convergent critique of the exclusionary nature of the so-called human subject situated at the centre of Western philosophy.[46] Re-thinking law through a posthuman lens and working to dismantle the dominant subject situated at the heart of the legal system would have radical implications for how the law is envisaged.[47]

43. ibid 90.
44. R Braidotti, *The Posthuman* (Polity Press, Cambridge 2013) 82.
45. Braidotti supra (n 5).
46. On critical race studies, the postcolonial and posthumanism see, eg: R Amaro, 'Afrofuturism' in R Braidotti and M Hlavajova (eds), *Posthuman Glossary* (Bloomsbury, London and New York 2018); Bignall and Rigney supra (n 15); Bignall, Hemming and Rigney supra (n 15). On gender and posthumanism see, eg: R Braidotti, *Posthuman Feminism* (Polity Press, Cambridge forthcoming 2021); Otto and Jones supra (n 11); C Åsberg and R Braidotti (eds), *A Feminist Companion to the Posthumanities* (Springer International, Cham 2018); Jones supra (n 6); Wilcox (2016) supra (n 6); Wilcox (2017) supra (n 6); S Alaimo, *Bodily Natures: Science, Environment, and the Material Self* (Indiana University Press, Bloomington 2010); S Alaimo and S Heckman, *Material Feminisms* (Indiana University Press, Bloomington 2008); K Barad, 'Posthumanist Performativity: Toward an Understanding of how Matter Comes to Matter' (2003) 28(3) Signs: Journal of Women and Culture in Society 801; D Haraway, *Simians, Cyborgs and Women: The Reinvention of Nature* (Routledge, New York and Oxford 1991). On critical disability studies and posthumanism see, eg: Heathcote supra (n 6); D Goodley, R Lawthom and K Runswick-Cole, 'Posthuman Disability Studies' (2014) 7 Subjectivity 341. On critical animal studies and posthumanism, see, eg: P MacCormack, 'Introduction' in P MacCormack (ed), *The Animal Catalyst: Towards Ahuman Theory* (Bloomsbury, London and New York 2014); JT Maher, 'Legal Technology Confronts Speciesism, or, We Have Met the Enemy and He is Us' in P MacCormack (ed), *The Animal Catalyst: Towards Ahuman Theory* (Bloomsbury, London and New York 2014); Y Otomo and E Mussawir (eds), *Law and the Question of the Animal: A Critical Jurisprudence* (Routledge, Oxford 2013). On critical environmental studies/posthumanism see: S Mentz, 'Blue Humanities' in R Braidotti and M Hlavajova (eds), *Posthuman Glossary* (Bloomsbury, London and New York 2018); S Alaimo, *Exposed: Environmental Politics and Pleasures in Posthuman Times* (University of Minnesota Press, Minneapolis and London 2016).
47. Davies supra (n 7).

Posthuman theory is a vast and varied field. In this article, I am primarily interested in posthuman theories of new materialism. New materialism is part of the posthuman convergence between post-anthropocentrism and post-humanism.[48] However, new materialism, which broadly seeks to re-situate the importance of matter in Western thought, lies more squarely within post-anthropocentrism. Drawing on new materialism within the wider frame of posthuman theory ensures that critiques of humanism are not lost when undertaking the new materialist shift. Leaning into posthuman theory brings together the question of who is seen as a subject and questions of matter. This avoids the risk in some strands of new materialist thinking (which have been subject to criticism) that in seeking to re-centre ontology, epistemology is sometimes sidelined, producing a theory of matter that, ultimately, thinks about matter alone.[49] For critics, this neglect of epistemology results in an inadequate account of how new materialist perspectives apply in a world where inequalities between humans remain.[50] Posthuman theory, in bringing together critiques of both humanism and anthropocentrism, ensures that the question of matter's significance can be considered without risking the displacement of important epistemological turns that have come about through feminist, queer, critical race, postcolonial and crip theory, among others.[51]

What I am terming here as 'posthuman theories of new materialism' include a broad range of theories: from theories of 'vibrant matter';[52] 'onto-epistemology';[53] 'agential-realism';[54] or 'vitalist materialism'.[55] While the following paragraphs by no means provide a comprehensive review of this field, I have sought to provide an overview of some core arguments with the aim of applying these theories to IEL and, specifically, to RoN.

3.1 Posthuman theories of new materialism and IEL

Posthuman theories of new materialism challenge dominant understandings of subjectivity, stressing both the 'force of living matter' and the ways in which 'nature-culture' has already been complicated by techno-scientific discovery.[56] For example, Jane Bennett, in her work on 'vibrant matter', challenges the binding of 'subjectivity' to the fantasy of 'human uniqueness'[57] and the 'fantasy that "we" are really in charge of those "its"'.[58] Bennett characterizes matter as an 'actant',[59] challenging the idea

---

48. Braidotti supra (n 5).
49. R Braidotti, 'A Theoretical Framework for the Critical Posthumanities' (2019) 36(6) Theory, Culture & Society 31, 42–3.
50. See ibid 42–3; S Choat, 'Science, Agency and Ontology: A Historical Materialist Response to New Materialism' (2017) Political Studies 1; Alaimo (2010) supra (n 46) 178–88.
51. See: D Haraway, *Staying with the Trouble: Making Kin in the Chthulucene* (Duke University Press, Durham 2016); Alaimo (2010) supra (n 46).
52. J Bennett, *Vibrant Matter: A Political Ecology of Things* (Duke University Press, Durham and London 2010).
53. K Barad, *Meeting the Universe Halfway: Quantum Physics and the Entanglement of Matter and Meaning* (Duke University Press, Durham and London 2007).
54. ibid.
55. Braidotti supra (n 44) 55.
56. ibid 3.
57. Bennett supra (n 52) ix.
58. ibid x.
59. ibid viii.

that objects are opposite to subjects through a focus on 'thing-power'.[60] Bennett notes that humans are part of a shared, 'vital materiality'.[61] Humans impact upon, and are impacted by, things, yet humans are also 'a particularly potent mix of minerals'.[62] Bennett, and posthuman theory more broadly, thus challenges the idea that agency is something held by humans alone but, rather, states that 'the locus of agency is always a human-nonhuman working group'.[63]

Challenging the centrality of humans as subject and matter as object is vital. Such centrality has long worked to uphold ideas that humans dominate the environment, justifying exploitation.[64] This in turn has prevented adequate understanding of the various non-human powers that circulate in the world.[65] Dismantling the subject/object binary that dominates Western thought is essential work, particularly when it comes to understanding 'the environment' and therefore IEL. This dismantling is also required if cultures of domination and extraction are to be challenged.

Posthuman new materialist theory centres the agency of matter, situating 'the cultural' within a wider collective of human and non-human interactions. Bruno Latour's work on Actor-Network Theory[66] is used to argue that the world is a network, a crisscrossing of multiple assemblages, both human and non-human, in which nature and culture are overlapping as opposed to distinct.[67] Such theories seek to create a world that could adequately account for that fact that, as Carolyn Merchant argues,

> The relation between humans and the nonhuman world is … reciprocal. Humans adapt to nature's environmental conditions; but when humans alter their surroundings, nature responds through ecological changes.[68]

Posthumanist theory can embrace such dynamics of reciprocity, but also renders visible deeper, more complex levels of entanglement: humans and non-humans are situated in co-emergent relationalities. In this sense, agency is never 'pure' or 'absolute' but rather, agency is always distributed, always conditioned by entanglements between agential 'beings', human, non-human and matter alike.[69] This, however, is a world where, as Haraway writes, '[n]othing is connected to everything; everything is connected to something'.[70] The repercussions of such relationalities directly challenge IEL's imagined separation of humans, non-humans, and environments into different legal spheres.[71]

60. ibid 2.
61. ibid 14.
62. ibid 11.
63. ibid xvi.
64. ibid ix.
65. ibid ix.
66. B Latour, *Reassembling the Social: An Introduction to Actor-Network Theory* (Oxford University Press, Oxford 2007).
67. See: V Kirby, 'Natural Convers(at)ions: Or, What if Culture Was Really Nature All Along?' in S Alaimo and S Hekman (eds), *Material Feminisms* (Indiana University Press, Bloomington 2007) 225.
68. C Merchant, *Ecological Revolutions: Nature, Gender and Science in New England* (University of North Carolina Press, Chapel Hill 1989) 8.
69. S Alaimo, 'Trans-Corporeal Feminisms and the Ethical Space of Nature' in S Alaimo and Hekman (eds), *Material Feminisms* (Indiana University Press, Bloomington 2007) 246.
70. Haraway supra (n 51) 31.
71. These theories also share some common concerns with Earth jurisprudence, which likewise identifies how humans, non-humans and matter are all interconnected, albeit from a

Posthuman theories of matter itself also have implications for IEL. As Grear argues,

> If matter has escaped its imposed (imagined) inertia – if matter begins to evade categorisations, to over-spill linear conceptions of causality, to generate meanings – then matter necessarily challenges the previous *taken for granted* of environmental law.[72]

In short, posthuman understandings disrupt the object/subject binary that underlies IEL, challenging human exceptionalism and the idea that humans, non-humans and environments can ever be understood in a disconnected way. To give a more concrete example, drawing on the work of Marcus Taylor: currently the law tends to view a river as an object. Environmental laws accordingly focus on regulating and conserving the use of river water, the river itself being seen as a static object able to be tamed by human actions.[73] Yet if one takes a posthuman approach, human and non-human connections can be more easily seen, as well as the ability of the river itself, to act. Taylor uses the example of a drought in 2012 in the Deccan Plateau in India, explaining how the water initially dried up and noting the wider factors that caused this (including climate change as well as over-consumption and water pollution, thus reducing the availability of clean water elsewhere). In response, local communities began to extract more groundwater to meet their needs, undermining small cattle farming practices that relied upon groundwater. This caused farmers to sell their cattle, increasing vulnerability in the area. In response, wealthier people began to use technology to drill deeper, extracting water and creating a further shortage for all. These people then sold the water to the farmers at a higher price.[74] This example shows the multiply related ways in which environments and humans interact with, and react to, one another as elements in an assemblage. A posthuman understanding allows all these factors and connections to be made analytically visible in a different way: the river is no longer a static object but a living actant which is in connection with human actants, responding to them in its own distinctive and lively manner. The human subject of human rights and the environment becomes 'repositioned as just one partner'[75] in a 'spatial and temporal web of interspecies dependencies'[76] in which lively matter is, itself, an actant, a 'subject' for which the law must adequately account.

An environmental law that is receptive to the epistemic shift required to take account of the insights of posthuman theory might allow for the casting aside of

---

radically different starting point: eg T Berry, *The Great Work: Our Way into the Future* (Bell Tower, New York 1999); C Cullinan, *Wild Law: A Manifesto for Earth Jurisprudence* (Green Books, Cambridge 2003); A Naess, *Ecology of Wisdom* (Penguin, London 2016); C Cullinan, *Wild Law: A Manifesto for Earth Justice* (2nd edn Green Books, Cambridge 2011); P Burdon, *Earth Jurisprudence: Private Property and the Environment* (Routledge, Oxford and New York 2017); N Rogers and M Maloney (eds), *Law as if Earth Really Mattered* (Routledge, Oxford and New York 2017).
72. Grear supra (n 9) 92 (emphasis in original).
73. M Taylor, *The Political Ecology of Climate Change Adaptation: Livelihoods, Agrarian Change and the Conflicts of Development* (Routledge, Oxford and New York 2015).
74. ibid. See also: B Ohdedar, 'The Human Rights to Water in India: In Search of an Alternative Commons-Based Approach in the Context of Climate Change' in T Haller et al., *The Commons in a Glocal World: Global Connections and Local Responses* (Routledge, Oxford and New York 2019). With thanks to Birsha Ohdedar for the suggested example.
75. Grear supra (n 9) 92.
76. D Haraway, *When Species Meet* (University of Minnesota Press, Minnesota 2008) 11.

'the eco-destructive assumptions and ideological closures of the Anthropocene-Capitalocene',[77] allowing, instead, for a more liveable law of a different imaginary in which relations are tangled, tentacular and co-emergent: a law, to use Donna Haraway's words, for the Chthulucene.[78]

It is clear that posthuman theory will have radical implications for IEL, offering the potential to challenge and possibly to resolve some of the core tensions raised by critical IEL scholars. This potential arises precisely because posthuman theory challenges the same dominant Western epistemological frames that underlie IEL itself – that is, anthropocentrism, humanism and the division of nature/culture and subject/object – and offers instead a more empirically faithful account of 'the world'.

4 THE RIGHTS OF NATURE: A WAY FORWARD?

Over the past few decades, nature has begun to be recognized both as having rights and as being a legal person in certain contexts.[79] RoN laws are 'emerging in response to extreme pressure on ecosystems, and on communities that live and rely on them'.[80] The call for the environment to have legal rights and/or personhood, allowing it to bring claims in law on behalf of 'itself', could challenge the anthropocentrism of IEL.

RoN has much in common with posthuman legal theories. A RoN approach has the potential to provide a more integrated account of the environment, with RoN laws directly challenging 'the values of dominant political and economic systems, which view humans as separate from nature, treat the elements of nature as objects for human exploitation, and prioritize exponential economic growth over ecosystem functioning'.[81] This aim very much aligns with posthuman theory and with its call for a greater understanding of the connection between human and non-human entities. Allowing nature as an actant and seeing nature as a connected ecosystem that encompasses multiple human and non-human interests legally able to have its rights presented in courts could help to tackle some of the shortcomings identified by critiques of IEL. However, crucially, the effectiveness of RoN in reaching these aims will depend on how nature and its rights are defined.

As noted earlier, RoN have been recognized in a variety of domestic contexts in multiple different ways[82] but have yet to be implemented at the international level. Some states have, however, begun to push for the international recognition of RoN. In 2009, the Bolivian President called on the UN General Assembly (UNGA) to adopt a Universal Declaration of the Rights of Mother Earth (UDRME).[83] In 2010,

---

77. Grear supra (n 9) 95.
78. See: Haraway supra (n 51).
79. Post-anthropocentric conceptions of environmental governance have a long history. Much is left to be said about the relationship between these bodies of thought and RoN. See, eg: CD Stone, *Should Trees have Standing? Law, Morality and the Environment* (3rd edn, Oxford University Press, Oxford and New York 2010); Berry supra (n 71); Naess supra (n 71); Burdon supra (n 71); Rogers and Maloney supra (n 71).
80. CM Kauffman and L Sheehan, 'The Rights of Nature: Guiding our Responsibilities through Standards' in S Turner et al. (eds), *Environmental Rights: The Development of Standards* (Cambridge University Press, Cambridge 2019) 343.
81. ibid 356.
82. DR Boyd, *The Rights of Nature: A Legal Revolution that could Save the World* (EWC Press, Toronto 2017).
83. Evo Morales, 'Address by H.E. Mr. Evo Morales Ayma, the President of the Plurinational State of Bolivia', 64th Session of the General Assembly of the United Nations (2009).

Bolivia then hosted the World People's Conference on Climate Change and the Rights of Mother Earth where around 35 000 people from over 140 countries[84] wrote the citizens' UDRME.[85] The text asserts the rights of nature, which includes the role of humans and pays particular attention to the multiple power dynamics that structure the climate change debate, calling for the 'decolonization of the atmosphere' while noting the links between the ways in which the environment is exploited and capitalist and patriarchal structures.[86] At the UN level, annual intergovernmental negotiations have been held since 2009 on constructing a non-anthropocentric understanding of sustainable development. Several UN General Assembly Resolutions and UN Secretary General Reports have now been produced that call for the recognition of RoN.[87] A series of UNGA Interactive Dialogues have also been held on Harmony with Nature.[88] In 2015, the UNGA called for the creation of an expert report on Earth Jurisprudence, establishing a global network of experts.[89] The Expert Report on Earth Jurisprudence that followed was released in 2016.[90] The Report recognizes the 'fundamental legal rights of ecosystems and species to exist, thrive and regenerate'.[91] In 2017, the UNGA Dialogue focused on applying Earth Jurisprudence to the Sustainable Development goals.[92] In terms of setting international standards, the jurisprudence of the citizen-led (and therefore non-binding) International Tribunal for the Rights of Nature, which applies the UDRME to real cases, is also of use.[93] Overall, and notwithstanding such developments, however, RoN have yet to be seriously considered within international law. Seeking to situate RoN within IEL will require considerable continued advocacy, but also offers potential, precisely because definitions have yet to be set.

To understand what RoN could include/exclude there is a need to analyse their application in domestic law. As noted above, Indigenous peoples have been central in obtaining RoN in various contexts. For example, Indigenous peoples played a key role in the recognition of RoN in Ecuador's 2008 constitution.[94] The constitution 'celebrates' nature, with nature being defined as 'Pachamama', referring to the sacred deity revered by Indigenous peoples of the Andes.[95] In New Zealand, Indigenous peoples have also played a central role in the recognition of RoN. Here, RoN have been recognized through two agreements which came about following long negotiations processes with local Māori activists (the Whanganui *iwi* in relation to the Whanganui

---

84. Figures on delegates from: Kauffman and Sheehan supra (n 80) 347.
85. World People's Conference on Climate Change and the Rights of Mother Earth, April 22nd 2010, Bolivia, People's agreement <https://pwccc.wordpress.com/support/> last accessed 23 November 2020.
86. ibid.
87. For a full list of these, see: UN Harmony with Nature, 'UN Documents on Harmony with Nature' <http://harmonywithnatureun.org/unDocs/> last accessed 23 November 2020.
88. See: UN Harmony with Nature, 'Interactive Dialogues of the General Assembly' <http://www.harmonywithnatureun.org/dialogues/> last accessed 23 November 2020.
89. United Nations, UNGA Res A/RE/S/70/208 (2015), 3–4.
90. United Nations, UNGA Res A/71/266 (2016).
91. ibid 7.
92. UNGA, 'Report of the Secretary-General' (2017) UN Doc A/72/175.
93. Rights of Nature Tribunal <https://www.rightsofnaturetribunal.org/> last accessed 23 November 2020.
94. See: Eisenstadt and Jones West supra (n 17).
95. Republic of Ecuador, Constitution of 2008, trans. Georgetown University, Preamble <https://pdba.georgetown.edu/Constitutions/Ecuador/english08.html> last accessed 23 November 2020.

river or Te Awa Tupua and the Tūhoe *iwi* in relation to the Te Urewera forest).[96] However, as also noted above, Indigenous people have not been involved in all instances of RoN recognition. For example, Indigenous groups are not involved in the proposed 'right of nature' Bill in the Philippines,[97] nor in the initial recognition of RoN in India (subsequently overruled by the Supreme Court).[98] It is clear, however, that Indigenous legalities have been central in the recasting of legal concepts that has led to the emergence of the recognition of RoN.[99]

In 2008, Ecuador became the first country to recognize RoN constitutionally. Ecuador's constitution outlines nature rights as being inherent to the Earth itself, a legal recognition and status that applies nationally. This broad national coverage differs from other RoN provisions, which focus on specific ecosystems.[100] For example, in New Zealand, the Whanganui River (Te Awa Tupua) and the Te Urewera forest[101] have had their legal personality recognized.[102] Here, however, the relevant laws define the boundaries of the two ecosystems and thus legal personality is only recognized in relation to these two specific areas – not nationwide. The latter is a more common approach to the application of RoN in domestic law, with the High Court of Uttarakhand in India too, for example, recognizing the legal personhood of the Ganges and Yamuna Rivers alone.[103]

From a posthuman perspective, recognition of RoN within a bounded area alone runs the risk of perpetuating fragmentation (depending on the construction of 'an area'). Thinking about the development of posthuman theory-informed international RoN standards, RoN would require an entanglement-responsive approach recognizing the juridical implications of distributed agency and interconnection. Seeing nature as agentic, and accounting for the intimate connections between human and non-human lives and 'environments', would address core problems outlined above concerning IEL – namely its anthropocentric underpinnings and its fragmented nature. And, arguably, this kind of agency and connection must be recognized globally. Recognizing RoN within a bounded area alone potentially denies such interconnections beyond those boundaries.

RoN provisions differ in their content, but they do share at least one key commonality: the linking of the health and well-being of the environment to that of the people who live there such that the provisions allow people to bring legal claims on behalf of nature. In coming to the Te Awa Tupua agreement, for example, the Whanganui *iwi*

---

96. Te Awa Tupua (Whanganui River Claims Settlement) Act 2017 (New Zealand); Te Urewera Act 2014 (New Zealand).
97. L Chavez, 'Philippine Bill Seeks to Grant Nature the Same Legal Rights as Humans' (2019) Mongaby <https://news.mongabay.com/2019/08/philippine-bill-seeks-to-grant-nature-the-same-legal-rights-as-humans/#:~:text=A%20coalition%20in%20the%20Philippines,confer%20legal%20personhood%20on%20nature.&text=The%20bill%20is%20part%20of,their%20protection%20amid%20intensifying%20threats> last accessed 4 March 2021.
98. First recognized by the High Court of Uttarakhand in: *Mohd. Salim v State of Uttarakhand and Others*, Writ Petition (PIL) No. 126 of 2014 (March 20, 2017), with the decision being overruled by the Supreme Court of India later that year. See: *The State of Uttarakhand and Ors. v Mohd. Salim & Ors.*, Supreme Court of India, Petition for Special Leave to Appeal No. 016879/2017.
99. See: O'Donnell et al. supra (n 14).
100. Kauffman and Sheehan supra (n 80) 344.
101. For a further discussion of this context see: Kauffman and Sheehan supra (n 80) 354–5.
102. Supra (n 96).
103. Supra (n 98).

argued that they are connected to the environment they live in and that the river is alive, and an ancestor. The Te Awa Tupua Act recognizes the river as a legal person with 'all the rights, powers, duties and liabilities of a legal person'.[104] To uphold the river's interests, a guardian body (Tu Pou Tupua) must be appointed and is authorized to speak on behalf of the river.[105] The guardian body is made up of one *iwi* representative and one Crown representative. The river and the people are deemed to be inseparable,[106] meaning that harming the river is, by law, harming the *iwi*. Similarly, the Te Urewera Act recognizes Māori ties to the forest and the Māori view that the forest is a living being. This Act also created a Board to serve as the guardian of the forest's interests, recognizing the legal personality of Te Urewera.[107]

Similarly, in Ecuador, the constitution states that humans are an inherent part of nature, linking RoN to the right to a healthy environment.[108] Furthermore, Article 71 of the constitution states that all 'persons, communities, peoples and nations can call upon public authorities to enforce the rights of nature'.[109] In the US, similarly, RoN provisions link local communities to nature. A development at the state-based (regional) level, there are now well over 40 such RoN local laws.[110] These developments have primarily emerged through the work of local environmental activists. RoN in the US therefore tend to be linked to community rights, with nature being framed as integral to human welfare.[111]

Obviously, the focus on community or people's rights within RoN (in any of the abovementioned formulations) could be seen as a human-centred approach. It might be assumed, therefore, that a posthuman approach would necessarily read such a human community focus as anthropocentric. However, posthuman theory suggests not the displacement of culture for or by nature but, rather, the need to focus on the nature-culture continuum.[112] By drawing out the entanglements between humans, non-humans, and 'the environment', a more reciprocal dynamic can be made central for the law, which will need to balance these sometimes-competing interests, but to do so from a starting point that does not, *ab initio*, assume them to exist in atomistic competition or to pre-exist such enquiry as privileged agentic subject versus objectified

---

104. Te Awa Tupua Act supra (n 96).
105. ibid.
106. ibid Article 69(2).
107. For a further discussion of this context see: Kauffman and Sheehan supra (n 80) 354–5. For more both on this specific case and on the rights of rivers, see: E O'Donnell, *Legal Rights for Rivers: Competition, Collaboration and Water Governance* (Routledge, London and New York 2020). See also: Boyd supra (n 82) 131–57.
108. Republic of Ecuador supra (n 95).
109. ibid Article 71.
110. By mid-2017, at least 43 US local governments had adopted some form of RoN ordinances. Craig Kauffman and Pamela Martin compiled data on these cases. See footnote 9 in Kauffman and Sheehan supra (n 80).
111. See, eg: City of Pittsburgh, Code of Ordinances, Title 6, Article 1, ch 618, 'Marcellus Shale Natural Gas Drilling Ordinance' (2010) <https://library.municode.com/pa/pittsburgh/codes/code_of_ordinances?nodeId=COOR_TITSIXCO_ARTIRERIAC_CH618MASHNAGADR> last accessed 23 November 2020. For more on this, see: Kauffman and Sheehan supra (n 80) 346–7.
112. D Haraway, 'A Cyborg Manifesto: Science, Technology, and Socialist-Feminism in the Late Twentieth Century' in D Haraway, *Simians, Cyborgs and Women: The Reinvention of Nature* (Free Association Books, London 1991) 149, 151; C Åsberg, 'Feminist Posthumanities in the Anthropocene: Forays into the Postnatural' (2017) 1(2) Journal of Posthuman Studies 185.

matter. Whether or not existing RoN approaches always achieve this is, however, another question.

RoN provisions have been applied through different means, in different contexts. One clear division discernible is the difference between models that recognize the rights of nature (as in Ecuador) and provisions that recognize nature's legal personality. In New Zealand a legal personality model has been used. This is because the *iwi* do not emphasize the concept of rights because, to *iwi*, nature is not property but rather a living, 'spiritual' entity as well as a 'physical entity',[113] an ancestor.[114] Accordingly, the concept of guardianship is therefore promoted. The preference for the guardianship approach, in part, explains the difference between provisions in New Zealand and, say, Ecuador.[115] The different models result in different procedures. Unlike Ecuador's RoN laws, New Zealand's laws do not award inherent rights. Rather, legal personality is instilled in the river and forest. This grants the river and the forest (through their guardians) procedural access rights in New Zealand's legal system but does not give them special rights per se. The natural systems thus have the mediated right to petition the court or to receive reparations, for example, but do not have the right to be protected in and of themselves.[116]

The differences between how RoN provisions have been designed also impacts what happens when RoN clash with other rights. Ecuador, being one of the first states to recognize RoN, has some of the most developed jurisprudence in this area, but the recognition of RoN in Ecuador has in practice been highly contested and environmental damage remains rampant, particularly in relation to industrial activity and oil extraction.[117] Many provisions have yet to be adequately defined and applied.

Under the Constitution of Ecuador, nature has 'the right to integral respect for its existence and for the maintenance and regeneration of its life cycles, structures, functions and evolutionary processes'.[118] In addition, it is stated that '[n]ature has the right to be restored' and that the state 'shall apply preventative and restrictive measures on activities that might lead to the extinction of species, the destruction of ecosystems and the permanent alteration of natural cycles'.[119] Nature rights are not, however, absolutely protected: the constitution situates sustainable development as core, seeking to balance environmental needs against development needs.[120] Central, however, is Article 395.4, which states that, 'In the event of doubt about the scope of legal provisions for environmental issues, it is the most favorable interpretation of their effective force for the protection of nature that shall prevail'.[121] This, however, is not always the outcome, and RoN laws have, since 2008, developed within a highly politicized context.[122]

---

113. Te Awa Tupua Act supra (n 96), Article 13(a).
114. CM Kauffman, 'Managing People for the Benefit of the Land: Practicing Earth Jurisprudence in Te Urewera, New Zealand' (2020) 27(1) ILSE: Interdisciplinary Studies in Literature and Environment 1.
115. See: C Kauffman and PL Martin, 'Constructing Rights of Nature Norms in the US, Ecuador, and New Zealand' (2018) 18(4) Global Environmental Politics, 43, 57.
116. See: Kauffman and Sheehan supra (n 80) 346.
117. For more on the tension between the recognition of RoN and mineral mining in Ecuador, see: Eisenstadt and Jones West supra (n 17).
118. Republic of Ecuador supra (n 95) Article 71.
119. ibid Articles 72 and 73.
120. See, eg: ibid Article 395; see also: Article 408.
121. ibid Article 395.4.
122. Kauffman and Sheehan supra (n 80) 349.

Nevertheless, despite contestation, there are signs of real progress. Several cases have established a standard that killing any animal that is part of an endangered species constitutes a RoN violation.[123] Other judgments have focused on government construction projects, concluding that such projects cannot impede the ability of ecosystems or species to regenerate.[124] The disruption of migration and breeding patterns has also been ruled as violating RoN[125] and the government has been ordered to control illegal mining.[126] RoN have also been enforced in other contexts, for example, in 2011, following the government's removal of several shrimp companies from ecological reserves, one company sought to sue the government, arguing that their removal infringed their economic interests as well as their property rights and the right to work.[127] In 2015, the Constitutional Court ruled on this case, declaring that because natural rights are transversal, they impact on all other rights, including property rights. The Court stated that all actions of the state and individuals must be in accordance with the rights of nature,[128] proclaiming that this position reflects 'a biocentric vision that prioritizes nature in contrast to the classic anthropocentric conception in which the human being is the centre and measure of all things, and where nature was considered a mere provider of resources'.[129] Thus, the courts in Ecuador have sought to use RoN to challenge anthropocentrism with the transversal application of RoN and their ability to challenge other rights. While such approaches and standards could provide key normative inspirations when setting global RoN standards, it is salutary that the setting of standards in Ecuador took considerable effort, especially when it came to challenging economic interests,[130] and that this struggle is still very much ongoing.[131]

---

123. See, eg: Judgment No. 09171-2015-0004, Ninth Court of Criminal Guarantees, Guayas Province, Republic of Ecuador (23 April 2015) 55–9. See also: Kauffman and Sheehan supra (n 80) 350; and: Judgment No. 2003-2014 – C.T., National Court of Justice, Specialized Chamber of Criminal, Military Criminal, Criminal Police and Transit Cases, Republic of Ecuador (7 September 2014); C Kauffman and PL Martin, 'Constructing Rights of Nature Norms in the US, Ecuador, and New Zealand' (2018) 18(4) Global Environmental Politics 43.
124. Judgment No. 11121-2011-0010, Provincial Court of Justice, Loja Province, Republic of Ecuador (30 March 2011). See: Kauffman and Sheehan supra (n 80) 350–1.
125. Judgment No. 269 – 2012, Civil and Mercantile Court, Galápagos Province, Republic of Ecuador (28 June 2012). See: Kauffman and Sheehan supra (n 80) 351.
126. Constitutional Protective Action No. 0016-2011, Twenty-Second Criminal Court, Pichincha Province, Republic of Ecuador (20 May 2011). See: Kauffman and Sheehan supra (n 80) 352.
127. Judgment No. 166-15-SEP-CC, Case No. 0507-12-EP, Constitutional Court of Ecuador, Republic of Ecuador (20 May 2015) 2. See: Kauffman and Sheehan supra (n 80) 353.
128. Judgment No. 166-15-SEP-CC, Case No. 0507-12-EP, Constitutional Court of Ecuador, Republic of Ecuador (20 May 2015) 12. See also: Kauffman and Sheehan supra (n 80) 353.
129. Judgment No. 166-15-SEP-CC, Case No. 0507-12-EP, Constitutional Court of Ecuador, Republic of Ecuador (20 May 2015) 10 – trans. from Kauffman and Sheehan supra (n 80) 353.
130. For more on this see: Kauffman and Sheehan supra (n 80) 357.
131. For more on this evolving history and the various challenges faced in Ecuador, see: CM Kauffman and PL Martin, *The Politics of Rights of Nature: Strategies for Building a More Sustainable Future* (MIT Press, Cambridge MA 2021). RoN laws in Ecuador are still developing. For example, in 2014, RoN were codified into a new Penal Code and Ecuador's 2018 Environmental Code also included RoN provisions. While these are promising steps, unfortunately both codes remain vague at the level of application. See: Republic of Ecuador, Penal Code, Organic Law, 2014; Republic of Ecuador, Environmental Code, 2018. With thanks to Craig Kauffman for his insights on the Penal and Environmental Code in Ecuador. See also: Kauffman and Sheehan supra (n 80) 353–4.

In New Zealand, the Te Awa Tupua Act does not derogate from existing private rights in the Whanganui River.[132] The Act states that any actor, public or private, must 'have particular regard to' the interests of the river[133] and must recognize the values of the Te Awa Tupua, which include treating the river as a living entity.[134] Thus, as Craig M Kauffman and Linda Sheehan note, through giving legal personhood to nature (but not giving nature rights per se), the New Zealand system has been set up so that 'decisions on how to balance the rights of ecosystems against the rights of other legal persons (e.g. individuals and corporations) in a given situation will need to be made'.[135] Currently, the hierarchy of rights between these multiple competing interests is unclear. Standards will likely develop over time, much as in Ecuador. These Acts, therefore, while being key for Māori rights, are carefully constructed to ensure that they are framed around the neoliberal legal order. The Acts allow for recognition through a legal personhood framework, thereby drawing on the existing options with New Zealand's settler-colonial legal framework, avoiding the outright prioritization of RoN over, for example, corporate rights to exploit nature.[136] It remains to be seen, however, how a court would rule in the instance of a clash between property rights and nature rights.[137]

A key emerging RoN standard in the US that might prove central when seeking to set out posthuman theory-informed international RoN standards is the right of nature to flourish.[138] Kauffman and Sheehan argue that

> the right to flourish switches the emphasis from preventing permanent damage to ensuring some level of well-being for an ecosystem. This would require a more restrictive definition of which human impacts are acceptable, and thus stricter standards based on measurements of the well-being of ecosystems.[139]

Overall, the right for nature to flourish could come to set an important RoN standard. Calling for the right to flourish goes beyond merely restoring nature but, rather, could be a step towards recognizing nature's full agency in a way that is more akin to Bennett's new materialist understanding of the agency of matter. Such a right would contrast with the more limited understanding of nature's legally defined rights, which does not – inherently – allow for a wider understanding of the agency of matter itself. It is clear from this review of their success and limitations thus far that RoN challenge powerful political and economic interests, making the question of their implementation highly politicized. There are signs, arguably, that recognition of RoN globally could be one way of potentially dismantling the subject/object dichotomy at the heart of IEL. RoN could also provide a way to challenge the more top-down,

---

132. The situation of the forest is a little different as it was formerly a national park. For more on this see: Kauffman and Martin supra (n 115) 52.
133. Tw Awa Tupua Act supra (n 96) Article 15(3).
134. ibid Article 13.
135. Kauffman and Sheehan supra (n 80) 354.
136. Otto and Jones supra (n 11).
137. For more information on the history of the law in New Zealand, see: Kauffman and Martin supra (n 115) 56–8.
138. Kauffman and Sheehan supra (n 80) 347. See, eg: Ordinance of the City Council of Santa Monica establishing Sustainability Rights, 12 March 2012, <https://www.smgov.net/departments/council/agendas/2013/20130312/s2013031207-C-1.htm#:~:text=(a)%20All%20residents%20of%20Santa,sustainable%20climate%20that%20supports%20thriving> last accessed 23 November 2020.
139. Kauffman and Sheehan supra (n 80) 347.

state-led approach taken within IEL, allowing multiple stakeholders to have a greater say in environmental protection. While there is clearly growing international interest in RoN, the question of standards and implementation remains a lively field of contestation and tensions. However, domestic examples of application – such as those outlined above – could, and arguably do, suggest standards that could and should be considered as models for a way forward.

5 POTENTIALS AND PITFALLS OF A POSTHUMAN THEORY-INFORMED RIGHTS OF NATURE APPROACH

Above, I analysed some of the flaws in existing IEL, noting the ways in which posthuman theory might be used to provide a much-needed onto-epistemic shift. I have also outlined how RoN might provide one way to re-think IEL through the notion of the posthuman.

RoN and posthuman theory align across several vectors. For one, both seek to recognize the agency of nature-matter. Both therefore confront the subject/object binary that underpins Western thought, challenging human exceptionalism. However, while inherent links between RoN and posthuman theory have been suggested,[140] from a legal studies perspective, it becomes clear that it is not a given that a RoN approach will inherently produce a posthuman approach to IEL. After all, these projects, while related, are distinct and it is true to say that posthuman theory and RoN have not yet extensively been brought into mutual conversation. In the next few pages, I will seek to analyse the potentials and risks of a posthuman theory-informed RoN approach, focusing on the issues of representation, universalism and global inequalities.

5.1 Who represents nature?

Posthuman theory posits that nature has agency.[141] However, if RoN are to be upheld at law, humans must put forward nature's claims on its behalf. Humans can seek to represent nature drawing on a variety of tools, which may include, for example, Earth jurisprudence[142] or the application of scientific knowledge. However, these tools are by no means neutral and they do not always provide clear answers. Take the application of scientific knowledge, for example: while the application of the 'right to science' in international environmental law may, indeed, as Anna-Maria Hubert argues, create a more 'effective, equitable and democratically legitimate and accountable process',[143] exactly what science says for the purpose of understanding what is best for nature is contestable. To give a concrete example of how science, despite drawing on a variety of recognized methods to seek to ensure rigour, is

---

140. See, eg, artist Ursula Biemann and architect Paulo Tavares' fantastic project on 'Forest Law'. See: 'Ursula Biemann and Paulo Tavares: BAK' (2015) Frieze, Issue 175 <https://www.frieze.com/article/ursula-biemann-paulo-tavares> last accessed 13 April 2021. While not discussing RoN directly, Jessie Hohmann makes a similar point, arguing that new materialism may be used to push rights beyond their current framing, towards the more-than-human. See: Hohmann supra (n 8) 12–14.
141. Bennett supra (n 52).
142. See, eg: supra (n 71).
143. A Hubert, 'The Human Right to Science and Its Relationship to International Environmental Law' (2020) 31(2) European Journal of International Law 625, 625.

contestable, one can look to deep-sea mining. While deep-sea mining, or what is termed 'exploitation', has not yet been legally authorized, the Mining Code, which would authorize such exploitation, is currently under draft.[144] There is an obligation under international law to ensure that adequate environmental impact assessments (EIAs) are conducted before mining can go ahead.[145] Scientists argue, however, that the standards currently set for conducting EIAs are too low,[146] noting how the measures used to conduct EIAs in international waters lag behind international standards applicable to other environments and within other areas of international law.[147] There is no defined minimum scope for conducting a valid EIA in international law.[148] Accordingly, while EIAs have been conducted,[149] the concern is that the standards set when conducting such EIAs are inadequate.[150] Commenting specifically on the EIAs that have been conducted on deep-sea mining, Holly J Niner et al. argue that these EIAs lack the 'statistical power' required in order to be adequate or accurate.[151]

What this example shows is that it is not always clear what is best for nature. While one group of scientists might argue that any harm to ecosystems caused by deep-sea mining will be minimal, another challenges that stance. This lack of certainty makes it difficult (at least drawing on the 'authority of science') for humans to represent nature at all. From a posthuman perspective, however, this dilemma becomes ever more complex. As posthuman theorist Vicky Kirby has argued, to 'represent nature' is to risk re-inscribing a humanist and anthropocentric blueprint through a human framing of what nature is and wants. As Kirby states, nature does not need a 'human scribe to represent itself, to mediate or translate its identity'.[152] Nature is self-organizing and has a language of its own, comprised of a series of networks.[153] Yet if the law is to protect nature's rights, nature will require human representation. This is a problem: humans do not always know what is best for nature[154] and are tied to humanist and

144. See: International Seabed Authority, 'The Mining Code' <https://www.isa.org.jm/mining-code> last accessed 12 April 2021.
145. Pulp Mills on the River Uruguay (Argentina v Uruguay), International Court of Justice, Judgment of 20 April 2010. More specifically in relation to the law of the sea, the need for EIAs was affirmed in: Responsibilities and Obligations of States Sponsoring Persons and Entities with Respect to Activities in The Area, International Tribunal for the Law of the Sea, Advisory Opinion of 1 February 2011, paras 124–50.
146. HJ Niner et al., 'Deep-Sea Mining with No Net Loss of Biodiversity – An Impossible Aim' (2018) 5 Frontiers in Marine Science 1; Flora and Fauna International, 'The Risks and Impacts of Deep-Sea Mining to Marine Ecosystems' 7 <https://cms.fauna-flora.org/wp-content/uploads/2020/03/FFI_2020_The-risks-impacts-deep-seabed-mining_Executive-Summary.pdf> last accessed 12 April 2021; JM Durden et al., 'Environmental Impact Assessment Process for Deep-Sea Mining in "The Area"' (2018) 87 Marine Policy 194.
147. Harden-Davies et al. supra (n 13).
148. Pulp Mills on the River Uruguay supra (n 145) para 205.
149. See: Bundesanstalt für Geowissenschaften und Rohstoffe, 'Environmental Impact Assessment' 2018 <https://isa.org.jm/files/files/documents/EIA_BGR_0.pdf> last accessed 12 April 2021; Global Sea Mineral Resources, 'Environmental Impact Assessment' 2018 available to download at <https://www.isa.org.jm/minerals/environmental-impact-assessments> last accessed 12 April 2021.
150. Harden-Davies et al. supra (n 13).
151. Niner et al. supra (n 146) 7. For a discussion of the inadequacies of existing processes as well as proposals on how to make the process more robust, see: Durden et al. supra (n 146).
152. Kirby supra (n 67) 232.
153. ibid 232.
154. ibid 232.

anthropocentric blueprints of thought when working within the dominant Eurocentric framework of international law.

This representational necessity presents a conundrum: if 'the world' really is 'a witty agent' with an 'independent sense of humor'[155] as Donna Haraway argues, how can that wit, that agency, ever be fully understood by humans, let alone represented non-reductively by them in court? However, this may be a Western problem. Haraway's human subject and the body of knowledge that she and most posthuman theory primarily draws on is Global North-centric. Some Indigenous cosmovisions, as I will outline shortly, are not necessarily presented with the same conundrum of representation.

Bennett, likewise primarily writing from a Western, US perspective, when discussing the need to create a political system that includes matter, is all too aware of this dilemma concerning human understanding and representation. '[T]hing power', she states, is that which 'we cannot know' and which 'refuses to dissolve completely into the milieu of human knowledge'.[156] Posthuman neo-materialisms thus present an impossibility: the need to include matter/'nature' in understandings of the world and the impossibility of humans ever being able to fully understand it. However, while there is something about matter and 'nature' that will always exceed human knowledge, this does not mean that matter should remain sidelined or objectified.[157] Rather, posthuman theory points to the need to remain 'perceptually open', to accept that not all can be known but seek to know and understand what can, as Bennett argues.[158] Rosi Braidotti argues that 'we need to devise a new vocabulary, with new figurations to refer to the elements of our posthuman embodied and embedded subjectivity'.[159] Accordingly, not only must matter be included in thought, accepting the limits of current understandings, but there is a need to remain open to change, to new languages and figurations.[160]

Turning at this point towards Indigenous cosmovisions and practices of relationality might yield clues towards such new languages and figurations. The question of how nature is represented has been central to the framing of provisions in New Zealand. For example, during the Te Urewera negotiations, the Tūhoe *iwi* were keen to ensure that the focus was on the return of the land to its pre-settler dignity, not on them gaining ownership or property rights over it. For the Tūhoe *iwi*, nature is not and cannot be property. As the CEO of Te Uru Taumatua (the organization representing the Tūhoe *iwi*), Kirsti Luke, argued in 2013,

> Ownership and the owning of Te Urewera has been a mechanism to destroy belonging and care, and therefore community. Ownership granted entitlement without having earned it ... Ownership does not value kinship with the things around us ... it breeds very transactional relationships between humans and the land ...[161]

In this instance, to respect this non-ownability, a legal personality model was applied: no one owned Te Urewera, and legal personality was deployed as 'an imperfect approximation of recognizing the forest as a whole, living, spiritual being but likely the best

---

155. Haraway supra (n 46) 199.
156. Bennett supra (n 52) 3.
157. ibid 3.
158. ibid 14.
159. Braidotti supra (n 44) 82.
160. Bennett supra (n 52) 111.
161. K Luke, Presentation at the United Nations Interactive Dialogue of the General Assembly on Harmony with Nature, United Nations Headquarters, New York, Monday, April 23, 2018, as quoted in Kauffman supra (n 114) 6.

possibility within a European legal framework'.[162] Earth jurisprudence suggests a similar solution, noting that an ecosystem's natural order is so complex that humans are incapable of fully understanding it, and concluding that humans should seek to structure their systems to best fit this natural order, rather than trying to dominate nature.[163]

Yet even if nature can be acceptably represented, to some degree at least, other problems arise in relation to any approach relying on legal personhood. There are risks in seeking to challenge the liberal framework of the law by calling upon legal constructs so intimately and ultimately dependent upon an anthropocentric, individualistic account of the legal subject.[164] By trying to work within the system, even when seeking to include a new subject, one risks merely extending the existing paradigm without actually challenging it sufficiently. In other words, by calling for inclusion without a wider paradigm shift, there is a risk, as Braidotti argues (in relation to the inclusion of animals as subjects), that '[h]umanism is actually being reinstated uncritically under the aegis of species [and materialist] egalitarianism'.[165] While egalitarianism is not directly at issue in the case of legal personhood for Te Urewera, it is at least likely that the underpinnings of the very construct called upon need to be re-thought. In short, there is a risk that calling for nature to be recognized as a subject within the current legal system, perhaps particularly at the international level, will reinforce or legitimize the very same system that makes such resort necessary. This dilemma does not mean, however, that RoN and posthuman approaches should be abandoned. Rather, as feminist theorists of international law have argued with respect to gender justice, there is a need for multiple strategies at multiple levels, seeking to foster legal change from within the system while also seeking to re-think the system itself.[166] In this sense, RoN may play a 'transitional role'[167] but need not be the end game. While RoN may have been 'unthinkable just a few decades ago',[168] they are now 'gaining momentum',[169] and as such approaches become more accepted, the space for more radical ideas of what RoN can be, or for ideas beyond RoN, will also open up.[170]

The realities of power dynamics must also be recognized here. For example, Indigenous groups have, in some instances, and as outlined above in the context of New Zealand, adopted a strategy of working within the system while trying to bring their own knowledge to bear on that system. While there are indeed limitations to such an

---

162. Kauffman supra (n 114) 7.
163. ibid 10.
164. On the legal subject, see: N Naffine, 'Women and the Cast of Legal Persons' in J Jones, A Grear, RA Fenton and K Stevenson (eds), *Gender, Sexualities and Law* (Routledge, Oxford 2011) 15; A Grear, '"Sexing the Matrix": Embodiment, Disembodiment and the Law – Towards the Re-gendering of Legal Rationality' in J Jones, A Grear, RA Fenton and K Stevenson (eds), *Gender, Sexualities and Law* (Routledge, Oxford 2011) 39; Sydney Parfitt supra (n 31).
165. Braidotti supra (n 44) 78–9.
166. Jones supra (n 6); C Charlesworth, G Heathcote and E Jones, 'Feminist Scholarship on International Law in the 1990s and Today: An Inter-Generational Conversation' (2019) 27(1) Feminist Legal Studies 79; F Bird, '"Is This a Time of Beautiful Chaos?" Reflecting on International Feminist Legal Methods' (2020) 28(2) Feminist Legal Studies 179.
167. G Garver, 'Are Rights of Nature Radical Enough for Ecological Law?' in K Anker et al. (eds), *From Environmental to Ecological Law* (Routledge, Oxford and New York 2021) 100.
168. Boyd supra (n 82) 222.
169. ibid 223.
170. See also Youatt who proposes a new model for thinking about legal personhood through a model of human-nonhuman personification: R Youatt, 'Personhood and the Rights of Nature: The New Subjects of Contemporary Earth Politics' (2017) 11 International Political Sociology 39.

approach, and such negotiations are a far cry from adopting Māori jurisprudence throughout New Zealand, the negotiations have arguably represented an important milestone in the settler-colonial state and pressed back, albeit imperfectly, incompletely and contingently, against the dominant onto-epistemology (albeit that the risks of system-legitimation noted above still persist).

Perhaps one way in which RoN can be thought of beyond the liberal individual subject would be through challenging the meaning of rights themselves. Rights have predominantly been applied in law to bounded, individual legal subjects – a perennial challenge.[171] Garver, for example, asks whether rights of nature (as rights) can be radical enough to create an ecological law?[172] It is relatively clear that if RoN are framed through current dominant legal understandings of rights, their impact will be limited. However, rights can be re-thought. As Iván Vargas-Roncancio asks, drawing on ethnographic research focusing on indigenous cosmovisions: what happens if rights are granted 'to relationships instead of substances and or/persons?'[173] Arguably, if rights are granted to relationships, the framing shifts. Rights are currently balanced against one another, a framing that for RoN 'essentially equips nature for battle with other rights holders'.[174] Clearly, existing liberal conceptions of rights are part of the currently dominant 'divisive, reductionist and atomistic' system which does not account for the interconnections between matter, humans and non-humans.[175] However, if rights are granted to relationships, the framing of relational dynamics opens up, promising a shift beyond the problematic theoretical underpinnings of existing applications of rights.[176] RoN, if so conceived and adequately developed both theoretically and jurisprudentially, have the potential, arguably, not only to challenge IEL, but to address the entire way in which law and jural relations are currently understood.[177]

5.2 Universalism, colonialism and global inequalities

Since sovereign will[178] and the lack of a universal system for environmental protection[179] are two of the core challenges faced by IEL, it is tempting to think that seeking to create a universal RoN frame for environmental protection is required. However,

---

171. R Kapur, *Gender, Alterity and Human Rights: Freedom in a Fishbowl* (Edward Elgar, Cheltenham 2018). On the limits of human rights and reimagining them from a new materialist perspective, see: A Grear, 'Human Rights and New Horizons? Thoughts toward a New Juridical Ontology' (2018) 43(1) Science, Technology & Human Values 129.
172. Garver supra (n 167).
173. Vargas-Roncancio supra (n 17) 122.
174. Garver supra (n 167) 91.
175. ibid 91.
176. On the liberal underpinnings of rights and alternative framings, see: Kapur supra (n 171).
177. Youatt makes a similar argument, noting the need to emphasize the connections between the human and non-human. Youatt, however, calls for legal personhood to be considered, not rights, suggesting that legal personhood has a stronger potential to recognize such connections. However, if rights are framed as relational (see the next paragraph), it seems rights framings could indeed be compatible with Youatt's framing. See Youatt supra (n 170).
178. For example, Aguila and Viñuales highlight that a key barrier which stands in the way of more radical environmental protection provisions being adopted in the Global Pact is, in fact, state sovereignty. State sovereignty, they conclude, and the foregrounding of the state in international law, will therefore likely result in the provisions of the Global Pact going little beyond existing provisions in IEL. See: Aguila and Viñuales supra (n 26) 8.
179. UN General Assembly supra (n 24).

there are vast problems with the concept of universalism that could haunt any application of RoN. Feminist and postcolonial theorists have long problematized international law's claim to be universal (and its purported neutrality), noting the ways in which it both disguises and reproduces the gendered and racialized power hierarchies upheld by the law.[180] After all, many international legal principles were created at a time when much of the world was colonized and when only European states had a say on what international law was.[181] Thinking specifically about Indigenous peoples, while Indigenous people have long interacted between peoples and nations, often 'going beyond the nation-state in order to advance their position and pursue justice',[182] they were and often still are excluded from shaping, making and participating in international law.[183]

IEL has also had to tackle the problems posed by structural injustices associated with universalism, most notably when seeking to balance environmental protection with the economic needs of different actors with varying levels of economic power.[184] Many provisions have been built into IEL that seek to manage this tension. For example, the concept of common but differentiated responsibility underpins many environmental law treaties, seeking to ensure that the economic development needs of some states are balanced against the wealth of others when deciding differing responsibilities to address climate change. Another example of how IEL seeks to balance this tension can be seen in the principle of sustainable development, which notes the need to exploit natural resources in a manner that is sustainable and in which economic objectives are taken into consideration to ensure that states, and especially states with stronger development needs, can continue to draw on their natural resources.[185] However, such approaches ultimately allow environmental exploitation to continue.[186] While sustainable development seeks to account for economic imbalances (many of which are the result of colonialism and the ways in which European powers

---

180. See: A Anghie, *Imperialism, Sovereignty and the Making of International Law* (Cambridge University Press, Cambridge 2012); C Charlesworth and C Chinkin, *The Boundaries of International Law: A Feminist Analysis* (Manchester University Press, Manchester 2000); H Charlesworth and C Chinkin, *The Boundaries of International Law: A Feminist Analysis* (Manchester University Press, Manchester, 2000).
181. A Anghie, 'Finding the Peripheries: Sovereignty and Colonialism in Nineteenth-Century International Law' (1999) 40(1) Harvard International Law Journal 1.
182. M McMillan and S Rigney, 'The Place of the First Peoples in the International Sphere: A Logical Starting Point for the Demand for Justice by Indigenous Peoples' (2016) 39(3) Melbourne University Law Review 981, 992.
183. S James Anaya, *Indigenous Peoples in International Law* (2nd edn, Oxford University Press, Oxford 2000); McMillan and Rigney supra (n 182) 994–7.
184. See: S Alam et al. (eds), *International Environmental Law and the Global South* (Cambridge University Press, Cambridge 2015).
185. Sustainable development is made up of several components, including the general need to exploit resources in a manner which is 'sustainable', the need to preserve resources for future generations, the equitable use of resources between states and the need to consider economic and development objectivities. Sustainable development was concretized recently through its use in the 2015 Paris Agreement to the UN Framework Convention on Climate Change (UNFCCC) and the 2017 Resolution of the UN General Assembly, 'Our Ocean, Our Future: Call to Action', 6 July 2017, UNGA Res. 71/312. See also: R Gordon, 'Unsustainable Development' in S Alam et al. (eds), *International Environmental Law and the Global South* (Cambridge University Press, Cambridge 2015) 50.
186. On the politics of IEL from a Global North/South perspective, calling for a more nuanced understanding of Global North/South relations in IEL, see: Natarajan and Khoday supra (n 31).

profited, and continue to profit from, the extraction of resources from the places they once colonized) there are risks presented by this approach, which is used by states to justify environmental damage. As Usha Natarajan and Kishan Khoday note, while sustainable development does challenge ideas of economic growth, it is seldom used 'to call for less development'.[187] Taking this argument further, they argue that the concept of sustainable development, in the end, ensures that the status quo remains, helping to 'naturalize and obfuscate the process whereby some people systemically under-develop others', resulting in the continued deepening of global inequalities.[188]

Ultimately, such realities point to the need to challenge existing economic power imbalances. One way this might occur could be through the payment of reparations by states that benefited from the colonial extraction of the natural resources of those they colonized. Ultimately, however, the entire global capitalist system must be challenged if global economic imbalances are to shift and if the extractivist model upon which the global order is based upon is to be re-modelled. While much may be learnt from Marxist approaches to international law,[189] drawing on Indigenous jurisprudential models and experiences of environmental governance which challenge the nature/culture binary that underpins Western thought and embracing RoN approaches do hold out some hope of forging a less oppressive imaginary. Emerging literature on the commons and on new materialist onto-epistemologies for commoning might also provide a way in which to re-think the links between capitalism and the Anthropocene[190] (or the Capitalocene as Moore, among others, names it[191]). More could be learnt from looking towards work on radical alternatives to development[192] and to ideas around 'degrowth'[193] (which was importantly mentioned as a possible global solution for environmental issues for the first time at the international level in July 2020[194]). It is into this mix of critiques, possibilities and risks that RoN emerges as one way of rethinking law. The tensions between the aims and the current application of RoN need to be constantly re-thought in the search for international RoN standards and approaches in the search for a way forward that does not collapse into the same nature/culture framework which permeates IEL.

187. Natarajan and Khoday supra (n 31) 589.
188. ibid 589.
189. See: Tzouvala supra (n 2); Baars supra (n 2); R Knox, 'Marxist Approaches to International Law' in A Orford and F Hoffmann (eds), *The Oxford Handbook of the Theory of International Law* (Oxford University Press, Oxford 2016); S Marks, 'Human Rights and Root Causes' (2011) 74 Modern Law Review 57; C Miéville, *Between Equal Rights: A Marxist Theory of International Law* (Pluto Press, London 2006).
190. See: A Grear, 'Resisting Anthropocene Neoliberalism: Towards New Materialist Commoning?' in A Grear, and D Bollier (eds), *The Great Awakening: New Modes of Life Amidst Capitalist Ruins* (Punctum Press, Brooklyn NY 2020); Ohdedar supra (n 74); Neimanis supra (n 39).
191. J Moore, 'The Capitalocene, Part I: On the Nature and Origins of Our Ecological Crisis' (2017) 44(3) The Journal of Peasant Studies 594.
192. A Kothari, 'Radical Well-Being Alternatives to Development' in P Cullet and S Koonan (eds), *Research Handbook on Law, Environment and the Global South* (Edward Elgar, Cheltenham 2019).
193. For more on defining degrowth, see: J Hickel, 'What Does Degrowth Mean? A Few Points of Clarification' (2020) Globalizations 1.
194. See: United Nations, Report of the Secretary General on Harmony with Nature, 28 July 2020, UN Docs A/75/266.

6 CONCLUSION

I have argued that there are clear problems with IEL, which is essentially anthropocentric, separating human, non-human, and environmental interests into separately demarcated legal spheres, while prioritizing human interests over all others. I have sought to highlight posthuman legal theory's challenge to the anthropocentrism of IEL, and have suggested that those seeking to apply posthuman legal theory could greatly benefit from engaging with RoN approaches, drawing on some links between their respective aims. In turn, I have sought to understand what RoN could learn from posthuman theory.

To offer this reflection, I outlined some developing RoN standards in various domestic jurisdictions, with an eye towards the development of international standards. Drawing on the lessons learnt from domestic applications of RoN, several key challenges were highlighted including, for example, the core tension visible between economic interests and nature's rights. I then moved on to discuss some of the broader issues that haunt the application of both RoN and posthuman legal theory, focusing on the challenges presented by representation and universalism. Noting the problems with promoting universal concepts in an unequal world, I highlighted the need to situate RoN within the wider context of global economic inequalities, emphasizing the need to challenge global economic imbalances. This challenge must continue both through and beyond RoN.

On the question of representation, I drew on posthuman new materialist theory to argue that there is a central need to remain 'perceptually open'[195] and to devise new vocabularies,[196] recognizing the limits of the RoN project, while seeking to promote imaginative change.

To conclude, and as I noted in the course of my reflections, there are always risks in working within the liberal legal system in that, by working within the system and seeking to improve it, one risks legitimizing the system itself. This is a problem that all critical thinkers face: when seeking to apply critical thought, there is a risk that part of the radicality of that thought can be lost in application.[197] However, I suggest that critical change must occur both within a system as well as from outside to be effective. Implementing RoN standards is, as I have argued, a strong place to start when seeking to re-think IEL in a posthuman register. It is essential, with all that is now urgently at stake, that those seeking to apply posthuman legal theory to IEL engage with RoN approaches and that, in turn, the insights of posthuman theory are used to contribute to the development of international RoN standards.

ADDENDUM

Between this article being written and its publication, the Human Rights Council, on 8 October 2021, recognized a new right to a clean, healthy and sustainable environment for the first time. While the recognition of this right is to be highly applauded, as noted in this article, the framing of the right remains problematically anthropocentric. See: Human Rights Council, 2021, A/HRC/48/13.

195. Bennett supra (n 52) 14.
196. Braidotti supra (n 44) 82.
197. Feminist approaches to international law provide a good example here; while feminist approaches have been successful in adding women's concerns to existing international legal frames, such as within international human rights law, the transformative elements of feminist approaches which seek, for example, to challenge the gendered foundations of the international legal system itself, have been somewhat left behind in the focus on the inclusion of women. See: Jones supra (n 6); Charlesworth, Heathcote and Jones supra (n 166); Bird supra (n 166).

Response-abilities of care in more-than-human worlds

Marie-Catherine Petersmann*
Postdoctoral Researcher, Department of Public Law and Governance, Tilburg Law School

This article rethinks the doctrines of responsibility and protection in international environmental law in light of notions of response-abilities *and* care *in more-than-human worlds. Inspired by the intersecting strands of new materialist, relational and posthuman literatures, and informed by critiques of them by decolonial, indigenous and black scholars, the analysis works with onto-epistemologies of becoming that posit an inseparability of being, knowing and acting with(in) the Anthropocene/s. Through the notion of* response-abilities of care, *the article reconfigures how the destructive and the restorative relations between humans and nonhumans could be construed beyond a narrow understanding of state sovereignty, territorial jurisdiction, liberal human-centred notions of individuated agency and the strict causal nexus between victim and perpetrator. The analysis concludes by reflecting on how law could remain open to emergent, unfolding and contingent potentialities of entangled human-nonhuman relations, and questions law's capacity to recognize and respond to the agency and alterity of nonhumans. These configurations exceed the schema of responsibility and protection that organizes even international environmental law's most progressive theories and practices, such as granting 'rights to nature'.*

Keywords: *responsibility, protection, response-abilities, care, becoming-with, Anthropocene*

1 INTRODUCTION

Living in the 'Anthropocene' implies living in times when 'many conditions and processes on Earth are profoundly altered by human impact'.[1] Particular human activities have become a geophysical force capable of disrupting the relative ecological stability that has sustained life on Earth. Anthropogenic disruptions like global warming, and the current COVID-19 pandemic, are daunting examples of disastrous events caused by particular modes of living and inhabiting more-than-human worlds. In these

---

*   m.c.petersmann@tilburguniversity.edu. I would like to thank Hans Lindahl, Anna Grear and Dimitri Van den Meerssche for helping me think through and structure the argument, and my colleagues at Tilburg Law School for their constructive feedback when I presented an earlier draft at the 'Constitutionalizing in the Anthropocene' research seminar. I also want to thank the two wonderful reviewers who helped me sharpen my thinking and critique, and Samvel Varvastian, Ivan Vargas, Emille Boulot and Rose Campbell for their fantastic editorial work.
1.   The formalization of the concept by the Anthropocene Working Group (AWG) still needs to be approved by the International Commission on Stratigraphy. On the AWG's findings, see <http://quaternary.stratigraphy.org/working-groups/anthropocene/> accessed 7 November 2020.

unfolding human-caused disasters, CO_2 and SARS-CoV-2 act as powerful nonhuman agents, which, in turn, are disrupting the relative stability of political and legal orders. The entangled human-nonhuman agency at play in these intertwined phenomena displaces modernist views of human subjects separated from nonhuman objects. The reception of the 'Anthropocene' thesis in the humanities has therefore been described as a major 'event' that destabilizes modernist cuts between humans and nonhumans at work in social theory.[2]

Despite its wide deployment, the 'Anthropocene' is a controversial term, the definition, starting date and causes of which remain largely contested.[3] What is at stake in those critiques is the problematic reassertion of universality through an *Anthropos-cene* that re-establishes a new form of 'planetary humanism' that risks erasing histories of violence and dispossession of the wretched of the modern world and disavows the multiple worlds inhabited with(in) 'Anthropocenes'.[4] This article therefore uses the semiotic construct of 'Anthropocene/s' to capture both the singularity implied by the 'planetary condition' associated with the 'Anthropocene' and the plurality of multiple ways of inhabiting, experiencing and engaging with(in) more-than-human worlds that unfold in 'Anthropocenes'.[5]

Against this backdrop, the article interrogates what it would mean for law and legal theory to recognize the entangled human-nonhuman agency that the Anthropocene/s foregrounds. My argument aligns with those strands of critique that think with and against the Anthropocene to revisit the presuppositions of Western modernity – a modernity grounded in an image of 'nature' as an object amenable to 'human' mastery and control.[6] Both the human subject and the natural world produced by Western modern taxonomies are here questioned and suspended. To this end, the article

---

2. Cf. C Hamilton, C Bonneuil and F Gemenne (eds), *The Anthropocene and the Global Environmental Crisis: Rethinking Modernity in a New Epoch* (Routledge, 2015).
3. See eg N Clark and B Szerszynski, *Planetary Social Thought: The Anthropocene Challenge to the Social Sciences* (Polity, 2020); K Yusoff, *A Billion Black Anthropocenes or None* (The University of Minnesota Press, 2019); SL Lewis and MA Maslin, *The Human Planet: How We Created the Anthropocene* (Yale University Press, 2018); H Davis and Z Todd, 'On the Importance of a Date, or, Decolonizing the Anthropocene' (2017) 16:4 An International Journal for Critical Geographies 761.
4. For a compelling critique of the erasure of structurally dispossessed, dehumanized and desubjectivized indigenous, black, creole and other 'inhumans' associated with the 'geologically white' Anthropocene, see Yusoff supra (n 3); and Clark and Szerszynski supra (n 3) (especially Chapter 5: 'Inhuman Modernity, Earthly Violence') at 100–22.
5. My approach thereby aligns with, eg, J Amoureux and V Reddy, 'Multiple Anthropocenes: Pluralizing Space–Time as a Response to "the Anthropocene"' (2021) Globalizations. Clark and Szerszynski also convincingly define 'planetary social thought' as a double interrogation regarding a 'planetary multiplicity' on the one hand – or how the Earth, through its dynamic processes, is continuously nudged into transformation by human and nonhuman forces – and 'earthly multitudes' on the other hand – or how the Earth is inhabited differently, with distinct modes of engaging, experiencing, knowing and imagining it. See Clark and Szerszynski supra (n 3). The plural use of 'Anthropocenes' also enables accounting for the different '-cenes' that have been suggested, including the Plantationocene, the Capitalocene or the Chthulucene. See, eg, D Haraway, 'Anthropocene, Capitalocene, Plantationocene, Chthulucene: Making Kin' (2015) 6 Environmental Humanities 159.
6. On the modern nature/culture divide and the need to overcome it, see P Descola, *Par delà nature et culture* (Gallimard, 2005); B Latour, *We Have Never Been Modern* (Harvard University Press, 1993). The deployment of modern 'mastery' reached beyond the so-called 'natural'

engages with intersecting strands of new materialist and posthumanist literatures that view the human as relationally entangled with nonhumans,[7] thereby giving rise to post- or in-human approaches to subjectivity in more-than-human worlds.[8] While post- or in-human theories have come of age and transitioned from the critical margins to become widely established across the humanities, they have tended to overlook, ignore or neglect antecedent decolonial critiques. As Zakiyyah Iman Jackson remarked, '[i]t has largely gone unnoticed by posthumanists that their queries into ontology often find their homologous (even anticipatory) appearance in decolonial philosophies that confront slavery and colonialism's inextricability from the Enlightenment humanism they are trying to displace'.[9] The turn(s) to materiality, relationality and agency discussed throughout this article align, therefore, with decolonial and indigenous authors who view nonhuman agency in non-modernist terms,[10] and with critical Black scholars who call for 'poetics of relation' as processes of being, moving and being moved with(in) a 'chaotic' world.[11] In doing so, the article acknowledges the critiques of

---

environment and had the 'body' and the 'other' as equally important sites of operation. See J Singh, *Unthinking Mastery: Dehumanism and Decolonial Entanglements* (Duke University Press, 2018).

7. The literature I draw upon focuses on process-orientated onto-epistemologies of becoming, where the human subject is relationally embedded in the materiality of the world. This perspective is shared among posthumanist approaches, new materialisms, actor-network theory, speculative realism and object-oriented ontology. See R Braidotti, *Posthuman Knowledge* (Polity, 2019); G Harman, *Object-Oriented Ontology: A New Theory of Everything* (Pelican Books, 2018); G Harman, *Towards Speculative Realism: Essays and Lectures* (Zero Books, 2010); D Coole and S Frost (eds), *New Materialisms: Ontology, Agency, and Politics* (Duke University Press, 2010); B Latour, *Reassembling the Social: An Introduction to Actor Network-Theory* (Oxford University Press, 2005).

8. Yusoff uses the category of the 'inhuman' to overcome the exclusively white subjectivity of the 'human' in modern thought and open up the possibility of a redescription of relations between multiple subjectivities. In Yusoff's words: '[t]he Anthropocene is a project initiated and executed through anti-Blackness and inhuman subjective modes, and it cannot have any resolution through individuated liberal modes of subjectivity and subjugation', Yusoff supra (n 3) at 63.

9. ZI Jackson, 'Review: Animal: New Directions in the Theorization of Race and Posthumanism' (2013) 39:3 Feminist Studies 681. See also ZI Jackson, *Becoming Human: Matter and Meaning in an Antiblack World* (New York University Press, 2020).

10. See J Rosiek, J Snyder and S Pratt, 'The New Materialisms and Indigenous Theories of Non-Human Agency: Making the Case for Respectful Anti-Colonial Engagement' (2020) 26:3–4 Qualitative Inquiry 331; ID Vargas Roncancio, 'Conjuring Sentient Beings and Relations in the Law: Rights of Nature and a Comparative Praxis of Legal Cosmologies in Latin America', in K Anker et al. (eds), *From Environmental Law to Ecological Law* (Routledge, 2020) 119. I refrain, however, from speaking '*for* indigenous peoples' or describing '[*their*] ecological imagination', in line with the call raised by some indigenous scholars. See Z Todd, 'Indigenizing the Anthropocene' in H Davis and E Turpin (eds), *Art in the Anthropocene: Encounters Among Aesthetics, Politics, Environments and Epistemologies* (Open Humanities Press, 2015) 244, at 251–2. I also do not romanticize indigenous ways of inhabiting that world nor call for 'becoming indigenous', as is increasingly observed in governing discourses relating to the Anthropocene. See D Chandler and J Reid, *Becoming Indigenous: Governing Imaginaries in the Anthropocene* (Rowman & Littlefield, 2019).

11. See É Glissant, *Poetics of Relation* (University of Michigan Press, 1997). For contemporary scholars who, building on Glissant's poetics, suggest distinct socialities and collective modes of being, thinking and acting to thrive in an anti-black world, see F Moten's trilogy on *Consent Not to Be a Single Being*.

new materialist and posthumanist ontologies voiced by scholars working within the fields of Native/Indigenous and Black studies, and thinks with their politics of refusal.[12]

In evaluating legal dilemmas in light of these 'onto-epistemological' reconfigurations, the article diffracts the disciplinary commitments of international environmental law, thereby opening up new avenues of inquiry and critique.[13] It does so by situating, unpacking and problematizing the international legal doctrine of state responsibility for environmental protection. More specifically, the article explores which understandings of *responsibility* and *protection* are available to international legal thinking, and what it would mean to align these concepts to notions of *response-ability* and *care* as articulated in new materialist, relational and posthumanist literatures. Fundamentally, it is the underlying logic of international environmental law that this article seeks to challenge, rather than offering reformist or doctrinal fixes to be incorporated into existing legal frameworks.

The article is divided into three parts. I first identify a set of onto-epistemological reconfigurations of human and nonhuman relations that overcome modernist legacies of a putative disconnection between humans and nonhumans. While the analysis focuses on insights drawn from new materialism, posthumanism and object-oriented ontology – strands of theory that also have clear divergences from each other – it also considers insights from biology on a 'symbiotic view of life', demanding 'sympoietic' forms of thinking and acting. The second and third parts elaborate how the doctrinal legal notions of *responsibility* and *protection* expressed in international environmental law fit uncomfortably with the onto-epistemological reconfigurations explored in the first part. More specifically, the second part juxtaposes Haraway's call to cultivate 'response-ability' as a form of collective knowing and doing and Barad's agential realist form of 'responsible intra-action' with the ideal of responsibility in international environmental law – a normative trope restricted by conceptual and material coordinates of state sovereignty, territorial jurisdiction and strict liability. I use the concept of 'response-ability' in the singular to build on Haraway's neologism and to refer to an ethical, political and juridical commitment that can materialize into different practices, modalities and expressions – distinct 'response-abilities'. The third part of the article, in turn, explores how speculative ethics of care in more-than-human worlds,

---

12. Fundamental here is the erasure of racist anti-blackness that informs the 'human', and which is reproduced by expansive post-human approaches. See A Karera, 'Blackness and the Pitfalls of Anthropocene Ethics' (2019) 7:1 Critical Philosophy of Race 32; TL King, 'Humans Involved: Lurking in the Lines of Posthumanist Flight' (2017) 3:1 Critical Ethnic Studies, 162; ZI Jackson, 'Outer Worlds: The Persistence of Race in Movement "Beyond the Human"' (2015) 21:2/3 GLQ: A Journal of Lesbian and Gay Studies 215. See also TL King, J Navarro and A Smith (eds), *Otherwise Worlds: Against Settler Colonialism and Anti-Blackness* (Duke University Press, 2020).

13. 'Onto-epistemology' refers to the 'study of practices of knowing in being' in line with Barad, for whom '[p]ractices of knowing and being are not isolable; they are mutually implicated'. Indeed, 'we know because we are of the world. We are part of the world in its differential becoming. The separation of epistemology from ontology is a reverberation of a metaphysics that assumes an inherent difference between human and nonhuman, subject and object, mind and body, matter and discourse'. K Barad, *Meeting the Universe Halfway: Quantum Physics and the Entanglement of Matter* (Duke University Press, 2007) at 185. A methodology of 'diffraction' is used to read insights from distinct fields or issues into one another and explore the tensions and insights that arise when they interfere with each other. See Karen Barad, 'Diffracting Diffraction: Cutting Together-Apart' (2014) 20:3 Parallax 168–87.

as advocated by Puig de la Bellacasa, could help rethink notions of environmental protection under international environmental law. The latter tend to be limited to the realm of the 'human environment', constrained by direct causality between the harm suffered and the remedy to be provided by the perpetrator, and tied to temporal, spatial and subjective criteria ill-suited to a 'sympoietic' view of life. Contraposing the doctrine of states' *responsibility to protect* the(ir) environment with *response-abilities of care* in more-than-human worlds helps to reconstrue both the destructive and the restorative relations between humans and nonhumans.

2 BEING, ACTING AND THINKING WITH(IN) THE ANTHROPOCENE/S

The Anthropocene constitutes a profoundly disorienting 'event'.[14] In an attempt to prevent or fix it, international environmental lawyers tend to focus their attention on regulatory and institutional reforms in order to 'continue to try and maintain the current Holocene-like state'.[15] In traditional international environmental law, 'nature' has primarily been regulated as a source for wealth generation – as 'natural resources' – while the 'natural environment' has mainly been construed as a passive object of human protection and control.[16] For example, the rules on deep-seabed mining deploy extractive qualifications of 'nature' as a 'resource' to be allocated and exploited in regulated ways.[17] Today, the modernist belief in a controllable 'natural environment' persists to such an extent that prominent international environmental scholars continue to contemplate whether the 'organization of the Anthropocene is in our hands'[18] – a question itself imbued with enduring ideals of instrumentalist voluntarism oriented towards 'environmental management in the Anthropocene'.[19]

These legal schemes and normative aspirations for regulated exploitation, control and managed protection of the environment are permeated with an image of human

---

14. C Bonneuil and J-B Fressoz, *L'Evénement Anthropocène: La Terre, l'histoire et nous* (Broché, 2016).
15. LJ Kotzé and RE Kim, 'Earth System Law: The Juridical Dimensions of Earth System Governance' (2019) 1 Earth System Governance, at 2 and 10.
16. U Natarajan and K Khoday, 'Locating Nature: Making and Unmaking International Law' (2014) 27 Leiden Journal of International Law 573, at 575. The inverted commas serve to acknowledge how 'nature' has been conceptualized in competing ways in environmental law, infused by a vision of settlement and development, a wilderness-seeking Romanticism, a utilitarian attitude trying to manage nature for human benefit and a twentieth-century ecological view. See J Purdy, *After Nature: A Politics for the Anthropocene* (Harvard University Press, 2015).
17. On this extractive perspective in international law, see I Feichtner and S Ranganathan (eds), 'Symposium: International Law and Economic Exploitation in the Global Commons' (2019) 30 European Journal of International Law 541. For a historical account of this extractive relation to the Earth, see also PJ Usher, *Exterranean: Extraction in the Humanist Anthropocene* (Fordham University Press, 2019).
18. J Viñuales, 'The Organization of the Anthropocene: In Our Hands?' (2018) 1 Brill Research Perspectives in International Legal Theory and Practice 1.
19. See D Schlosberg, 'Environmental Management in the Anthropocene', in T Gabrielson et al. (eds), *The Oxford Handbook of Environmental Political Theory* (Oxford University Press, 2016) 193.

mastery over an inert 'nature', which is directly inherited from Enlightenment thinking.[20] The relative stability of the Holocene and the related conception that 'nature' is amenable to human comprehension and control are therefore part and parcel of international environmental law's edifice.[21] Living with(in) the Anthropocene/s, however, signals the 'end of the modern world' and its ideals of stability, predictability and control.[22] Far from a natural world mastered by humans and their juridical tools,[23] the 'defiant',[24] 'uncontrollable'[25] or 'unconstructable'[26] 'nature' at play in social ordering calls for different ways of engaging with and relating to more-than-human worlds.[27]

Against this backdrop, the literature portraying the Anthropocene/s as an onto-epistemological rupture with modernist Enlightenment thought puts forward a relational sensibility that repositions humans with(in) a 'vibrant material world'.[28] In this 'web of materiality', all matter – living and non-living – is entangled.[29] While grounded in different inquiries, with distinct emphases and interventions, new materialist, relational and posthumanist theories share an analytical focus on the dynamism of matter and the entanglement of human and nonhuman, living and non-living

20. Cf. N Wolloch, *History and Nature in the Enlightenment: Praise of the Mastery of Nature in Eighteenth-Century Historical Literature* (Routledge, 2016). Indeed, as modern international law is of European origins, its concept of sovereignty evolved in ways that mirror the Enlightenment understanding of 'nature'. Natarajan and Khoday supra (n 16) at 586.
21. D Vidas et al., 'International Law for the Anthropocene? Shifting Perspectives in Regulation of the Oceans, Environment and Genetic Resources' (2015) 9 Anthropocene 1, at 4.
22. The 'end of the world' is a recurrent trope in critical Anthropocene studies to signify the end of the modernist split between humans and nonhumans and the mastery of the former over the latter. See AL Tsing, *The Mushroom at the End of the World: On the Possibility of Life in Capitalist Ruins* (Princeton University Press, 2015); D Danowski and E Viveiros de Castro, *The Ends of the World* (Polity, 2016); D Chandler, K Grove and S Wakefield, *Resilience in the Anthropocene: Governance and Politics at the End of the World* (Routledge, 2020). On the universalization of the experience of black and indigenous peoples when claiming that 'the world' (in singular) has ended, see S Fishel and L Wilcox, 'Politics of the Living Dead: Race and Exceptionalism in the Apocalypse' (2017) 45 Millennium: Journal of International Studies 340.
23. Latour speaks of 'provincializing modernity' as a European task *par excellence* and posits the 'Globe' – and hence 'globalization' and 'global' law – as paradigmatic colonial object and processes. B Latour, '*Onus Orbis Terrarum*: About a Possible Shift in the Definition of Sovereignty' (2016) 44 Millennium: Journal of International Studies 305. See also S Ramaswamy, *Terrestrial Lessons: The Conquest of the World as Globe* (University of Chicago Press, 2017).
24. Cf. C Hamilton, *Defiant Earth: The Fate of Humans in the Anthropocene* (Polity, 2017).
25. Cf. H Rosa, *The Uncontrollability of the World* (Polity, 2020).
26. Cf. F Neyrat, *The Unconstructable Earth: An Ecology of Separation* (Fordham University Press, 2018, trans. DS Burk).
27. This entails a turn to aesthetics and affects. See D Matthews, 'Law and Aesthetics in the Anthropocene: From the Rights of Nature to the Aesthesis of Obligations' (2019) Law, Culture and the Humanities 1. Other examples include De Lucia's attempt at rethinking the encounter between law and nature through an aesthetics of wonder. See V De Lucia, 'Rethinking the Encounter Between Law and Nature in the Anthropocene: From Biopolitical Sovereignty to Wonder' (2020) 31 Law and Critique 329.
28. Cf. J Bennett, *Vibrant Matter: A Political Ecology of Things* (Duke University Press, 2010); S Vermeylen, 'Materiality and the Ontological Turn in the Anthropocene: Establishing a Dialogue between Law, Anthropology and Eco-Philosophy' in LJ Kotzé (ed), *Environmental Law and Governance for the Anthropocene* (Hart Publishing, 2017) 141.
29. M Davies, *Law Unlimited: Materialism, Pluralism and Legal Theory* (Routledge, 2017) at 66.

entities. Far from constituting a homogeneous style of theory and practice – and at times covering incompatible trajectories – these strands of thought aim at a distinct understanding of ontology, epistemology, ethics and politics to overcome anthropocentrism and discursive idealism.[30] They share an aspiration for practices of humility and care across species, acknowledging a mutual vulnerability that spans 'the entire living order' while also recognizing that not all inter- and intra-species vulnerabilities are the same, nor are they equally recognized or cared for.[31] As Tsing puts it, this shared but differential precariousness entails a project of 'collaborative survival', since '[s]taying alive – for every species – requires livable collaborations'.[32]

This sense of cross-species collaboration resonates with Margulis' theory of 'symbiogenesis', which she developed to define life-making and life-sustaining processes through the relating of 'holobionts' – or entities composed of a host and all other species living in or around it.[33] Barad's neologism of 'intra-action' is useful here to understand the functioning of holobionts – and hence how life unfolds on Earth. Instead of traditional 'interactions', which assume separate individual agencies that precede each action, the concept of 'intra-action' signifies the mutual constitution of entangled human-nonhuman agencies.[34] The intra-activity of holobionts displaces metaphysics of individualism. In line with Barad's agential realist account, (holobiontic) matter is here viewed as 'a dynamic expression/articulation of the world in its intra-active becoming'.[35] Holobionts, in other words, are assemblages created and sustained by the entangled agencies of different species. Contemporary biologists are therefore advocating a 'symbiotic view of life' as a new paradigm for biology, which establishes this symbiotic condition at the level of insular individuality itself, since animals and plants are composites of many species living, developing and evolving together.[36] As Gilbert, Sapp and Tauber evocatively put it: '[w]e are all lichens'.[37] Indeed, the Covid-19 pandemic brought to the fore how human bodies

---

30. Cf. CN Gamble, JS Hanan and T Nail, 'What is New Materialism?' (2019) 24:6 Angelaki 111; V Kirby, 'Matter Out of Place: "New Materialism" in Review' in V Kirby (ed), *What If Culture was Nature all Along?* (Edinburgh University Press, 2017) 1–25. On the disavowal of race in new materialisms, see also supra (n 12).
31. AP Harris, 'Vulnerability and Power in the Age of the Anthropocene' (2014) 6 Washington and Lee Journal on Energy, Climate and Environment 98, at 126. On how vulnerability and care are shaped by relations of power, see also V Browne, J Danely and D Rosenow (eds), *Vulnerability and the Politics of Care: Transdisciplinary Dialogues* (Oxford University Press, 2021).
32. Tsing speaks of precarity as an 'earthwide condition' that enables us to appreciate the 'patchy unpredictability' that is the condition of our time. Tsing, supra (n 22) at 2, 4 and 5.
33. L Margulis, *Symbiotic Planet: A New Look at Evolution* (Basic Books, 1998) at 35–7. See also M-C Petersmann, 'Sympoietic Thinking and Earth System Law: The Earth, its Subjects and the Law' (2021) 7 Earth System Governance.
34. Barad, supra (n 13) at 33.
35. ibid at 392–3.
36. SF Gilbert, J Sapp and AI Tauber, 'A Symbiotic View of Life: We Have Never Been Individuals' (2012) 87 The Quarterly Review of Biology 325. The documentary *Symbiotic Earth: How Lynn Margulis Rocked the Boat and Started a Scientific Revolution* (dir. John Feldman, 2017) offers a great visual account of a symbiotic view of life.
37. Gilbert et al. supra (n 36) at 336. As composite organisms, 'being lichens' stresses the need to suspend a sense of insular individuality. On the blurring of sharp lines between species, see also J Dupré, 'Metaphysics of Metamorphosis: The Swarming, Ever-Changing Character of the Living World Challenges our Deepest Assumptions about the Nature of Reality' [2017], at <https://aeon.co/essays/science-and-metaphysics-must-work-together-to-answer-lifes-deepest-questions> accessed 7 February 2021.

live with over 380 trillion viruses – some more disruptive than others – as part of a holobiont, and makes manifest how symbiotic continuities and multispecies dependencies are inescapable.[38] Such perspectives on human-nonhuman entanglements call for a relational onto-epistemology that captures the symbiotic nature of how life unfolds through co-constitutive agencies between species.[39] These cross-species alliances – and the contact zones triggered between traditionally distinct disciplines of 'natural' and 'social' sciences – not only question whether 'we have ever been modern', but question whether 'we have ever been individuals' as well[40] – two presuppositions at the heart of international environmental law.

Ontologically speaking, the condition of being is therefore itself a condition of living-with.[41] As object-oriented philosopher Morton puts it, the nature of coexistence between humans and nonhumans is symbiotic – the real, in other words, is defined by entities related in symbiosis, where it is 'unclear which is the top symbiont … who is the host, and who is the parasite'.[42] What Morton calls the 'symbiotic real' is characterized by asymmetrical and non-total interconnections between entities across space and time. In light of this collective making of life and its limitless potentialities, a symbiotic view acknowledges the infinite possibilities of becoming that these encounters can generate.

Crucially, however, entanglement should not be mistaken for an absolute inseparability of all beings, nor an understanding that there are no differentiated power relations between humans and nonhumans. As Barad emphasizes, 'agential separability' implies both 'differentiating and entangling' without 'producing (absolute) separation'.[43] Humans and nonhumans, in their intra-active becoming, continuously engage in emergent, dynamic and iterative 'boundary-making practices that produce "objects" and "subjects" and other differences out of, and in terms of, a changing relationality'.[44] In these dynamics of intra-activity, questions of 'space, time and matter are intimately connected' and 'entangled with questions of justice'.[45] As such, these onto-epistemological reconfigurations gesture towards a distinct practice of inquiry,

---

38. K Birrell and T Lindgren, 'Anthropocenic Pandemic: Laws of Exposure & Encounter' [2021] at <https://criticallegalthinking.com/2021/01/04/anthropocenic-pandemic-laws-of-exposure-encounter> accessed 24 February 2021. See also B Latour, *Où suis-je ? Leçons du confinement à l'usage des terrestres* (La Découverte, 2021) at 63–4.
39. An observation already established by Kropotkin as early as 1902. See P Kropotkin, *Mutual Aid: A Factor of Evolution* (The Anarchist Library, 1902).
40. Latour (n 6); and Gilbert et al. supra (n 36).
41. CA Jones, 'Symbiontics: A View of Present Conditions from a Place of Entanglement' [2020] at <https://brooklynrail.org/2020/07/criticspage/Symbiontics-a-view-of-present-conditions-from-a-place-of-entanglement> accessed 3 February 2021.
42. T Morton, *Humankind: Solidarity with Nonhuman People* (Verso, 2017) at 1.
43. K Barad, 'Quantum Entanglements and Hauntological Relations of Inheritance: Dis/continuities, SpaceTime Enfoldings, and Justice-to-Come' (2010) 3 Derrida Today 240–68, at 265 (emphases omitted). See also section 3 below.
44. Barad, supra (n 13), at 93. Note that from an object-oriented ontology (OOO) perspective, the claim that objects in a relation do not preexist it but emerge through it, is untenable. For OOO, (hyper)objects are never entirely deployed, and potential relations between (hyper) objects are always withdrawn or held in reserve. See Harman (2018), supra (n 7) at 53 and 258; and T Morton, *Hyperobjects: Philosophy and Ecology after the End of the World* (University of Minnesota Press, 2013).
45. Barad, supra (n 13) at 236. Barad speaks of 'spacetimematter relations'.

one that 'involves transformations not just of our ways of knowing but also of our ways of being, feeling, committing, and living in the world'.[46]

As is argued in the next section, the 'entangled relations of difference'[47] that are enacted through intra-actions entail asymmetrical power relations, with some actants bearing more 'response-ability' than others. The departure from presumptions of pre-existing, independent, closed off entities – units, relata, subjects, objects – and insistence that 'relata do not preexist relations' but emerge through specific intra-actions,[48] creates a rupture with onto-epistemologies of fixed and bounded systems – whether these are understood as 'nature' or 'society', 'states' or 'individuals', 'humans' or 'nonhumans'. Such relational onto-epistemologies also entail a break from the schemes of anthropocentric agency and direct causality central to international environmental legal thought and practice.

Does international environmental law's notion of state responsibility leave room for such collective forms of being, acting and becoming, while remaining sensitive to differential and asymmetrical response-abilities? Could this legal domain be opened up to onto-epistemologies of becoming that offer 'a metaphysics grounded in connection, challenging delusions of separation'?[49] In the next section, I critically explore the doctrine of state responsibility for environmental protection. My juxtaposition of this doctrine with a notion of response-abilities of care in more-than-human worlds is not intended to propose a new norm to be incorporated in international environmental law's extant framework, but to question the latter's onto-epistemological premises and presuppositions.

3 FROM STATE RESPONSIBILITY TO INTRA-ACTIVE RESPONSE-ABILITIES

Under international law, a state is responsible for an internationally wrongful act, provided that the action or omission that led to the illegal act can be attributed to the state's conduct or effective control.[50] These rules of state responsibility are difficult to apply to transboundary environmental harms, the spatial, temporal, subjective and causal ramifications of which are often impossible to fully comprehend.[51] The attribution of such harms to individuated states is therefore particularly difficult to prove.[52] Against this backdrop, a legal infrastructure has been established to safeguard environmental protection through forms of preventive, institutional and managerial collaborations. A network of international cooperation provides, for example, for states to share information and best practices, to undertake early consultations on environmental risks and impact assessments, to immediately notify affected states of existing problems, to provide

46. Rosiek et al. supra (n 10) 335–6.
47. Barad, supra (n 13) at 236.
48. ibid at 139–40.
49. K Wright, 'Becoming-With' (2014) 5 Environmental Humanities 277, at 278.
50. International Law Commission, Draft Articles on Responsibility of States for Internationally Wrongful Acts, with commentaries in the *Yearbook of the International Law Commission*, 2001, Vol. II, Part Two, UN doc. A/CN.4/SER.A/2001/Add.1, Articles 1 and 2.
51. I follow Morton in defining environmental harms as 'hyperobjects' that are 'massively distributed in time and space' and therefore viscous, nonlocal, temporally undulated, phased and interobjective. Morton, supra (n 44).
52. See A Nollkaemper et al., 'Guiding Principles on Shared Responsibility in International Law' (2020) 31:1 European Journal of International Law 15.

technological and financial support, or agree to set limitations on the use of certain pollutants in order to jointly reduce environmental impacts.[53] States must also monitor their activities and ensure that the latter do not cause environmental harms both within their territory and areas under their effective control, as well as in other states' territories. In the case of environmental harms, however, the question of attribution is inevitably challenging, and the conundrum it raises has been the object of extensive scrutiny and criticism on the part of international environmental legal scholars.[54] This problem of attribution of states' responsibility for environmental harms has increasingly been addressed in light of resulting human rights violations, as is exemplified by the 'rights turn' in climate litigation.[55]

In recent scholarship, proposals have also been advanced to expand responsibility for internationally wrongful acts to private (transnational) corporations and to extend the jurisdictional scope beyond territorial boundaries. As Seck puts it, '[w]hile the "international community" has taken steps to negotiate and implement numerous global environmental treaties, these initiatives are premised on the idea of a bounded regulatory state that is able and willing to control corporate conduct effectively within its borders'.[56] Not only is territorial limitation problematic, but, as Seck notes, 'the invocation of extraterritoriality … risks undermining its objective, as it reinforces the myth of the bounded autonomous state while simultaneously endorsing the need to regulate across borders'.[57] My objective here is not to rehearse the critique of the attribution of wrongful acts based on a narrow understanding of state jurisdiction and territorial or effective control. Instead, I seek to build on Seck's argument against 'a vision of the territorially bounded sovereign state as an independent, autonomous being, which … is not only unhelpful, but undermines the critical importance of building mutually supportive relationships that acknowledge the reality of our ecological interdependence'.[58] This dominant vision of the state reinforces a legal infrastructure wherein each state is imagined to be individually responsible for the protection of the(ir) environment in a predetermined, fixed and bounded spatial grid, and where the state interacts with other equally independent and autonomous states to this end. Indeed, the jurisdiction and responsibility of states is still embedded in a spatial imaginary circumscribed by cartographic coordinates of longitude and latitude, delimited by borders and internal sovereignty, and based on the norm of non-intervention in domestic affairs.[59]

Such modernist state theorization fits uncomfortably with the spatiality and entangled materialities that are suggested as new taxonomies to make sense of the

---

53. See Viñuales and Dupuy who characterize the 'conceptual matrix' of international environmental law as divided between 'prevention' and 'balancing' principles. JE Viñuales and P-M Dupuy, *International Environmental Law* (Cambridge University Press, 2017).
54. See M Wewerinke-Singh, *State Responsibility, Climate Change and Human Rights Under International Law* (Hart, 2019).
55. J Peel and HM Osofsky, 'A Rights Turn in Climate Change Litigation?' (2018) 7 Transnational Environmental Law 37. See also M-C Petersmann and C McKinnon, 'Is Climate Change a Human Rights Violation?' in M Hulme (ed), *Contemporary Climate Change Debates: A Student Primer* (Routledge, 2019) 160.
56. SL Seck, 'Moving Beyond the E-word in the Anthropocene', in U Özsu et al. (eds), *The Extraterritoriality of Law: History, Theory, Politics* (Routledge, 2019) at 49.
57. ibid at 50.
58. ibid at 58.
59. N Rajkovic, 'The Visual Conquest of International Law: Brute Boundaries, the Map, and the Legacy of Cartogenesis' (2018) 31 Leiden Journal of International Law 267.

Anthropocene/s. The 'post-modern' theorization of territory is equally problematic since it further marginalizes physical and material worlds by focusing on 'de-territorial' or 'supra-territorial' forms of globalization.[60] Both the rigid modernist understanding of fixed territorial boundaries and the tendency towards de-territorialized thinking in 'post-modern' legal theory are countered today by approaches aimed at *terrestrializing* the more-than-strategic and more-than-human dynamism of the Earth.[61] This materialist turn in territorial theorizations addresses the non-static, vertical and volumetric qualities of terrestrial space, exploring new heights and depths from the atmosphere to the subterranean.[62] It works with 'ecological boundaries' alongside biogeochemical cycles[63] and suggests a distinct spatiality for geopolitics.[64] Such revitalized materialist insights highlight the limits of the juristic ideal of a static, fixed and predetermined definition of territorial jurisdiction on which the attribution of responsibility for wrongful acts rests. Under international (environmental) law, in sum, territorial boundaries tend to exist as a 'pre-given political knowledge', in relation to which 'much of international lawyers' work is to take note of boundaries and divide powers and issues between states in a similarly straightforward, either-or fashion'.[65]

In addition to these concerns about extra/territorial jurisdiction and responsibility, and the inadequacy of a schematic centred upon bounded, independent and autonomous interacting states – modelled on an image of an independent, autonomous and liberal individual[66] – one must also account for the differential responsibilities of state actors. As has long been argued in the literature on environmental colonialism and global environmental justice, while developing countries have suffered an overwhelming burden of environmental harms whilst negligibly contributing to their

---

60. See P Zumbansen et al. (eds), *Beyond Territoriality: Transnational Legal Authority in an Age of Globalization* (Martinus Nijhoff Publishers, 2012); D Bethlehem, 'The End of Geography: The Changing Nature of the International System and the Challenge to International Law' (2014) 25 European Journal of International Law 9.
61. M Usher, 'Territory *Incognita*' (2019) 44 Progress in Human Geography 1019, at 1024–32. See also B Latour, *Down to Earth: Politics in the New Climatic Regime* (Polity, 2018); as well as Part V on the 'Terrestrial' in Latour and Weibel, supra (n 35). For a fascinating visual expansion of traditional cartographies by taking into account materialist, relational and posthuman insights, see A Arènes, A Grégoire and F Aït-Touati, *Terra Forma: Manuel de Cartographies Potentielles* (Éditions B42, 2019).
62. Usher, ibid at 1035.
63. On delineating 'ecological boundaries' along biogeochemical cycles, see P Szigeti, 'A Sketch of Ecological Property: Toward a Law of Biogeochemical Cycles' (2021) 51:1 Environmental Law 41.
64. On geopolitics accustomed to the 'critical zone' (the Earth's outer layer, crust or envelope – from vegetation canopy to the soil and groundwater – that supports and encloses all discovered life), see Latour, supra (n 61). For a visual grammar of the infinitely complex and interwoven geochemical cycles born in the critical zone, see also A Arènes, B Latour and J Gaillardet, 'Giving Depth to the Surface: An Exercise in the Gaia-graphy of Critical Zones' (2018) 5 The Anthropocene Review 120.
65. P Szigeti, 'In the Middle of Nowhere: The Futile Quest to Distinguish Territoriality from Extraterritoriality' in Özsu et al., supra (n 56). For Szigeti, the arbitrariness of the extra/territorial division exposes the weakness of the traditional grounds for jurisdiction in international law, which calls for a reformulation of jurisdictional doctrine from the ground up. Szigeti advocates for 'ecological boundaries' along biogeochemical cycles. Szigeti, supra (n 63).
66. Seck, supra (n 56) at 58.

causes – as is clearly evidenced by historical emissions of greenhouse gases – developed countries have suffered such effects to a lesser extent whilst bearing a higher degree of responsibility for their causes.[67] It is precisely to account for developing and developed states' differential vulnerabilities to climate harms and for their unequal capability to respond to climate change effects, as well as to reflect differential historic responsibilities for climate harming emissions, that the principle of 'common but differentiated responsibilities and respective capabilities' (CBDRRC) was enshrined, for example, in the UN Framework Convention on Climate Change.[68] Yet, while the CBDRRC principle focuses on states' responsibility for past harms by foregrounding historical emissions, concerns for more-than-human worlds must also account for future harms.[69] As Chakrabarty reminds us:

> Whether we blame climate change on those who are retrospectively guilty – that is, blame the West for their past performance – or those who are prospectively guilty (China has just surpassed the United States as the largest emitter of carbon dioxide, though not on a per capita basis) is a question that is tied no doubt to the histories of capitalism and modernization. But scientists' discovery of the fact that human beings have in the process become a geological agent points to a shared catastrophe that we have all fallen into.[70]

This concern over a 'shared' catastrophe,[71] signals an additional conundrum regarding the attribution of responsibility for environmental harms over time, which demands a simultaneous accounting for multiple, complex and conflicting temporal regimes.[72] The modern linear and progressive temporality inherent in cause-and-effect thinking that determines the attribution of responsibility under international

---

67. S Mason-Case and J Dehm, 'Redressing Historical Responsibility for the Unjust Precarities of Climate Change in the Present', in B Meyer and A Zahar (eds), *Debating Climate Law* (Cambridge University Press, 2021); C Gonzalez, 'Global Justice in the Anthropocene' in Kotzé, supra (n 28) at 219; S Caney, 'Two Kinds of Climate Justice: Avoiding Harm and Sharing Burdens' (2014) 22 The Journal of Political Philosophy 125; and A Agarwal and S Narain, *Global Warming in an Unequal World: A Case of Environmental Colonialism* (Centre for Science and Environment, 2003).
68. UN Framework Convention on Climate Change (UNFCCC), A/RES/48/189 (20 January 1994), Articles 3–4.
69. Important here is the need to account for postcolonial 'modernized' futures that developing states demand, in light of the injustices they historically suffered by bearing most of the effects of socio-ecological harms whilst contributing less to their causes. D Chakrabarty, 'Planetary Crises and the Difficulty of Being Modern' (2018) 46 Millennium: Journal of International Studies 259, at 272.
70. D Chakrabarty, 'The Climate of History: Four Theses' (2009) 35 Critical Inquiry 197, at 218. For Chakrabarty, this 'all' relates to his concept of planetary subjects as 'species beings', which refers to 'a figure of "continuity" that connects [humans] to other species and to processes we may consider planetary', thereby dissolving 'the figure of the autonomous human subject who remains the mainstay of political [and legal] thought'. Chakrabarty supra (n 69) at 282.
71. I put 'shared' in inverted commas here to stress that what concerns us all concerns us differently. This 'shared' catastrophe is only a future threat for some whilst a long-experienced living condition for others. See Fishel and Wilcox, supra (n 22).
72. See Bonneuil's essay on 'regimes of planetarity', which shows how the Anthropocene shakes our frameworks of temporality and the 'modern' and 'presentist' 'regimes of historicity', as characterized by François Hartog. C Bonneuil, 'Der Historiker und der Planet: Planetaritätsregimes an der Schnittstelle von Welt-Ökologien, Ökologischen Reflexivitäten und Geo-Mächten' in F Adloff and S Neckel (eds), *Gesellschaftstheorie im Anthropozän* (Campus, 2020) 55.

environmental law is indeed insufficient. Many environmentally harmful effects suffered today are related to past activities or events with longue durée effects, which manifest in unforeseeable ways and surface at unpredictable times.[73] While the doctrine of inter-generational equity captures a sense of responsibility for environmental harms against future generations, it tends to express a temporal ideal of nearness that seeks to safeguard the rights of today's generation's children and grandchildren.[74] There is, however, a disjunction between this image of the near future and deep time concerns – a discrepancy also observable in climate litigation, where the articulation of future projections tends to be limited to a tangible expansion of the present or of a future close at hand.[75] In contrast, a deep time perspective 'operates as the horizon of questions of meaning, self-understanding, and responsibility raised when … we expand our historicity to a geological scale'.[76] Yet, thinking about responsibility at Earth magnitude should not detract from accounting for the historical responsibility of humans with 'anthropological differences'.[77] Indeed, (deep time) future-oriented outlooks risk erasing the past, thereby sacrificing, overshadowing or forgetting the damned of the modern world.[78] Living with(in) the Anthropocene/s demands an account of the conflicting temporalities of historical reckonings, political decision frames and deep time concerns. A discrepancy between these temporal and spatial

---

73. By way of illustration, following the dumping of several hundreds of thousands of tons of chemical weapons following World War II these weapons are surfacing three-quarters of a century later in fishing nets and washing up on beaches, while continuing to poison the bottom of the deep seas, with everlasting consequences on oceans' health. See A Neimanis, 'Held in Suspense: Mustard Gas Legalities in the Gotland Deep', in I Braverman and ER Johnson (eds), *Blue Legalities: The Life & Laws of the Seas* (Duke University Press, 2020) 45. The nonlocal, temporally undulated, phased and interobjective nature of such environmental harms are characteristics of 'hyperobjects'. See Morton, supra (n 44).

74. This bias towards temporal nearness is evidenced in the following quote by Knox, as former UN Special Rapporteur on human rights and the environment: 'the line between future generations and today's children shifts every time another baby arrives … It is critical, therefore, that discussions of future generations take into account the rights of the children who are constantly arriving, or have already arrived, on this planet. *We do not need to look far to see the people whose future lives will be affected by our actions today. They are already here*', 2018 Report on 'Children's Rights and the Environment' (A/HRC/37/58), para 68 (emphases added).

75. In the *Urgenda* case, for example, the timeframe at stake oscillated between the present ('by 2020') and a future set 'by 2050', which casts the temporal span as a shadow of the present – or a 'near' and 'foreseeable future' as referred to by the court. *Urgenda Foundation v The Netherlands* [2015] Verdict, The Hague District Court C/09/456689/HA ZA 13-1396 (2015), para 38.

76. D Wood, *Deep Time, Dark Times: On Being Geologically Human* (Fordham University Press, 2018), at 60–61.

77. 'Anthropological differences' are here meant as naturalized differences that 'have the capacity to *limit the right to have rights*' and '*universally* create[] a relationship of domination or exclusion', Balibar, 'Ontological Difference, Anthropological Difference, and Equal Liberty' (2020) 28:1 European Journal of Philosophy 3, at 6–7 (emphases in the original).

78. For a compelling critique of suggestions to (re)make the future without unmaking the ontological constraints of the present and the past, see D Chandler in 'Black Anthropocene' (who invokes 'the need to repair' through denouncing and accounting for and with what has been disavowed in the making of modernity) and F Neyrat in 'We the People Concerned with Time: Ecopolitics and Sovereignty in the Anthropocene' (who urges us to care 'for past generations, the sacrificed ones, the damned of the Anthropocene'), in Working Papers, 'Constitutionalizing in the Anthropocene', Workshop, Tilburg University, 2020 (on file with author).

scales and those at work in international environmental law is evident. This discrepancy limits the legal intelligibility of the materialities and injustices of the Anthropocene/s.

Thinking with Haraway's concept of 'response-ability' can provide inspiration for a reorientation of the trajectory of legal thought towards the kinds of relational onto-epistemologies introduced in the second section of this article. Indeed, an openness to continuously unfolding 'times that remain at stake' is well captured in Haraway's call to cultivate 'response-ability' as a practice of ongoing collective knowing and doing, where the duty to respond to harms is inherently joined with the question of differentiated ability.[79] Haraway calls for responsible action in full recognition of specifically endowed abilities to respond to 'shared' yet differential afflictions.[80] Enacting 'response-ability' implies both an awareness that not all actants are equally responsible and able to respond to shared harms – a sensitivity also inherent to the principle of CBDRRC[81] – and an acknowledgment of distributed agency between humans and nonhumans. Practices of 'response-ability', Haraway notes, help open passages for a praxis of care 'in ongoing multispecies worlding',[82] without, however, reducing or minimizing differences in the destructive impact of actants.[83] As Haraway remarks: '[w]e are all responsible to and for shaping conditions for multispecies flourishing in the face of terrible histories, but not in the same ways. The differences matter – in ecologies, economies, species, lives'.[84] As a practice of 'tentacular thinking and doing',[85] 'response-able' state and non-state actors – human and nonhuman, corporate and other forms of techno-industrial agents – should be responsive to harms that know no absolutely fixed causal, subjective, spatial and temporal limits.

'Response-ability', in this sense, is embedded in what Haraway calls a process of 'ongoingness', where accountabilities are extensive and permanently unfinished.[86] What Haraway proposes here is an ecology inspired by a feminist ethic of 'response-ability' in which questions of species difference are always conjugated with attention to affect, entanglement and rupture.[87]

---

79. D Haraway, *Staying with the Trouble: Making Kin in the Chthulucene* (Duke University Press, 2016) at 55.
80. How to (determine how to) *respond* is an equally important question – one that will not be unpacked in this article, however.
81. Supra (n 68). See also L Rajamani, 'The Reach and Limits of the Principle of Common but Differentiated Responsibilities and Respective Capabilities in the Climate Change Regime', in N Dubash (ed), *Handbook of Climate Change and India: Development, Politics and Governance* (Oxford University Press, 2011).
82. This aligns with Haraway's observations on the Chthulucene. Whilst acknowledging the Euro-centred globalizing forces that shaped the Capitalocene, Haraway opts for the term 'Chthulucene' to define the world we live in: 'unlike either the Anthropocene or the Capitalocene, the Chthulucene is made up of ongoing multispecies stories and practices of becoming-with in times that remain at stake, in precarious times, in which the world is not finished and the sky has not fallen – yet', Haraway, supra (n 79), at 55.
83. ibid at 105.
84. ibid at 116. Haraway's take resonates here with Braidotti's 'we-are-all-in-this-together-but-we-are-not-all-one-and-the-same'. Braidotti, supra (n 7) at 54.
85. Haraway uses 'tentacular' as a metaphor to capture at the same time its Latin etymological roots of 'to feel' and 'to try', and plays with figurative symbols such as spiders or octopuses as examples of critters with 'many-armed allies' and 'myriad tentacles' that exist collaboratively through expansive nets and networks. Haraway, supra (n 79) at 30–31.
86. ibid at 132.
87. ibid at 68.

Haraway's concepts of 'response-ability' and 'ongoingness' find resonance in Barad's agential realist understanding of 'intra-actions', which, as mentioned earlier, express agential separability yet never produce absolute separation between 'subjects' and 'objects' of inquiry, knower and known.[88] With every new encounter, an entity intra-actively becomes other – it emerges anew from that intra-action. As such, humans and nonhumans come to matter and affect each other through their intra-active encounters. Agential separability accounts for the enduring patterns of differences, inclusions and exclusions in how the world unfolds and is configured, which produces divergent abilities to respond to such patterns. How humans differ among themselves and from other nonhumans, in other words, matters for the intra-active relations that compose them and which compose the world in its becoming.[89] It is in this important sense, Barad reminds us, that '[w]e are responsible for the world of which we are a part, not because it is an arbitrary construction of our choosing but because reality is sedimented out of particular practices that we have a role in shaping and through which we are shaped'.[90]

For Barad, therefore, the agency of individual components cannot be isolated. Response-abilities for intra-actions take place *within* and *as part of* the world in its differential becoming. As a mutual constitution of entangled human-nonhuman agencies, every intra-active relation enacts an onto-epistemology anew.[91] The knowing/being binary is thereby dismantled and reconfigured with(in) each new intra-active relation.

This dismantling of binaries is well captured by what indigenous scholar Watts refers to as a theoretical understanding of the world through 'Place-Thought'.[92] This non-binary, relational onto-epistemology rejects the liberal humanist conception of the subject and problematizes any understanding of responsibility that 'begins and ends with a willful subject who is destined to reap the consequences of his actions'.[93] A sense of intra-active 'response-ability' exceeds both individualism and holism – abstractions that dissolve through the continuous reconfigurations of subjects and

---

88. Barad's 'agential realism' is a 'new ontology, epistemology, and ethics, including a new understanding of the nature of scientific practices', which 'entails a rethinking of fundamental concepts … including the notions of matter, discourse, causality, agency, power, identity, embodiment, objectivity, space, and time'. Barad, supra (n 13) at 25–6.
89. As Barad repeatedly asserts, attending to such issues is 'an integral part of questioning the constitution of the nature-culture dichotomy and the work it does: not only *that* it matters, but *how* it matters and *for whom*'. Barad, supra (n 13), at 87 (emphases in the original).
90. ibid at 390. 'Ethics', Barad notes, 'is therefore not about right response to a radically exterior/ized other, but about responsibility and accountability for the lively relationalities of becoming of which we are a part', at 393.
91. As Barad insists, this does 'not merely mark the epistemological inseparability of observer and observed [but also marks] the *ontological* inseparability of agentially intra-acting components', ibid at 33 (emphasis in the original).
92. 'Place-Thought' is based on the premise that land is alive and thinking, and that humans and nonhumans derive agency through the extensions of these thoughts. V Watts, 'Indigenous Place-Thought and Agency amongst Humans and Non-humans (First Woman and Sky Woman go on a European World Tour!)' (2013) 2:1 Decolonization: Indigeneity, Education and Society 20 at 21. See also CF Black, *The Land is the Source of the Law: A Dialogical Encounter with Indigenous Jurisprudence* (Routledge, 2011).
93. Barad, supra (n 13), at 172.

objects in a world of perpetual becoming.[94] In line with a symbiotic view of life, fixed, permanent and predetermined categories of 'human' and 'nonhuman' are discarded, as any fixity would inhibit possibilities for the iterative reconfiguring of human-nonhuman formations, and the schemes of response-abilities emerging with(in) them.[95] As Barad puts it: '[r]esponsibility – the ability to respond to the other – cannot be restricted to human-human encounters when the very boundaries and constitution of the "human" are continually being reconfigured and "our" role in these and other reconfigurings is precisely what "we" have to face'.[96]

Crucially, however, while Barad's agential realism and posthuman ethics of worlding focuses on an 'understanding that we are not the only active beings', this understanding 'is never justification for deflecting that responsibility onto other entities'.[97] The agentic decentring and deformation of the 'human' does not deflect responsibility to 'nonhumans', but rethinks responsibility through the 'more-than-human'. Recognizing nonhuman agency, Barad insists, does not reduce human accountability: 'on the contrary, it means that accountability requires that much more attentiveness to existing power asymmetries'.[98] A redistribution of agency and accountability for response-abilities in more-than-human worlds, in sum, does not suspend or defer a reckoning with the disproportionally higher 'response-ability' of certain humans and their way of inhabiting and experiencing the Anthropocene/s at the expense of others.

While breaking from modernist modes of knowing and being, such ontoepistemologies do not remove exercises of human agency from scrutiny. The notion of intra-active 'response-ability' reconfigures understandings of subjectivity, agency and causality as well as the bounded temporal and spatial registers in which these are embedded. In contrast to the insulated agency of state or non-state entities – to which stable notions of responsibility can be tied – the onto-epistemological premises of intra-active response-abilities envisage an ongoing, continuously unfolding and open responsiveness to the entanglements of self and others where subjects, objects, matter, space and time are iteratively produced and performed in 'a nonlinear enfolding of spacetimemattering'.[99]

Juxtaposing the doctrinal notion of states' responsibility to protect the(ir) environment with intra-active response-abilities of multiple and differentiated agencies shows the limits of the narrow conceptual understanding of human-nonhuman

---

94. As Barad puts it: '[h]olding the category "human" ("nonhuman") fixed (or at least presuming that one can) excludes an entire range of possibilities in advance, eliding important dimensions of the workings of agency'. Instead of frozen or fixed entities, Barad sees 'an ongoing performance of the world in its differential dance of intelligibility and unintelligibility', ibid at 178 and 149.
95. Barad further notes: 'it is a mistake to presume an a priori distinction between humans and nonhumans and foreclose the drawing of boundaries between the human and the nonhuman from critical analysis', ibid at 216. Yet, this 'is not to suggest that there really are no boundaries or that what is at stake is a postmodern celebration of the blurring of boundaries', ibid at 380.
96. ibid at 392.
97. ibid at 218 and 392.
98. ibid at 219. See also the critiques of new materialists and posthumanists' turn(s) to 'more-than-human' onto-epistemologies by decolonial, indigenous and black scholars, who caution against a flattening and disavowing of the historically enacted differences between human subjects along specific 'colour lines' that are perpetually reproduced in the political economy of capitalism, supra (n 12).
99. Barad, supra (n 13), at 244 and 393–4.

relations underpinning international environmental law. This understanding, I argue in the next section, informs an equally limited conception of *protection* of the human environment under international environmental law, which should be displaced by a notion of *care* in more-than-human worlds.

4 FROM ENVIRONMENTAL PROTECTION TO CARE IN MORE-THAN-HUMAN WORLDS

Under international law, concerns for environmental protection first emerged by focusing on the 'human environment', the protection of which would preserve and enhance 'the condition of man, his physical, mental and social well-being, his dignity and his enjoyment of basic human rights'.[100] As the title of the 1972 Stockholm Conference on the Human Environment epitomizes, international law's approach to environmental protection put human interests at the centre of environmental concerns.[101] Narratives of environmental protection have since evolved towards more ecocentric,[102] acentric,[103] or Earth-centric[104] visions to guide normative regulations, understood as serving the benefits of more-than-human worlds rich in biodiversity.[105] The recognition of 'rights of nature' across various jurisdictions is often mentioned as an emblematic example of the progressive ecological reorientation of environmental protection.[106] Protecting so-called 'natural' entities by granting them rights tends to be viewed as a way of overturning humans' extractive approach to 'natural resources' and, by some, as a veritable 'legal revolution that could save the world', as stated by the current UN Special Rapporteur on human rights and the environment.[107] Yet, the extension of human rights to 'natural' entities might enhance their legal protection, but risks sacrificing their nonhuman agency and alterity by anthropomorphizing

---

100. UNGA A/RES/2398 (XXIII), Problems of the Human Environment (3 December 1968), preamble.
101. Stockholm Declaration on the Human Environment (16 June 1972) UN Doc.A/Conf.48/14/Rev.1 (1973) 11 ILM 1416 (1972).
102. Earth Jurisprudence and ecological law have been suggested as 'ecocentric' laws. See P Burdon, 'The Earth Community and Ecological Jurisprudence' (2013) 3:5 Oñati Socio Legal Series 815. See also Anker, supra (n 10).
103. Critical Environmental Law has been suggested as 'acentric' law. See A Philippopoulos-Mihalopoulos, Critical Environmental Law as Method in the Anthropocene' in A Philippopoulos-Mihalopoulos and V Brooks (eds), *Research Methods in Environmental Law: A Handbook* (Edward Elgar, 2017) 131.
104. Earth System Law has been suggested as 'Earth-centric' law. See Kotzé and Kim, supra (n 15).
105. On the evolution of 'environmental protection' narratives in international law, see M-C Petersmann, 'Narcissus' Reflection in the Lake: Untold Narratives in Environmental Law Beyond the Anthropocentric Frame' (2018) 30:2 Journal of Environmental Law 235; and V de Lucia, 'Beyond Anthropocentrism and Ecocentrism: A Biopolitical Reading of Environmental Law' (2017) 8 Journal of Environmental Law 2.
106. See EL O'Donnell and J Talbot-Jones, 'Creating Legal Rights for Rivers: Lessons from Australia, New Zealand, and India' (2018) 23 Ecology and Society 7.
107. Cf. DR Boyd, *The Rights of Nature: A Legal Revolution That Could Save the World* (ECW Press, 2017).

and moulding the protection of 'natural entities' into a human rights template.[108] This approach inhibits intra-active response-abilities based on non-binary, de-essentialized and 'entangled relations of difference'.[109] Ultimately, the extension of liberal human rights to 'nature' hinges on a problematic human representation of the nonhuman.[110] Even in international environmental law's most ambitious protective schemes, in sum, nonhuman entities remain passive objects of human protection – an approach locked into a modernist idea of 'nature' as a mere site of masterful human intervention and control. To address these limits of environmental *protection*, I contend that a turn to *care* is key to the development of a praxis of response-abilities.

Attempts to transpose ethics of care to environmental concerns in international law are not new.[111] Ethics of care emerged in the 1980s as part of feminist theories – informed by intersectional gender, class and race politics – in the context of care work, whether in institutional or domestic settings.[112] The initial focus on individual self-care and collective care for the other expanded towards a sense of 'care for the world': a 'world as the array of material and immaterial conditions under which human beings live – both with one another and with a rich variety of nonhumans, organic and technological'.[113] Theorized as an affective connective tissue between an inner self and an outer world, care constitutes 'a feeling *with*, rather than a feeling *for*, others'.[114] As such, care goes hand in hand with the relational onto-epistemologies put forward in this article and must therefore be distinguished from its metonyms of compassion or empathy.[115] A relational disposition of care does not imply, to be clear, a symmetrical responsivity, let alone a balanced reciprocity. Nonhumans might

---

108. Arguably, the original referent of human rights – the white modern subject – is normatively reinforced instead of transformed each time rights are expanded to previously 'inhuman' categories such as indigenous, black, brown or LGBTQI+ subordinated groups. See, eg, R Kapur, *Gender, Alterity and Human Rights: Freedom in a Fishbowl* (Edward Elgar, 2020).
109. Barad, supra (n 13) at 236. On difference as a 'right to opacity' – a right not to be rendered transparent to modern subjects to fit into their cognitive schema and thereby dominate other modes of being based on essentialized Western ideals, see Glissant, supra (n 11) at 189–94. For a wonderful essay along these lines applied to more-than-human relations, see also B Morizot, *Manières d'être vivant. Enquêtes sur la vie à travers nous* (Actes Sud, 2020).
110. How the nonhuman is here uplifted through protection granted by modern subjects is reminiscent of how the colonial enterprise was couched in benevolent language to civilize 'inhuman' savages. For an early debate along those lines, see the 1550 Valladolid controversy between Bartolomé de Las Casas and Juan Ginés de Sepúlveda, referred to in JW Moore and R Patel, *A History of the World in Seven Cheap Things: A Guide to Capitalism, Nature, and the Future of the Planet* (University of California Press, 2018) at 36–7.
111. See the 2000 Earth Charter Principle 1 on 'Respect and Care for the Community of Life' at <https://earthcharter.org/wp-content/uploads/2020/03/echarter_english.pdf?x79755> accessed 3 February 2021.
112. See C Gilligan, *In A Different Voice* (Harvard University Press, 1982); J Tronto, *Moral Boundaries: A Political Argument for an Ethic of Care* (Routledge, 1994); V Held, *The Ethics of Care: Personal, Political, and Global* (Oxford University Press, 2005).
113. E Myers, *Worldly Ethics: Democratic Politics and Care for the World* (Duke University Press, 2013) at 17. See also Browne et al., supra (n 31).
114. HJK Hobart and T Kneese, 'Radical Care Survival Strategies for Uncertain Times' (2020) 38 Social Text 1, at 2 (emphases added).
115. On the differences between compassion and empathy (as emotions or values) and care (as activity or practice) and their legal receptivity, see J Herring, 'Compassion, Ethics of Care and Legal Rights' (2017) 13 International Journal of Law in Context 158. See also V Held, 'Morality, Care and International Law' (2011) 4 Ethics and Global Politics 173.

well not care about humans – the reverse being true as well – yet humans and nonhumans depend upon each other in their intra-active becoming. In this sense, practices of care allow us to envision what it means for beings embedded within more-than-human compositions to be, always intra-actively, thriving in entangled caring relations.

As such, care generates a different mode of engaging with more-than-human worlds by productively interrogating not only *who* and *what* to care about but also *how to (begin to) care* about being-in-the-world.[116] Unlike environmental protection schemes that regulate the use of products or activities through top-down, command-and-control management by identifiable centres of authority, an ethics of care is inherently open-ended and distributed. As Schrader puts it, 'what or who counts as a subject of care cannot be delimited in advance'.[117] Unlike the orthodox scheme of states' responsibility for environmental protection, working with care is a process that is not merely normative and prescriptive, but requires responsiveness to harms for which there might not be a pre-given script. In line with Haraway's 'ongoingness' and Barad's 'radically open future', care breaks free from cause-and-effect thinking and from its linear and progressive spatio-temporality. In contrast to the rationalism of liberal subjects and modernist assumptions of linear progress, care demands a suspension of a given futurity and of the commanding of pre-established (re)actions towards it.[118] The planning mentality of international environmental law – a mentality ill-suited for complex, unpredictable 'worlds of becoming'[119] – is here interrupted.

Puig de la Bellacasa's turn to speculative care is particularly productive for making sense of this shift from environmental protection to care in more-than-human worlds. 'Matters of care', as she puts it, do not require a 'translation into a fixed explanatory vision or a normative stance (moral or epistemological)', but a speculative ethical commitment to ways of knowing and caring that 'reaffect objectified worlds, restage things in ways that generate possibility for other ways of relating and living, connect things that were not supposed to be connecting across the bifurcation of consciousness'.[120] This speculative commitment to care opens up other possible worlds, politics

---

116. As Nixon contemplated, reflecting on Aldo Leopold's remark that 'we can be ethical only towards what we can see': 'how are we to act ethically toward human and biotic communities that lie beyond our sensory ken? How do we both make slow violence visible yet also challenge the privileging of the visible?', R Nixon, *Slow Violence and the Environmentalism of the Poor* (Harvard University Press, 2013) at 14–15.
117. A Schrader, 'Abyssal Intimacies and Temporalities of Care: How (Not) to Care about Deformed Leaf Bugs in the Aftermath of Chernobyl' (2015) 45 Social Studies of Science 665, at 671.
118. Indeed, '[i]ntra-actions always entail particular exclusions, and exclusions foreclose the possibility of determinism, providing the condition of an open future'. Barad, supra (n 13) at 177.
119. Cf. WE Connolly, *A World of Becoming* (Duke University Press, 2011), who advocates 'a story of becoming linked to experimental intervention in a world that exceeds human powers of attunement, explanation, prediction, mastery or control', at 10. Connolly's political philosophy resonates with Chandler's 'hacking' as an ontopolitical mode of governance in the Anthropocene. D Chandler, *Ontopolitics in the Anthropocene: An Introduction to Mapping, Sensing and Hacking* (Routledge, 2018) 141–86.
120. M Puig de la Bellacasa, *Matters of Care: Speculative Ethics in More Than Human Worlds* (University of Minnesota Press, 2017) at 60 and 65.

and legalities. This approach resonates with a 'non-correlationist'[121] understanding of human-world relations, inviting speculations about the world beyond immediate human experience and representation.[122] While spatio-temporal, subject-object 'abyssal distances' can separate 'us' from certain harms, a speculative commitment enables care beyond situated, embodied experience.[123] It entails a sense of care for what can be temporally, spatially and subjectively distant and (dis)continuous, for 'insensible worlds' that exceed immediate experiences and perceptions.[124] This means that response-abilities of care must be thought of 'in terms of what matters and what is excluded from mattering', or all other worlds or possible 'otherwise' that were not (yet) enacted.[125] As such, response-abilities of care resist the modernist drive of *being in charge* of environmental issues – by judging, predetermining and controlling *what*, *who* and *how* to protect the environment – and shifts towards *being involved* by remaining attentive to the unknown and open to the unknowable.[126] To return to Puig

---

121. What Meillassoux calls a (Kantian) correlationist thinking assumes that 'the correlation between thinking and being logically precedes any empirical statement about the world' and that one cannot, as a result, 'think that which cannot be associated with a relation-to-the-world'. Meillassoux uses the existence of 'arche-fossils' or 'fossil-matter' – namely 'matter indicating the existence of an ancestral reality or event that took place prior to life on Earth' – to show the possibility of 'thinking [scientifically] a world in which an event took place in a time and space that preceded any givenness [or being-world relation]'. Consequently, '[w]e are therefore obliged to break with the ontological requirement of the moderns, according to which to be is to be a correlate'. It is therefore possible to reconnect with a thought of the absolute: 'a Great Outdoor, not correlated to my thinking'. Q Meillassoux, *Après la finitude. Essai sur la nécessité de la contingence* (Seuil, 2006, réed. augmentée en 2012, préface d'A Badiou), at 32, 37, 26, 42, 51 and 53 (translated by the author).
122. Once again, affinities with Barad's displacement of 'representation' in favour of 'diffraction' come to light here. Barad critiques reflexivity for being founded on representationalism, which takes for granted the idea that 'representations reflect (social or natural) reality', thereby 'holding the world at a distance'. By contrast, they call for diffraction as a 'performative rather than representationalist' methodological approach for 'reading insights through one another in attending to and responding to the details and specificities of relations of difference and how they matter'. See Barad, supra (n 13) at 87–8 and 71. I am not suggesting here that Barad's agential realist critique of 'representation' aligns with a speculative realist approach based on 'non-correlationism' – a claim that would be antithetical to Barad's concept of 'entanglement'. On these distinctions, see also G Harman, 'Agential and Speculative Realism: Remarks on Barad's Ontology' [2016] at <www.rhizomes.net/issue30/harman.html> accessed 27 February 2021.
123. On 'abyssal distances', see Schrader, supra (n 117) at 683. This sense of 'abyssal intimacy' can then be understood, in Clark's terms (borrowing from Levinas), as 'a relation that enfolds within itself the condition of strangeness, the non-relation of unshared and incommunicable experience, even as it opens up the very possibility of being-together' – the formation of a bond. N Clark, 'Living Through the Tsunami: Vulnerability and Generosity on a Volatile Earth' (2007) 38 Geoforum 1127, at 1133.
124. K Yusoff, 'Insensible Worlds: Postrelational Ethics, Indeterminacy and the (k)Nots of Relating' (2013) 31 Environment and Planning D: Society and Space 208.
125. Barad, supra (n 13), at 220. Exclusions, for Barad, are constitutive of intra-active relations, which open possibilities whilst inevitably excluding others that would have been possible. On the importance of ethics of exclusion in Barad's agential realism, see G Hollin et al., '(Dis)entangling Barad: Materialisms and Ethics' (2017) 47:6 Social Studies of Science: An International Review of Research in the Social Dimensions of Science and Technology 918.
126. Puig de la Bellacasa, supra (n 120) at 90–91.

de la Bellacasa, it is about 'becom[ing] "obliged" to care in actual practice and relational arrangements, in messy material constraints rather than through moral dispositions'.[127]

This commitment to speculative care generates an ability to imagine other possible worlds, and acknowledges 'fugitive' and resistive socialities that disavow the modern world.[128] It takes us beyond the extant world of modernity and the subjectivities upon which it is grounded, to perform alternative ways of being, acting and thinking with(in) the Anthropocene/s. Against this backdrop, rethinking the legal doctrines of *responsibility* and *protection* through notions of *response-abilities* and *care* provides an opportunity to reconsider international environmental law and the world it enacts. Modes of legal theorizing responsive to such onto-epistemologies are already emerging. An expansion of our speculative sensorium of care in more-than-human worlds and the response-abilities that it entails would align, for example, with Matthews' call to reorient international law towards the concept of *obligation* – or the sense of feeling obliged – against the 'ever-expanding and diversifying "rights-talk"' in order to emphasize a 'being-in-community'.[129] As the etymological root of the word 'obligation' (*ligare*) suggests, obligations are ultimately concerned with 'binding beings'.[130] The emerging field of 'law *for* the Anthropocene'[131] also testifies to an increasing interest in alternative onto-epistemologies for worlds-otherwise, in which 'we' would engage with, relate to and feel (legally) obligated towards more-than-human worlds in different, symbiotic ways.[132] Adding to this field of literature that interrogates how legal thought and practice could operate with such ways of being, acting and knowing with(in) the Anthropocene/s, response-abilities of care in more-than-human worlds can help us think beyond the legal responsibility of states to protect the(ir) environment as given under international environmental law.

---

127. ibid at 204.
128. The notion of 'fugitive sociality' – the 'incalculably varied everyday enactments of the fugitive art of social life' as an ongoing refusal of standards imposed from elsewhere – comes from S Harney and F Moten, *The Undercommons: Fugitive Planning & Black Study* (Minor Compositions, 2013) at 73. Judy speaks of *poiēsis-in-black* to refer to such performances of thinking-in-action and thinking-in-disorder that are not subjugated to but fugitive from 'the universal history that would fix the fate of the self providentially, putting it in its proper place in the cosmic order of things'. RA Judy, *Sentient Flesh: Thinking in Disorder, Poiēsis in Black* (Duke University Press, 2020) at 423.
129. See Matthews, supra (n 27); De Lucia, supra (n 27); or A Akhtar-Khavari, 'Restoration and Cooperation for Flourishing Socio-Ecological Landscapes' (2020) 11:1–2 Transnational Legal Theory 62, who draws on the concept of symbiosis to outline a novel cooperative restoration paradigm for environmental law.
130. Matthews, supra (n 27) at 10. On the theoretical purchase of obligations and the 'ligatures of law', see also K McGee, 'For a Juridical Ecology of Ligatures', in B Latour, S Schaffer and P Gagliardi (eds), *A Book of the Body Politic: Connecting Biology, Politics and Social Theory* (Fondazione Giorgio Cini, 2020) 175.
131. A Grear, 'Legal Imaginaries and the Anthropocene: "Of" and "For"' (2020) 31 Law and Critique 351.
132. See the special issue curated by K Birrell and D Matthews, 'Re-storying Laws for the Anthropocene: Rights, Obligations and an Ethics of Encounter' (2020) 31 Law and Critique 233.

5 CONCLUSION

In this article, I have explored how the doctrinal notions of responsibility for and protection from environmental harms, as constituted under international environmental law, configure human-nonhuman relations in ways that reinforce modernist understandings that are ill-attuned to the realities that the Anthropocene/s foreground. I have refrained from deploying a reformist, regulatory and interventionist gaze that seeks to problem-solve particular environmental issues through command-and-control management or more ambitious international environmental norms. Instead, my contribution has been aimed at interrogating these prevalent practices and disciplinary commitments, which, I have argued, perpetuate a modernist mindset that views 'nature' as a site amenable to human intervention and control. In the face of globally shared – yet unequally distributed – planetary predicaments, the driving impulse in international environmental law is to enhance and secure state *responsibility* for environmental *protection*. It is this mode of engagement that I have sought to diffract.

In doing so, my analysis has built on the literature that affirms the Anthropocene/s as a condition to live with(in), and which attempts to make sense of the 'desedimentation' of the modern world.[133] The argument took as an onto-epistemological default position a sense of being and living in modernist ruins, with(in) fragile, symbiotic and contingent more-than-human worlds. Adopting an affirmative perspective, I framed the Anthropocene/s as a generative event – an opportunity for ways of being, acting and living *beyond* or *besides* modernity.[134] Indeed, affirmative approaches are seen as liberating critical thought from the constraints of modernist and anthropocentric thinking by displacing the 'arrogance of human-centred perspectives' that focus on identifying possible ways out from supposedly temporal crises and thereby securing the 'modern' world before it is too late.[135] Scholars affirming the Anthropocene/s find something liberating in the realization that there is no escape from it, that it 'cannot be secured, governed or engaged with in traditional ways'.[136] Perhaps counter-intuitively, Anthropocene/s are welcomed in celebratory terms, with the ruins of the world as it was conceived in modernity being embraced, rather than mourned. A generative sense of being and becoming with(in) more-than-human worlds invites us to value human (im)potentiality,[137] and unleashes

---

133. See K Thiele, 'Affirmation', in M Bunz, BM Kaiser and K Thiele (eds), *Symptoms of the Planetary Condition: A Critical Vocabulary* (Meson Press, 2017) 25. 'Desedimentation' here refers to the de-essentializing of differences among humans and nonhumans and the critical reconfiguration of the hierarchies by which they are articulated in relation to one another. I borrow the concept from ND Chandler, *X – The Problem of the Negro as a Problem for Thought* (Fordham University Press, 2013), for whom 'to desediment' is to 'make tremble by dislodging the layers of sedimentated premises that hold [the system] in place', at 137.
134. See the work on 'paraontology' as an escape from the fixity of racial ontology – *qua* modern ontology – that structures white supremacy and the world as such. 'Paraontology', then, is a mode of being that eschews the Western ontological demands of modern subject-world relations. See Chandler, supra (n 133) and Moten, supra (n 11).
135. P Bargués-Pedreny, 'From Critique to Affirmation in International Relations' (2019) 33 Global Society 1, at 7. See also D Chandler, 'The Death of Hope? Affirmation in the Anthropocene' (2019) 16:5 Globalizations 695.
136. Chandler, supra (n 119) at 4.
137. For Colebrook, '[t]he fact that we forget our *impotentiality* – that we treat humans as factual beings with a normality that dictates action – has reached crisis point in modernity,

an enhanced sense of humility, thereby opening up new forms of collective attachments and care.[138]

For international environmental law/yers, this exercise can seem profoundly disorienting, as it challenges the logic of law itself and its telos of providing order, stability and predictability. As instantiated by the rules on state responsibility, individuated actors must intervene to ensure the well-being of their citizens against the effects of predetermined environmental harms, with particular spatio-temporal delimitations and specific subjects and objects of protection in sight. A circumscription both of the harms – their effects on predefined subjects and objects – and of the actors involved – states held accountable by legal subjects – scaffolds the doctrine of state responsibility for environmental protection. A 'stable world' divided into delimited sites of authority and control and locked within a linear spatio-temporality is thereby taken for granted. But what if we alter our gaze and attempt to care in disordered, unstable and unpredictable more-than-human worlds, not intelligible to modernist registers of thought and practice? Far from producing a sense of doom, moving beyond the world *qua* modernity and its governing responses opens up different ways of engaging, relating and feeling response-able with others.

Fundamentally, I have not advanced the notion of response-abilities of care in more-than-human worlds as a new legal norm that should be recognized in an international environmental treaty ratified by states. My intervention is not meant to apply at the surface of international environmental law but at the depth of it: by questioning the onto-epistemological premises of extant international environmental laws that enact how states and non-state actors govern life on Earth and the human-nonhuman relations that constitute it. Thinking with response-abilities of care in more-than-human worlds can inspire a novel imagination and new sense of possible legal commitments. I side with Barad to justify this choice, since '[i]n an important sense, it matters to the world how the world comes to matter'.[139]

---

especially as we increasingly suspend the *thought* of our fragility for the sake of ongoing efficiency'. C Colebrook, *Death of the Posthuman: Essays on Extinction Vol. I* (Open Humanities Press, 2014) at 13.
138. L Head, *Hope and Grief in the Anthropocene: Re-conceptualising Human–Nature Relations* (Routledge, 2016) at 5–6. For Head, hope in the Anthropocene should be decoupled from the emotion of optimism about the world as we wish it to be. The affirmative dimension lies in the generative role of hope and grief as practice: '[i]f part of what we are grieving for, and what we must farewell, is our modern selves, it follows that a necessary intellectual and practical task is to imagine new kinds of selves', at 34. Note that while grief is individually experienced, mourning involves action and is carried out collectively both by human groups and by other animals. It is, as such, a 'process of renewing and remaking relationships after loss, and re-starting the commitment to life and to community'. T van Dooren and D Bird Rose, 'Keeping Faith with the Dead: Mourning and De-extinction' (2017) 38:3 Australian Zoologist 375, at 376.
139. Barad, supra (n 13) at 380.

Alter-transitional justice; transforming unjust relations with the more-than-human

Danielle Celermajer*
Department of Sociology and Social Policy, Sydney Environment Institute, University of Sydney

Anne Therese O'Brien**
Independent researcher

Drawing on the emerging field of multispecies justice, this article seeks to understand how the idea of transitional justice, capaciously understood, might be put to work to transform unjust relations between humans and the more-than-human. Reflecting on concerns in the literatures on animals and the environment concerning the cogency of addressing past wrongs against the more-than-human by using a justice framework, the article sets out a foundational agenda for transitional justice and a conceptual framework responsive to the ontological diversity of beings and communities other than humans. Focusing on soil specifically, the article explores the problem of developing transitional justice approaches for transforming relations that involve systemic violence where such violence is not acknowledged because the harmed being – soil – is not recognized as the type of community to which justice might be owed. To illustrate proto-transitional justice, the article considers both the work of regenerative farmers and emergent collaborations between farmers and visual artists to explore how engagements with the arts of relating to the more-than-human might move the as yet private transformations of relations with soil into a more public, albeit incipient, process of justice.

Keywords: *transitional justice, more-than-human, multispecies justice, soil integrity, regenerative agriculture, care, new materialism*

1 INTRODUCTION

When Robert Cover depicted law as 'a bridge linking a concept of reality to an imagined alternative',[1] he stipulated that the formal dimension of law, the *corpus juris*, is nourished by myths and narratives. By implication, the transformation of myths and narratives makes possible the transition from what *is* to what *might be*. Importantly for our topic, which concerns the prospect of addressing the systemic violence that characterizes

---

*   Danielle.celermajer@sydney.edu.au
** anneobr@gmail.com
1. RM Cover, 'Foreword: Nomos and Narrative' (1983) 97 Harvard Law Review 4, at 9. It was Charlotte Blattner's use of Cover's framing in her analysis of transitional justice for interspecies society that had us return to his work and recognize its pertinence for framing our arguments. See C Blattner, 'Drafting Principles for Transitional Justice for an Interspecies Society' (Harvard University 2019).

relations between humans and the more-than-human world, he also suggested that these myths and narratives 'build relations between the normative and the material universe'.[2]

This article emerges from our broader interest in justice for the more-than-human and, in particular, work that we have been undertaking in developing the field of multispecies justice.[3] To date, that field has for the most part been concerned with present and future relations, and with what type of institutional arrangements would better promote and protect justice for all humans, other animals and the environment. In light of a longstanding interest that one of us has had in how collectives deal with past systemic wrongs, here we extend this work and seek to understand how the idea of transitional justice, capaciously understood, might be put to work to think through how to build a bridge between the unjust reality of human relations with the more-than-human and new forms of relationship that would support the flourishing of humans *and* the more-than-human.[4] Given the vastness of the chasm between existing unjust and aspirational just relations between humans and beings other than humans, where Cover imagined a bridge, one might perhaps imagine an unmarked track between two different worlds: at one end, the unjust and violent reality that is comprehensively instantiated in dominant myths and across a comprehensive range of social, political, economic institutions, and at the other a possible future that has at best a tenuous hold even on the imagination.

Our goal is to explore and to suggest how this track might be forged, both at a relatively abstract level and then with respect to one particular part of the more-than-human world: soil. We have chosen soil for several reasons, which we will discuss below, but in the first instance precisely because it lies at the far side of the category of lifeforms that occur to (most) humans as morally considerable.[5] Indeed, despite the systemic harms that common human practices cause to soil, to a large extent, most people fail to register that such practices involve any wrongdoing. Soil ill fits within conventional notions of a moral subject, and hence presents a particular challenge to habitual imaginaries of what it might mean to enter into a set of transformative justice processes. At the same time, being inherently relational, soil offers a radical challenge for reimagining who and what might form part of a moral community, and for the types of myths, narratives and imaginaries that would be needed to nourish such a community.

The article commences with a theoretical discussion of transitional justice as a constitutive form of justice, paying particular attention to the 'imaginative stretch' that would be required to bring the idea of transitional justice to largely unacknowledged forms of violence against beings other than humans. In the next part of the

---

2. Cover (n 1). Throughout this article, we use the term 'systemic' to denote forms of violence that are produced and sustained by structures or institutions. Systemic violence is thereby embedded and normalized.
3. See D Celermajer, D Schlosberg, L Rickards, M Stewart-Harawira, M Thaler, P Tschakert, B Verlie and C Winter, 'Multispecies Justice: Theories, Challenges, and a Research Agenda for Environmental Politics' (2021) 30 Environmental Politics 119; D Celermajer, S Chatterjee, A Cochrane, S Fishel, A Neimanis, A O'Brien, S Reid, K Srinivasan, D Schlosberg and A Waldow, 'Justice through a Multispecies Lens' (2020) 19 Contemporary Political Theory 475.
4. See D Celermajer, *The Sins of the Nation and the Ritual of Apologies* (Cambridge University Press 2009).
5. The term comes from K Goodpaster, 'On Being Morally Considerable' (1978) 75 Journal of Philosophy 308. We choose this term rather than the more specific person before the law so as not to constrain ourselves at the outset to the commitments that the model of the person might entail.

article, we consider some of the principal debates that bear upon transitional justice for the more-than-human and the concerns that have been raised regarding the cogency of this endeavour. In particular, we take up the question of who or what can be morally considerable and the further question of who or what might enter into the processes involved in transitional justice. Reflecting on these debates and concerns, we then articulate a foundational agenda for transitional justice and set out a conceptual framework that we suggest is most suited to working beyond the human. In the fourth part of the article, we turn to soil and to the question of how to approach the business of transforming relations that are not only systemically violent, but that fail to acknowledge soil as the type of community to which justice might be owed. In the conclusion, we briefly consider a collaboration between regenerative farmers and visual artists and explore how their engagements with the arts of relating to the more-than-human might move the as yet private transformations of relations with soil into a more public, albeit incipient, process of justice.

2 THE CONSTITUTIVE WORK OF ACTS OF JUSTICE

With Cover's bridge in mind, one might locate 'acts of justice', such as court decisions, prosecutions and punishment, compensation, and symbolic forms of reparation along a scale that traverses the space between the pole where law reflects current reality, and the pole where it instantiates imagined alternatives. These acts might be doing the work of expressing broadly accepted standards of justice, those that embody existing agreements and so reflect the present constellation of power; or they may be doing the work of constituting new standards, those that reflect emerging agreements which are forged as different perspectives and interests rise in prominence and the constellation of power shifts.

To exemplify the former, consider a court finding that an individual is guilty of wilfully killing another person (where this does not take place in a sanctioned context such as war). The facts of the case might be under dispute, but the punishment meted out is unequivocally understood as an expression of the uncontested principle that killing another human is unjust. To exemplify the latter, consider a report by the UN Committee Against Torture indicating that violence against women in the private sphere constitutes a dereliction of the state's duty to prevent torture.[6] In articulating its authoritative interpretation, the Committee's act is constitutive of a new standard of justice because hitherto the category of torture had been confined to deeds committed by people acting in their public capacity as agents of the state. In this regard, advocacy for the legal recognition of certain categories of action as unjust (and not merely for the recognition of the injustice of specific instances of an accepted category) can be understood as an attempt to convince authoritative bodies (at the state and supra-state level) to act in this constitutive manner. That said, especially in contexts where people

---

6. See, for example, United Nations Committee Against Torture, 'Concluding Observations on the Fifth Periodic Report of Estonia, adopted by the Committee at its Fiftieth Session (May 6–31, 2013)', where the Committee urged Estonia to adopt comprehensive legislation on violence against women, including domestic violence and marital rape, and to establish effective complaint mechanisms. For background on the gendered nature of authoritative understandings of torture in international law see A Byrnes, 'The Convention Against Torture' in KD Askin and DM Koenig (eds), *Women and International Human Rights Law*, vol. 2 (Transnational Publishers Incorporated 2000).

disagree about fundamental norms, many acts of justice will fall somewhere between these poles, and people will disagree about whether the norm those acts express ought to be an accepted standard of justice.

In the field of transitional justice, acts of justice, particularly forms of symbolic reparation, are best understood as being constitutive, not simply of particular standards of justice, but of the basic norms bearing upon matters such as the standing and status of certain groups or identities and hence of the boundaries and contours of the ethical, legal and political community, and the appropriate or acceptable forms of conduct within the community. In this regard, such acts of justice operate at the boundary between the *corpus juris* and the background myths, narratives, or imaginaries.[7] To illustrate, take the example of political apologies for wrongs committed by the state, such as the Australian or Canadian apologies for the forced removal of Indigenous children from their families. The acts of apology did not simply register what everyone knew and accepted; they authoritatively constituted the practice of removal as being unambiguously wrong within this political community now and into the future.[8] To analogize the distinction that JL Austin drew with respect to language, such acts are not constative but performative.[9] They seek to bring something into existence and, it should be added, to move something out of existence.

A further implication of this constitutive character of transitional justice is that its temporality is neither linear nor straightforwardly progressive, but rather multidirectional and faltering. From a formal and positivist perspective, it would usually be the case that the explicit acts of wrongdoing that are the object of the reparative act (say the apology) belong to the past. However, the norms, the imaginaries and the epistemic logics – or in Cover's terms, the myths and narratives – that legitimated those wrongs persist. As one clearly sees in the case of the relationship between postcolonial states and Indigenous peoples, these 'wrongful myths, narratives and logics' continue to sustain other forms of wrongdoing such as police violence.[10] The apology for one class of wrongful action that those myths and narratives authorized contributes towards invalidating those very myths and narratives, but is unlikely to completely dispel them. This means that transitional justice mechanisms can be deployed, and indeed must be capable of being deployed, in contexts where violence or wrongdoing flowing from those myths and narratives persists.

---

7. Imaginaries, as we understand them, constitute our shared background, and it is through an imaginary that we experience ourselves and the world and form both our expectations and our projects. See C Taylor, *Modern Social Imaginaries* (Duke University Press 2004) 23. Following Lennon, imaginaries have affective and normative force. See K Lennon, *Imagination and the Imaginary* (Routledge 2015) 73.
8. Celermajer, *The Sins of the Nation* (n 4). Note authoritatively does not mean definitively or universally. Contestation persists.
9. JL Austin, *How to Do Things with Words* (Oxford University Press 1975).
10. C Cunneen, 'Colonial Processes, Indigenous Peoples, and Criminal Justice Systems' in S Bucerius and M Tonry (eds), *The Oxford Handbook of Ethnicity, Crime, and Immigration* (Oxford University Press 2014) 386. A powerful illustration of the layers of coloniality is illustrated by the fact that while the Royal Commission into Aboriginal Deaths in Custody in Australia documented in detail how the legacy of colonialism and ongoing colonial institutions infused all aspects of the criminal justice system, the Commission itself can be seen as a colonizing institution. See E Marchetti, 'The Deep Colonizing Practices of the Australian Royal Commission into Aboriginal Deaths in Custody' 2006 33(3) Journal of Law and Society 451–74.

The fact that transitional justice works in this constitutive mode, and that it is amenable to contexts of ongoing wrongdoing is critical when considering its applicability to the more-than-human, at least if the analysis is to speak to actual conditions and to lay a path for a realistic course of action, rather than setting out speculative ideals.[11] There can be no illusion that the systemic violence against animals and the environment is anywhere near its end. Indeed, if transitional justice is to have any purchase as a form of justice for the more-than-human, the constitutive dimension of transitional mechanisms will inevitably be radically amplified.

To illustrate, compare the deployment of transitional justice mechanisms during periods of political transition in the wake of a history of systemic racism with their hypothetical deployment in relation to the large-scale killing and abuse of animals in industrial farming. In the case of racism, the objective of the mechanisms such as political apologies, reparation schemes or Truth and Reconciliation Commissions is to instantiate norms of racial equality and respect within the polity.[12] Admittedly, it may be that majorities and stakeholders with institutional power continue to reject such norms and that racial discrimination and violence persist, but the condemnation of racist norms and acts has nevertheless been advocated by a significant (albeit previously marginalized) portion of the polity, and is well instantiated in supra-national standards such as international human rights law.[13] In the case of animal slaughter, the objective of our hypothetical transitional mechanisms would be (amongst others) to instantiate norms concerning animals' rights to life and to be free from torture. In this case, although a small minority of humans support these norms, they are virtually comprehensively rejected across the larger community, and their systemic violation is economically, socially, legally and politically institutionalized within the polity.[14] Nor can these norms find affirmation in international law, not even in international law that is routinely flouted. Whereas in the first case, at least certain forms of racialized violence will have been curtailed when transitional justice mechanisms are deployed, the acts being called into question in relation to the more-than-human persist and are likely to endure for the foreseeable future.

Adopting Cover's frame illuminates how transitional justice's character as justice in its constitutive dimension should not be seen as a weakness, as if it were a second best to the more established and constative dimensions of justice – the distributive, retributive

---

11. Our point is not to disparage abstract ideals of speculative theory but to clarify our approach.
12. See, for example, A Valls, 'Racial Justice as Transitional Justice' (2003) 36(1) Polity 53–71 and Celermajer, *The Sins of the Nation* (n 4). For a critical view with respect to apologies to Indigenous peoples, see J Corntassel and C Holder, 'Who's Sorry Now? Government Apologies, Truth Commissions, and Indigenous Self-Determination in Australia, Canada, Guatemala, and Peru' (2008) 9(4) Human Rights Review 465–89.
13. For example, in making its findings in relation to the forced removal of Aboriginal and Torres Strait Islander children, the Australian Human Rights Commission made reference to a number of international human rights standards, including the Convention on the Elimination of All Forms of Racial Discrimination and the Convention on the Prevention and Punishment of the Crime of Genocide. See Australian Human Rights and Equal Opportunity Commission, *Bringing Them Home: Report of the National Inquiry into the Separation of Aboriginal and Torres Strait Islander Children from their Families* (Sydney HREOC 1997), especially Chapter 13.
14. D Wadiwel, *The War Against Animals* (Brill 2015).

or compensatory. As Juan E Corradi put it in one of the earliest uses of the term, transitional justice is more than ordinary justice, 'because it aims beyond the simple ordering of human relations: it seeks to achieve moral and political regeneration'.[15] Especially in the context of the fragility and incipient nature of norms concerning wrongs against beings other than humans, and in the light of current realities, it is in its transitional mode that justice can do its most important and transformative work. At a later moment, other dimensions of justice might have their time. Nevertheless, for transitional justice to do its transformative work, it too needs to be critically scrutinized and cleansed of its anthropomorphism and of the assumptions that it encodes about the nature of the subject of (in)justice.

3 TOWARDS A CONCEPTUAL FRAMEWORK FOR TRANSITIONAL JUSTICE AND THE MORE-THAN-HUMAN

Our discussion so far has rested on two highly inclusive terms: transitional justice and the more-than-human. At the outset of this discussion, we continue to use these two terms without further specification so as to canvas some of the debates that have taken place at their interface. As the discussion proceeds, we will narrow in on each.

Broadly understood, transitional justice is concerned with the question of how to effect a social and political transformation from a political community whose past has been characterized by various forms of systemic violence, injustice and (in the human realm) violations of human rights, to one whose future is premised on and capable of sustaining just relations and social peace.[16] As transitional justice developed as a field of practice, various mechanisms came to be thought of as a type of 'toolkit' for transition: trials, truth or truth and reconciliation commissions, restitution and compensation, various forms of institutional reform, apology, memorials and a range of forms of symbolic reparation. The aims of transitional justice are generally framed in terms of their double temporality, being backward looking (accountability for wrongdoing in the past) and forward looking (establishing the normative and institutional conditions for sustainable peace and justice).

What is distinctive about transitional justice is, however, somewhat lost if it is conceptualized purely in terms of what the particular mechanisms might deliver: for example, accountability for wrongdoing, or compensation and restitution to enable victims to move forward in ways that the harms they suffered had impeded. Rather, these dimensions of accountability and reparation are folded into the larger aim of transforming the relationships that constitute the social order,[17] or in the terms we

---

15. JE Corradi, 'Toward Societies Without Fear' in JE Corradi and others (eds), *Fear at the Edge: State Terror and Resistance in Latin America* (University of California Press 1992) at 267. Notably, this excerpt is taken from a larger passage where Corradi was arguing that transitional justice is both more and less than ordinary justice. The reasons for its being less are principally concerned with the power dynamics of political transitions.
16. For overviews see M Minow, *Between Vengeance and Forgiveness: Facing History after Genocide and Mass Violence* (Beacon Press 1998); RG Teitel, *Transitional Justice* (Oxford University Press 2000); P Arthur, 'How Transitions Reshaped Human Rights: A Conceptual History of Transitional Justice' (2009) 31 Hum Rts Q 32.
17. That the form of relationships gives shape to the social order is perhaps best explained by the notion of the field. As Cassirer wrote, 'The field itself can no longer be understood as a

established at the outset of this article: transforming the myths, narratives and social imaginaries of the polity.

The centrality of relational transformation is illuminated in a slightly different characterization of transitional justice as a technology of moral repair, an approach articulated perhaps most clearly in the work of Margaret Urban Walker.[18] The moral repair approach does not reject the backwards-forwards temporality of transitional justice, nor suggest different mechanisms, but rather seeks to centre the work of transforming the relationship between the parties (individuals and collectives) who have been variously perpetrators, victims, beneficiaries and bystanders.[19] Consistent with Hannah Arendt's understanding of forgiveness as that form of action that makes possible a future that is not mere reaction to the past but allows for the authentically new to arise,[20] reorganizing relational dynamics is here understood to be the fundamental driver of the ultimate social and political transformation, albeit allowing that different actions might be most effective in bringing about this shift.[21] So, for example, whereas in the abstract, compensation might seem to do the work of enabling victims to pursue opportunities that had been curtailed by the wrongs committed against them and to live lives that had been damaged, contextualized within the overall framework of moral repair, compensation is expressive of a recognition that the prior relationship had been organized in a harmful and asymmetrical way and that (from an ethical point of view) it needs to be recalibrated.

Although, in practice, the field of transitional justice has been entirely focused on wrongs between humans, some have suggested that its three linked goals – providing accountability for the past, laying the foundation for a just future and repairing relationships – might be usefully brought to attend to the wrongs that humans have committed against the more-than-human world.[22] For the most part theoretical speculations have not explicitly assumed the frame of transitional justice, with the notable exception of Charlotte Blattner's comprehensive analysis of how transitional mechanisms might be brought to bear on interspecies relations, focusing on humans and animals other than humans.[23]

---

merely additive whole, as an aggregate of parts. The field is not a thing-concept but a relation-concept; it is not composed of pieces but is a system, a totality of lines of force'. E Cassirer, *The Logic of the Cultural Sciences* (Yale University Press 2000) 92.

18. MU Walker, *Moral Repair: Reconstructing Moral Relations after Wrongdoing* (Cambridge University Press 2006).

19. In this vein, although not including beneficiaries and bystanders, Minow writes: 'Building connections and enhancing communication between perpetrators and those they victimized, and forging ties across the community, take precedence over punishment or law enforcement.' Minow (n 16) 91–2. See also D Van Ness and KH Strong, *Restoring Justice* (Office of Justice Programs 1997).

20. H Arendt, *The Human Condition* (University of Chicago Press 2013) 237.

21. Walker (n 18).

22. Paul Taylor's *Respect for Nature* is frequently cited as the foundational text for suggesting that restitution ought to be done in relation to harms committed to beings other than humans, although he did not use the language of transitional justice and indeed has been strongly criticized in animal and environmental justice literatures for positing an understanding of restitution that enables ongoing abuse. See PW Taylor, *Respect for Nature* (Princeton University Press 1986). The most comprehensive treatment of traditional justice for animals we are aware of is Blattner (n 1).

23. Blattner (n 1).

In contemplating this shift from intra-human to human–more-than-human injustice, a number of objections have been raised.[24] Here, we focus on a family of objections which worry that beings other than humans do not have the requisite capacities to be parties to transitional justice. In its more basic form, the objection is that beings other than humans cannot be subjects of justice *per se* because they cannot be harmed in morally relevant ways.[25] The more onerous form of the objection is that even if the moral considerability of beings other than humans is recognized, they lack the capacities required for the distinctive type of relational transformation that lies at the heart of transitional justice.[26] Interrogating these objections will allow us to elaborate our own approach to transitional justice for the more-than-human.

For the purposes of this discussion, we deal quite briefly with the first form of the objection, not least because of the extensiveness of the debate concerning the moral considerability of the many types of beings who fall into the broad category of the more-than-human. Such debates range from classical claims about animals' sentience and their being subjects of their own lives, and hence having moral claims or rights,[27] through more complex questions concerning how to justify the moral considerability of lifeforms such as ecosystems or species, which cannot in any straightforward way be brought under the categories of sentient subjects or subjects of a life.[28] For the purposes of this discussion, we propose accepting the proposition that there are sound cases for claiming that a broad range of lifeforms other than humans – including

---

24. Our intention is not to provide a comprehensive inventory of objections, but to focus on those that motivate our position. For example, we do not consider the objection that restorative or reparative approaches implicitly enable ongoing abuse, an objection taken up in relation to animals in KS Emmerman, 'Sanctuary, Not Remedy: The Problem of Captivity and the Need for Moral Repair' in L Gruen (ed), *The Ethics of Captivity* (Oxford University Press 2014) and in relation to the environment in E Katz, *Nature as Subject: Human Obligation and Natural Community* (Rowman & Littlefield 1997). Nor do we consider the so-called baseline problem that queries which state of nature ought to be sought in restoration, as argued in M Oksanen, 'Ecological Restoration as Moral Reparation' (2008) 23 Proceedings of the XXII World Congress of Philosophy 99, and the related 'erroneous replacement' problem, which suggests that all restoration involves replacing what has been destroyed with a fake, as argued in R Elliott, *Faking Nature: The Ethics of Environmental Restoration* (Routledge 1997).
25. For a discussion of the Cartesian foundation of the exclusion of beings other than humans from the circle of moral subjects, see GL Francione, *Animals as Persons: Essays on the Abolition of Animal Exploitation* (Columbia University Press 2008).
26. For example, C Palmer, *Animal Ethics in Context* (Columbia University Press 2010). For a more extensive discussion of these and a range of other objections, see Blattner (n 1).
27. The classical statements on sentience as the basis for moral considerability is P Singer, *Animal Liberation* (Harper Collins 1975) and on being a subject of a life is T Regan, *The Case for Animal Rights* (University of California Press 2004). For an ecofeminist position see V Plumwood, *Feminism and the Mastery of Nature* (Routledge 1993).
28. An important line of development here has been the application of a capabilities approach, whereby harm is understood as an interruption in functioning. On the application of capabilities approaches to the environment see D Schlosberg, *Defining Environmental Justice: Theories, Movements, and Nature* (Oxford University Press 2007). On the argument for the application to ecosystems and species, see K Norlock, 'The Atrocity Paradigm Applied to Environmental Evils' (2004) 9 Ethics and the Environment 85. Claudia Card's application of this approach in C Card, *The Atrocity Paradigm: A Theory of Evil* (Oxford University Press 2002) has been taken up by scholars arguing for transitional justice approaches for animals, notably G Scotton, 'Interspecies Atrocities and the Politics of Memory' in A Woodhall and G Garmendia da Trindade (eds), *Political Approaches to Nonhuman Animal Issues* (Palgrave Macmillan 2017).

not only animals and trees, but also ecosystems, rivers and soils – can be harmed in morally relevant ways. Because, however, those cases, in some instances far more than others, are not broadly accepted, any approach to transitional justice will need to deal from the outset with the most basic constitutive dimensions of justice: that the lifeform in question is the type of being or beings or community that can be wronged in morally relevant ways, that humans' actions vis-à-vis those lifeforms constitute wrongs, and hence that humans have committed injustices against those beings.

The work of bringing polities to recognize certain acts as moral wrongs is by no means foreign to transitional justice in the intra-human realm, as we see with particular poignancy in the case of wrongs against Indigenous peoples. To return to our example of the Australian debate about an apology for the forced removal of Indigenous children from their families, the resistance to a national apology was driven to a significant extent by the insistence that the practice had been for the children's own good.[29] Similarly, the practice that has been adopted by various organizations in recent years of acknowledging that a meeting is taking place on unceded Indigenous land occurs within a context where neither legally nor socially are Indigenous land rights and the wrongful theft of Indigenous land broadly accepted. Those speech acts are performative in the sense that they are constitutive narratives in which the characters occupying the roles of perpetrator and victim of injustice are being recast.

Judith Butler was pointing to a similar failure to recognize certain people as subjects of justice when she drew a connection between the absence of mourning or grief over the killing of certain people, specifically those from countries with which the USA was at war, and the constitutional discounting of those lives.[30] Drawing on Butler's ideas, a number of scholars, including Chloe Taylor and James Stenescu, have explicitly connected the need to confront and challenge the widespread failure to recognize the moral significance of harm done to animals by using mourning and memorialization – key aspects of the toolkit of transitional justice.[31] Similarly, drawing on the literature on the mechanisms for denial,[32] Guy Scotton has argued that in a context where certain lives (in this case animal lives) are not accorded moral considerability, rituals and performances of mourning and memorialization can perform a constitutive function.[33] We refer to this work not to suggest that mourning and memorialization will always be the most appropriate transitional justice mechanisms to do the work of constituting certain beings as morally considerable,

---

29. For a detailed discussion see Celermajer *The Sins of the Nation* (n 4).
30. J Butler, *Frames of War: When is Life Grievable?* (Verso Books 2009). To link this back with the removal of Indigenous children, in parliamentary debates in Western Australia in 1904, JM Drew said, '[A] half-caste, who possesses few of the virtues and nearly all of the vices of whites, grows up to be a mischievous and very immoral subject ... it may appear to be a cruel thing to tear an Aborigine child from its mother, but it is necessary in some cases to be cruel to be kind.' Quoted in P Biskup, *Not Slaves, Not Citizens: The Aboriginal Problem in Western Australia 1898–1954* (University of Queensland Press 1973) 142.
31. J Stanescu, 'Species Trouble: Judith Butler, Mourning, and the Precarious Lives of Animals' (2012) 27 Hypatia 567; C Taylor, 'The Precarious Lives of Animals: Butler, Coetzee, and Animal Ethics' (2008) 52 Philosophy Today 60.
32. The classic text is S Cohen, *States of Denial: Knowing about Atrocities and Suffering* (John Wiley & Sons 2013). In the area of environmental harm and climate change specifically see KM Norgaard, *Living in Denial: Climate Change, Emotions, and Everyday Life* (MIT Press 2011).
33. Scotton (n 28).

but rather to indicate how others have thought about this connection. When we turn to harms against soil in the next part of the article, we will outline the case for recognizing that soil can be (and has been) harmed in morally considerable ways, and will trace some of the practices that are building recognition of soil's moral status.

Let us turn then to the more onerous objection and the one more specific to transitional justice *per se*. Even if it is accepted that beings radically different to humans *can* be harmed in a morally relevant sense, the objection remains that transitional approaches require not merely a subjective point of view, but more demandingly, a reflexive relationship with that harm: the subject must be aware of the harm as harm. As discussed below, it is thus contended, first, that transitional justice requires that those who participate in it should have quite demanding reflexive capacities or affordances, and, second, that beings other than humans do not (for the most part, if not entirely) have them. These putatively requisite capacities fall into two categories. First are those capacities or affordances required in order to experience harm as a moral wrong or as an injustice in a way that would make transitional approaches relevant or meaningful for the participant being/s. Second are the capacities and affordances required to participate in or to benefit from the transformative processes that transitional mechanisms seek to achieve: to have an experience whereby the awareness of harm as harm is replaced by an awareness of transcending or transforming that harm, not necessarily into an experience of justice, but into something akin to reconciliation or moral healing.[34]

Thus, for example, falling within the first category, Clare Palmer argues that animals 'lack concepts of justice, bear no grudges against either perpetrators or beneficiaries, and seek no satisfaction from either'.[35] In a similar vein, Donaldson and Kymlicka argue that 'most animal communities do not retain detailed intergenerational records of abusive treatment by humans'.[36] Palmer also thinks that animals lack the second set of capacities, arguing that they are incapable of obtaining satisfaction, as humans can, when they see that reparative action is taken in relation to harms they have suffered.[37]

Similar objections are raised with respect to the environment. Oksanen writes for example that nature cannot count as a victim in the morally relevant sense because it lacks 'the essential psychological and complex qualities that characterize the life and the experiences of human victims and the nature of human communality'.[38] Detecting a similar absence of a subject that one could meaningfully call the morally relevant victim, Katz also rejects the cogency of a reparative stance vis-à-vis nature.[39] In response to Almassi's claim that one can imagine reparative processes that would

---

34. Walker's writings certainly can be seen to give rise to this understanding. She writes, for example that moral repair 'involves the restoration or construction of confidence, trust, and hope in the reality of shared moral standards and of our reliability in meeting and enforcing them'. MU Walker, 'Moral Repair and its Limits' in TF Davis and K Womack (eds), *Mapping the Ethical Turn* (University of Virginia Press 2001) 120.
35. Palmer (n 26) 104. This is not a reason in Palmer's view not to take action that will alter the conditions to prevent future harms, but that the language of reparations ought not be used.
36. S Donaldson and W Kymlicka, *Zoopolis* (Oxford University Press 2016) 258.
37. C Palmer, 'Can We – and Should We – Make Reparation to "Nature"?' in WP Kabasenche, M O'Rourke and MH Slater (eds), *The Environment* (MIT Press 2012).
38. Oksanen (n 24).
39. E Katz, 'Replacement and Irreversibility: The Problem with Ecological Restoration as Moral Repair' (2018) 23 Ethics and the Environment 17.

rebuild trust between nature and humans,[40] Katz suggests that even if this is a metaphor, it is one 'strained beyond coherence'.[41]

A number of responses attempt to resist these objections. One is to call into question the assumption that the beings in question do not have the requisite capacities. In her comprehensive treatment of transitional justice for animals other than humans, Blattner takes this approach, mustering ethological research on animals' memories, awareness of death, experience of trauma, and capacity for reconciliation and forgiveness, as well as cautioning against projecting our assumptions into fields of knowledge about which we remain largely ignorant and have been shown to approach with dogmatic commitments.[42] As formulated, this response would still seem to limit the class of beings who might be involved, but Indigenous ontologies[43] or new animisms would suggest much more complex capacities for the whole of nature.[44] A second move is to argue that even if the ecological communities or beings who are the explicit object of harm (say, soils or rivers) lack the relevant capacities, these direct harms result in more indirect harms to others who do have the required capacities (including people).[45]

A third response is to move the focus away from the victim altogether and to argue that the object of the reparative acts is the transformation of the perpetrators. On this account, one need ask nothing of the victim, because what matters is that, by virtue of their involvement in reparative acts, those who habitually cause harm come to recognize their wrongs, and, through this moral encounter, become different types of people; people who would not commit such acts.[46]

A fourth and far more radical response from an ontological point of view is to move from focusing on the victim *or* on perpetrator to focusing on the relationship. Almassi gives the example of a fish restoration project in the Great Lakes region led by the Little River Band of Ottawa Indians, an Anishinaabe nation.[47] Describing the project, Holtgren, Ogren and Whyte write, 'The fish has been able to both heal old wounds and create new, sustainable relationships among people, even in a watershed

---

40. B Almassi, 'Ecological Restorations as Practices of Moral Repair' (2017) 22 Ethics and the Environment 19, at 24.
41. Katz (n 39) 21.
42. Blattner (n 1), see 35ff.
43. A Poelina, 'A Coalition of Hope! A Regional Governance Approach to Indigenous Australian Cultural Wellbeing' in A Campbell, M Duffy and B Edmondson (eds), *Located Research* (Springer 2020); RW Kimmerer, 'Learning the Grammar of Animacy 1' (2017) 28 Anthropology of Consciousness 128.
44. G Harvey, *Animism: Respecting the Living World* (Columbia University Press 2005); F Mathews, *For Love of Matter* (State University of New York Press 2003).
45. Card (n 28) makes this argument in relation to ecosystems and those who depend or live within them.
46. J Basl, 'Restitutive Restoration: New Motivations for Ecological Restoration' (2010) 32 Environmental Ethics 135; TE Hill, 'Ideals of Human Excellence and Preserving Natural Environments' (1983) 5 Environmental Ethics 211; W Throop, 'Environmental Virtues and the Aims of Restoration' in A Thompson and J Bendik-Keymer (eds), *Ethical Adaptation to Climate Change: Human Virtues of the Future* (2012). Smith objects that this focus on the perpetrator problematically marginalizes the good of the victim, but this seems to us to overlook the effect of transforming the perpetrator on the victim. See L Smith, 'On the "Emotionality" of Environmental Restoration: Narratives of Guilt, Restitution, Redemption and Hope' (2014) 17 Ethics, Policy & Environment 286.
47. Almassi (n 40).

where these relationships have been strained by settler colonialism'.[48] The radicality of this response lies in the ontological shift from subjects being the primary site of being, and then forming different types of relationships, to the relationship being the fundamental ontological unit. No particular capacities or affordances are required of distinct parties, because they (and their capacities and affordances) come into being only and always in relationship.

In reflecting on these objections and the various attempts to parse them, we can see that, except in the last case, there is a tendency to retain an ontological schema in which ideas (or reflexivity understood as residing in the realm of ideas) are valorised as the sole site of meaning-making and hence also of freedom. Thus, both the sense of harm as harm and the capacity to be engaged in transformation are assumed to take place in the realm of ideas and cognitive understanding (I *know* that I have been harmed and I *understand* that you are sorry). Transitional interventions effect moral repair, on this view, by transforming people's ideas and understandings about the principles or substantive demands of justice, about different identities and so on. To the extent that this emphasis on ideas remains tied to persistent ontological hierarchies – articulated from Plato through to representations of the great Chain of Being, to Descartes, to Kant and into contemporary humanisms that emphasize the capacity for complex linguistic moves – other beings are bound to fall short. Indeed, as Adorno wrote,

> Animals play for the idealist system virtually the same role as the Jews for fascism. To revile man as an animal – that is genuine idealism. To deny the possibility of salvation for animals absolutely and at any price is the inviolable boundary of its metaphysics.[49]

What, though, if we allow that both recognition of wrong as wrong and moral transformation can also occur through shifting embodied encounters and material relationships? Importantly, and consistent with a range of ontological positions such as Merleau Ponty's body-oriented phenomenology, new materialism and Actor Network Theory, this shift from 'ideas' to 'material' should not be taken to be coincident with the shift from a meaning-laden realm in which agency and freedom reside and reflexivity takes place, to a second, brute realm devoid of meaning except for that which the first bestows upon it.[50] To return to Cover, myths 'build relations between the normative and the material universe'.[51] To be clear, in adopting this ontological position we are not arguing that this move is a requirement of transitional justice for the more-than-human because the beings concerned lack language or reflexivity and hence are in deficit. Indeed, although the self-understanding of transitional justice in

---

48. M Holtgren, S Ogren and KP Whyte, 'Renewing Relatives: One Tribe's Efforts to Bring Back an Ancient Fish' (2015) Earth Island Journal 30(3). Available at <http://www.earthisland.org/journal/index.php/eij/article/renewing_relatives/>, quoted in Almassi (n 40) at 22.
49. TW Adorno, *Beethoven: The Philosophy of Music*, trans. E. Jephcott (Stanford University Press 1998) 80.
50. The three large bodies of theory noted here, Merleau Ponty's phenomenology, new materialism and Actor Network Theory (ANT) are by no means the same, but all three reject an ontology in which meaning (and the associated qualities of freedom, agency and so on) is invested only on one side of a fundamental dualism. See M Merleau-Ponty, *Phenomenology of Perception* (Routledge 1962); D Coole and S Frost, *New Materialisms: Ontology, Agency, and Politics* (Duke University Press 2010); and B Latour, 'Networks, Societies, Spheres: Reflections of an Actor-Network Theorist' (2011) 5 International Journal of Communication 15.
51. Cover (n 1).

the human realm has underplayed the role of embodied transformation and has largely seen shifts in material relationships as being representative of the primary 'normative' shift, we would reject this dualistic understanding.[52] Nevertheless, when we move to the question of relationships between humans and beings who either do not, or may not, have a form of consciousness or modes of communication that resemble that of humans, the emphasis on a presumed realm of reflexive ideas is neither sustainable nor, more importantly, ethically appropriate.

Thus, transitional justice for the more-than-human must be premised on an ecocentric and posthumanist framework. Grounding transitional justice in this way entails rejecting the automatic adaptation or extension of approaches that were developed solely with humans in mind when it comes to developing transitional justice for systemic wrongs against the more-than-human. Certainly, as Blattner cogently argues, the default assumption that animals (in the case she is analysing) lack the requisite affordances also needs to be met with significant scepticism.[53] From an ethical point of view, however, extensionist approaches impose logics within which more-than-human beings are from the outset encoded according to their proximity to or distance from the ideal of the human subject, within a hierarchical ordering in which they are doomed to be deficient. Indeed, if transitional justice for the more-than-human is to deal with the failure to recognize that morally relevant wrongs have been committed at all, then, as a field, transitional justice must also come to terms with the 'ur-problem' of the implicit equation of distinctly human affordances, not only with moral considerability but with the capacity to experience injustice and transformation.

Others have made a similar move in cognate fields. Considering what political deliberation involving animals might look like, for example, Donaldson and Kymlicka consider the practices undertaken at VINE Sanctuary, where animals gather when decisions are made. Although they 'cannot articulate their views in discussion, ... they are a presence, a reminder, and a check, on human deliberation'.[54] Going further, Donovan Schaefer argues that rather than starting with our conception of the human practice of religion as essentially ideational, belonging to a realm called 'spirit' as distinct from body, to allow the possibility of animal religion entails starting with animals' embodied experience of and resonance with the world they encounter.[55] Drawing on the material turn in religion, he quotes Vásquez' demand that we recognize 'that, although our experience of the world is mediated through our discursive

---

52. See D Celermajer, 'Mere Ritual? Displacing the Myth of Sincerity in Transitional Rituals' (2013) 7 International Journal of Transitional Justice 286.
53. Blattner (n 1).
54. S Donaldson and W Kymlicka, 'Farmed Animal Sanctuaries: The Heart of the Movement' (2015) 1 Politics and Animals 50, at 67. Isabelle Stengers makes a related argument about presence when she writes, 'We know that in laboratories in which experiments are performed on animals, all sorts of rites and ways of talking and referring to those animals exist, that attest to the researchers' need to protect themselves. ... The correlate of the necessity of "deciding" on the legitimacy of an experiment would then be the invention of constraints directed against these protective manoeuvres, forcing the researchers concerned to expose themselves, to decide "in the presence of" those that may turn out to be the victims of their decision'. I Stengers, 'The Cosmopolitical Proposal' in B Latour and P Weibel (eds), *Making Things Public: Atmospheres of Democracy* (MIT Press 2005) 994, at 997.
55. DO Schaefer, *Religious Affects: Animality, Evolution, and Power* (Duke University Press 2015).

and nondiscursive practices, we cannot reduce to human texts the materiality of our bodies and the world in which and through which we live'.[56]

In a similar vein, if transitional justice is to be brought into the sphere of relations between humans and the more-than-human world, its modalities must be adapted to the ways of being of those involved and not only the ways of being, knowing and transforming that humans occupy and narrate. In this regard, what remains of transitional justice is the search for acts that can catalyse transformation in relations that have been damaged. What falls away is the assumption that such acts must be meaningful in the ways that humans believe meaning-making occurs. The myths and narratives underpinning transitional justice itself must also be subject to transformation.

4 PRACTICES OF SOIL JUSTICE

As foreshadowed earlier, to explore how transitional justice might be taken up in relation to wrongs against beings other than humans, we focus here on soil. Even as beings such as animals and trees begin to show up as forms of life that might merit moral considerability, soil largely remains imagined as a lifeless substance or medium, a resource, and as such, an entity whose well-being matters only in so far as it effects the well-being of others.

For most human societies (with the exception of some Indigenous societies),[57] violence to soil is an everyday and unremarkable occurrence, just as soil itself is commonly considered a backdrop to more important things. Among societies practising industrial agriculture, violence to soil is normalized and even celebrated, with tilling widely lauded as a civilizational achievement. Where soil is harmed, the harm and its effects tend to appear slowly (if at all), more commonly through absence rather than presence. This challenges most humans' perceptive capacities, which more easily attune to the charismatic creatures that show emotion through more immediate facial and bodily expressions. Rob Nixon's concept of 'slow violence' is illuminating here. Slow violence is 'a violence that occurs gradually and out of sight, a violence of delayed destruction that is dispersed across time and space, an attritional violence that is typically not viewed as violence at all'.[58] As Nixon highlights, such violence does not bear the same phenomenal qualities or event forms of more compressed and dramatic

---

56. MA Vásquez *More than Belief: A Materialist Theory of Religion* (Oxford University Press 2011) 321, quoted in DO Schaefer, 'Do Animals Have Religion? Interdisciplinary Perspectives on Religion and Embodiment' (2012) 25 Anthrozoös 173.
57. There is evidence that some forms of tilling and other techniques of soil modification practised by Indigenous farmers and hunter gatherers cause significantly less erosion than conventional mechanized (mouldboard) ploughing. For example, G Rajaram et al. argue that the conservation tillage systems developed in the West have many characteristics of Indigenous tillage systems. They show this by highlighting examples of Indigenous tillage systems in India and the United States. See G Rajaram, DC Erbach and DM Warren 'The Role of Indigenous Tillage Systems in Sustainable Food Production' (1991) 8(1–2) Agriculture and Human Values 149–55. Analysis of fluvial sediments in South Eastern Australia by Portenga et al. shows that soil erosion rates from low-intensity, high-frequency Aboriginal burning regimes in the late Holocene were equal to background erosion rates from natural causes. See EW Portenga, DH Rood, P Bishop and PR Bierman, 'A Late Holocene Onset of Aboriginal Burning in Southeastern Australia' (2016) 44(2) Geology 131–4.
58. R Nixon, *Slow Violence and the Environmentalism of the Poor* (Harvard University Press 2011) 2.

types of violence, and is thus is less amenable to spectacle or to sparking moral concern.[59] Nixon observes that slow violence 'typically occurs in the passive voice – without clearly articulated agency'.[60] Often this is also because the actions that constitute such violence are embedded within much larger structural frameworks of action that have long been taken for granted, as inevitable parts of life.

Violence to soil involves damage to soil ecological and physical integrity, and thus its flourishing and ability to support biodiversity.[61] Soil typically harbours a staggering diversity of other lifeforms – species from all evolutionary domains – bacteria, archaea and eukarya – and accordingly, is vulnerable to myriad harms.[62] As ecological communities, relationships between species in soils develop over time, manifesting emergent properties, some of which can be understood as ecological functions. Violence to soil commonly involves high levels of disturbance: for example, ploughs that invert topsoil and compact the soil profile, or building impervious surfaces, such as roads, which also cause compaction. These actions sever soil's connectivity, collapsing pores and destroying fungal vessels that connect to plant roots and feed the soil food web. Exposed to the elements, vulnerable soil structures (micro and macro aggregates) degrade, reducing soil's water-holding capacity and leading to erosion.

Violence to soil is normalized by dominant conceptions of soil as primarily a raw material or a vessel, with value realized in its outputs, rather than soil being understood as something that is intrinsically valuable. In modern times, soil is seen as fungible, due to properties that afford exchange. Activities such as moving soil, buying soil and disposing of soil depend on its ability to be handled in bulk and moved in great volumes. When such perceptions of soil's fungibility are dominant and not tempered by appreciation for soil's less replaceable, living and more relational qualities, attitudes can prevail that amount to disregard for soil's particularity, fragility and needs.[63] To treat Earth Others solely as tools for use involves a type of violence, dispensing with the kind of ethical respect encoded in Kant's categorical imperative, which requires that we treat others (however, for Kant human others only) not simply as means but also as ends in themselves.[64] While soil's instrumental value to humans is a dimension of interdependence, recognition of soil's usefulness can crowd out appreciation of its own character and its own being in the world. Overly objectified understandings of soil that render it a passive receptacle of plant growth – indifferent to its connectivity being severed, rather than as a living community with capabilities in, within and for itself – can both drive and result from violent practices towards it.

In addition to narrow instrumental conceptions that provide implicit licence for violence towards soil, certain myths and narratives not only permit but celebrate

---

59. ibid 128–9.
60. ibid 136.
61. For a discussion of ecological integrity, capabilities and ecological justice, see D Schlosberg, *Defining Environmental Justice: Theories, Movements, and Nature* (Oxford University Press 2007) 153.
62. M Beare, D Coleman, D Crossley, P Hendrix and E Odum, 'A Hierarchical Approach to Evaluating the Significance of Soil Biodiversity to Biogeochemical Cycling' (1995) 170 Plant and Soil 5–22.
63. M Nussbaum sees fungibility as a key dimension of the objectification of women in her book *Sex and Social Justice* (Oxford University Press 1999).
64. This formulation of the categorical imperative appears in I Kant, *Groundwork for the Metaphysics of Morals* (Harper and Rowe 1964).

such violence. An influential narrative regarding technology is that the development of the plough helped to produce civilization (where civilization is understood as an unambiguously positive development). This narrative is used for two historical periods: the Neolithic revolution and the Green Revolution (mechanization) of modern agriculture. BBC economics journalist Tim Harford brings the two together in a radio series entitled *50 Things That Made the Modern Economy*:

> Four decades ago, the science historian James Burke … asked a simple question: Surrounded by the wreckage of modernity, without access to the lifeblood of modern technology, where do you start again? What do you need to keep yourself – and the embers of civilisation – alive? And his answer was a simple yet transformative piece of technology: a plough. And that's appropriate, because it was the plough that kick-started civilisation in the first place, and which – ultimately – made our modern economy possible.[65]

Here, Harford quotes a hyperbolic statement from the 1970s, without regard for the ways in which ploughs have been more critically evaluated in the decades since, particularly by farmers themselves. While there is no question that the plough has 'made' the modern economy in terms of influencing the ways in which the economy has developed (including the modes of exchange between soils and plants), the lifesaving credentials of ploughs – particularly as technologies of choice amid a world in ruin, are dubious. Such triumphalist discourses discourage more frank reflection across society on the harms that ploughs have caused soils and communities of diverse species, humans included, that depend on soils.

Greater ambivalence regarding the impact of ploughs can be found among farmers. A movement towards greater care for soil needs, containing a nascent respect for soil's flourishing (despite an overall instrumental justification for changed practices) has grown in recent decades, involving reduced tillage and increased plant diversity on farms. The adoption of conservation agriculture practices in cropland for example, increased globally by 10.5 million hectares each year between 2008–2009 and 2015–2016, reaching about 12.5 per cent of total cropland.[66] In Australia and across much of the world, farmers have increasingly adopted practices and technologies that account for the complex nutritional needs, physical structure, chemical sensitivity and biological liveliness of soil, with many beginning to conceive of soil differently: as deserving of care.[67]

No-till or low-till farming techniques involve the use of modified machinery for planting and harvesting that minimally impact upon soil structure. Refraining from conventional ploughing due to its capacity to harm the connectivity and fertility of soil, low-till practitioners know the importance of soil's structural and ecological integrity for healthy plant growth. Like museum conservators who adopt protocols for handling museum objects, such practitioners distinguish parts of soil that are appropriate to move, disturb or touch. They consider soil moisture and previous frequencies of disturbance when making these decisions. Tilling, where it is deemed

---

65. T Harford, 'How the Plough Made the Modern Economy Possible', BBC World Service, 27 November 2017 <https://www.bbc.com/news/business-41903076>.
66. Kassam et al. define Conservation Agriculture in relation to three interlinked principles: 'no or minimum mechanical soil disturbance, biomass mulch soil cover and crop species diversification'. See A Kassam, T Friedrich and R Derpsch, 'Global Spread of Conservation Agriculture' (2018) International Journal of Environmental Studies 1.
67. See, for example, the work of M Puig de la Bellacasa, 'Making Time for Soil: Technoscientific Futurity and the Pace of Care' (2015) 45(5) Social Studies of Science 691–716.

necessary, is more like a surgeon's knife and less like a twisting blade. This restraint is a practical form of recognition of soil's lateral connectedness: soil's fleshiness, its interwoven structure and the vulnerability of these connections. We might consider such practices as constituting a kind of spatial ethics with regard to the movement of bodies and tools (particularly machines) as they come into contact with soil.

Yet at the same time, in their most typical forms, low or no-till approaches tend to maintain monocultures, using large quantities of herbicides to eliminate self-sown species (instead of ploughing the soil for this purpose), and this can limit the diversity of soil dwellers.[68] While such practices demonstrate a type of sensitivity towards certain soil needs, for the most part, they are still justified and articulated in instrumental and technical terms rather than in more explicitly ethical registers. Soil's value is considered to be derivative of its ability to perform certain functions for humans, or other valued species.

Acknowledging shortcomings of conventional low-till approaches for soil health, numerous farmers are adopting more ecologically informed practices sometimes termed 'beyond no-till', such as pasture cropping, cover cropping, and controlled traffic farming. Simon Mattsson, a second-generation sugar cane grower near Mackay, Queensland, initiated major changes to his farming practice due to concerns about the declining productivity of the land, with sugarcane production declining 9 per cent every five years.[69] Harvests declined even after adopting several soil conservation measures such as cover crops, mulching and reduced tillage.[70] This decline prompted him to embark on a global journey to learn about soil biology, funded by a Nuffield Scholarship. In his travels Mattsson learned from regenerative farmers about practical ways to integrate crop and cover crop biodiversity into a commercial farming system.

Upon returning home, Mattsson made several changes. He reconfigured machinery to reduce its impact on the earth, using controlled-track technology to limit compaction of the soil to narrow zones under the tracks, in recognition of the sensitivity of soil structures to being damaged by machinery[71] especially after rain. He experimented with growing numerous plant species alongside the sugar cane: radish, turnip, soybeans, chickpea, vetch, oats, rye and sunflower. He now grows a commercial crop of sunflowers within one metre of the rows of sugar cane. The sunflower complements the sugarcane through being an annual plant that has a much faster growth rate compared to the sugar cane, shading the soil when the cane is young, and providing numerous other benefits (including its spectacular appearance when viewed from a distance, lending itself to a surprising artistic collaboration which also sheds light

---

68. S Sánchez-Moreno, J Castro, E Alonso-Prados, JL Alonso-Prados, JM García-Baudín, M Talavera and VH Durán-Zuazo, 'Tillage and Herbicide Decrease Soil Biodiversity in Olive Orchards' (2015) 35 Agronomy for Sustainable Development 691–700.
69. F Sheehan, 'Simon Mattsson – Cane and Cover Crops', Weekly Times. Reproduced by the Australian Biological Farming Conference 2018 <https://www.australianbiologicalfarmingconference.org/simon-mattsson.html> accessed 22 November 2020.
70. Reef Catchments (Mackay Whitsunday Isaac) Limited, *Case Study: Simon Mattsson* <https://hcmif3k7kt343pwrn2ytkt39-wpengine.netdna-ssl.com/files/2020/05/Mattsson-casestudy-FINAL1.pdf> accessed 22 November 2020.
71. The Research Council of Norway, 'Heavy Agricultural Machinery Can Damage the Soil, Nordic Researchers Find', ScienceDaily, 9 May 2011 <https://www.sciencedaily.com/releases/2011/05/110505083737.htm>.

on the work of justice to soil).[72] Having different types of plants growing together in a field means that the crops do not 'mine' the soil in the way that a monoculture does.[73] But, more importantly, the soil ecosystem is more diverse, because each type of plant attracts a different range of microbes via the sugars exuded by its plant roots.[74] These microbes help to build better soil structure, storing some of the sugars as long chain carbon compounds that can sequester carbon from the air.[75] Bob Cannard, a farmer interviewed in the documentary *Symphony of the Soil*, explains how diverse crops can feed the soil:

> In my gardens I grow two things all the time – 50% for people – which is the potato in this case, and 50% for nature – the soil improvement cycling crops. Very important – without a balance between the two, things will collapse. In my gardens and in the gardens of the future I believe, we need to recognize and feed nature as we feed humanity. I grow this mixed crop of soil improvement plants – you can call them weeds – they're mustards and vetches and clovers and a wide range of different plants in here.[76]

This description suggests acknowledgement of the need for distributive justice towards soil in farming, widening the range of beneficiaries of gardens' productivity so that the crops grown feed both humans and nonhumans. This approach challenges widely-held assumptions that cropping should involve humans harvesting the entire product of any given field, and that humans should compete according to a 'zero sum' calculus with the livelihoods of other species.[77]

Adopting a range of soil-sensitive practices and adapting these practices to signs of the condition of the soil, farmers can begin to inhabit attentive orientations to soil that are good bases for the recognition of soil as ethically significant, as an end in itself (in addition to as a means of making a living). Modifying practices iteratively upon receiving feedback from the land itself, farmers build a phronesis involving interpretive skills as well as greater receptivity and respect towards soil. Writing about Polyface Farm, where complex ecological relationships are woven into a farming enterprise, Romand Coles writes of a dynamic 'attentiveness from which new forms of understanding and practice begin to emerge that are more finely tuned to qualities of relationality, dynamics, interpenetration, complexity, fragility, reciprocity, and care than most of those that are dominant today'.[78]

---

72. L Ihlein, 'Sunset Symphony in the Sunflowers' (2017) <http://lucasihlein.net/Sunset-Symphony-in-the-Sunflowers> accessed 18 April 2021.
73. R Dybzinski, JE Fargione, DR Zak, D Fornara and D Tilman, 'Soil Fertility Increases with Plant Species Diversity in a Long-Term Biodiversity Experiment' Oecologia (2008) <http://www.cbs.umn.edu/sites/default/files/public/t2138.pdf> accessed 24 April 2021.
74. TR Turner, K Ramakrishnan, J Walshaw, D Heavens, M Alston, D Swarbreck, A Osbourn, A Grant and PS Poole, 'Comparative Metatranscriptomics Reveals Kingdom Level Changes in the Rhizosphere Microbiome of Plants' (2013) 7 ISME J. 2248–58.
75. CM Kallenbach, SD Frey and AS Grandy, 'Direct Evidence for Microbial-Derived Soil Organic Matter Formation and its Ecophysiological Controls' (2016) 7 Nature Communications 13630.
76. B Cannard, *Symphony of the Soil*, Dir. Deborah Koons (Lily Films, 2012), DVD.
77. This reference to livelihood as something that many species build comes from K Polanyi's *Livelihood of Man* (ed. HW Pearson, Academic Press 1977), which is explored by E Miller in *Reimagining Livelihoods: Life beyond Economy, Society, and Environment* (University of Minnesota Press 2019).
78. R Coles, *Visionary Pragmatism: Radical and Ecological Democracy in Neoliberal Times* (Duke University Press 2016) 101.

Consistent with our discussion above about reparation as a turn towards attending to the previously excluded and violated other, soil-sensitive farming often involves new practices of observing soil. This includes noting signs given by indicator species such as plants or parasitic nematodes and engaging in responsive tinkering to amend soil – in response to yellowing leaves, for example – noting responses within a time period in which any change would have produced an effect. Exploring receptive practices of care for worms, Abrahamsson and Bertoni write of the embodied learning involved in the work of incremental attunement:

> [T]his knowing takes the shape of a co-constructed, mutual, on-going and dynamic effort to attune your caring with the activities of the worms. Still, one that is not reciprocal in any egalitarian way, but rather sensitive to differences. 'Learning to speak worm', here, means learning to become attuned to the subtleties of the worms' relation with the wormery, with the food, with the bedding, with their environment. And food is a language that worms understand. It is a 'language,' but one that is not inflected in words, sentences and grammar, but in the utterance of practices, in the less codified tinkering of everyday life.[79]

A key form of tinkering that is assisting farmers in their interspecies interpretive work with soil is carried out by using tools such as microscopes, which provide glimpses of microbial life and clues as to its condition. Jan, a soil scientist and educator, provides farmers with low magnification microscopes as part of her workshops, and explained her motivation as one of sparking interest and motivation for independent inquiry:

> When [farmers] look at samples [of their soil] they see mites, springtails, other invertebrates. To know the soil is alive doesn't mean anything in particular but it starts [farmers] off. They then start asking other questions. They really have to shift their thinking, gain confidence to listen to their own environment, to know their own soil, don't rely on others to tell them what to do, and not follow recipes.[80]

Key to this work is helping farmers attune themselves to soil, renewing and redisclosing spatial and bodily understandings and assisting with the development and habituation of new practices which can help release the tight grip of control that can inhibit openness to more just interspecies relations in agriculture. Through spending greater time in careful observation, and attuning their bodies accordingly, practitioners can 'learn to be affected' by the condition of soil inhabitants, in modes of engagement that Bruno Latour has insightfully theorized.[81] Here he discusses an example of a 'longitudinal' wine tasting 'that allows you … to acquire a nose and a palate':[82]

> [T]hanks to the multiplication of instruments, we have become capable of registering new distinctions … The more instruments proliferate, the more the arrangement is artificial, the more capable we become at registering worlds. Artifice and reality are in the same positive column, whereas something entirely different from work is inscribed on the debit side: what we have there now is *insensitivity*.[83]

---

79. S Abrahamsson and F Bertoni, 'Compost Politics: Experimenting with Togetherness in Vermicomposting' (2014) 4 Environmental Humanities 134.
80. Interviewee 'Jan' in AT O'Brien, *Ethical Relationships to Soil in the Anthropocene* (PhD dissertation, Australian Catholic University 2017) 113–14.
81. For more on 'learning to be affected', see B Latour, 'How to Talk About the Body? The Normative Dimension of Science Studies' (2004) 10(2–3) Body & Society 205–29.
82. B Latour, *The Politics of Nature: How to Bring the Sciences into Democracy*, trans Catherine Porter (Harvard University Press 2004) 84.
83. ibid 85 (original emphasis).

Latour celebrates various ways in which interpretive skills can be enhanced through the careful use of the senses, and through employing certain tools. As technological means can enable humans to register subtleties and distinctions, they can help us to 'register worlds' where we might otherwise have difficulty doing so. For practitioners accustomed to prescriptive approaches to agriculture, learning of the mystery of soil communication through scientific instruments can be initially dissatisfying, since these tools provide fleeting clues but no definitive answers regarding what might be needed by the soil ecosystem. Action that flows from such observation is necessarily tentative, iterative and experimental. Nevertheless, this assertiveness feeds into the possibility of developing agricultural practice into more of a craft-based, open-ended receptive phronesis. Such approaches are slower than typical modern agricultural approaches, involving what Puig de la Bellacasa terms the 'pace of care'.[84] The interpretive difficulty of understanding soil heightens soil's alterity, reminding farmers of how much remains unknown in any interaction with soil organisms. Increased awareness of epistemic limits tempers aspirations to mastery and control in agroecosystems, calling into question the will to order and determine the lives of these unknowable species.

While the problem of extending human moral imaginations to comprehend injustices outside frames of reference conventionally considered to demarcate the domain of justice is not unfamiliar to the task of justice,[85] the high level of ontological difference between soils and humans presents considerable challenges for transitional justice to soils. And, although all processes of justice involve communicative gaps, such gaps are multiplied many times when it comes to soil. Public processes of transitional justice between humans often rely on intersubjective exchange between victims and perpetrators as a key element of the accountability process, bringing moments of identification and catharsis and heightening affective intensities. The lack of this kind of intersubjective exchange with soils means that, initially at least, efforts to do justice to soil might feel affectively dissatisfying.

Another challenge for transitional justice to soil is that little of the public discourse regarding soil conservation engages public ethics or the narratives that animate them. Education on soil conservation is commonly directed towards specialized audiences and concerned with alleviating cost pressures in farming enterprises, demonstrating business cases for farmers and explaining soil conservation scientifically. There is however a small but growing literature that seeks to engage the broader public regarding soil care. Public descriptions of soil that detail its aesthetically rich, surprising and interactive dimensions can do some work to help shift human relations that are stuck in control-oriented and static relations with soil. We can see this in the language encouraging care for soil by some writers and educators. David Montgomery writes, 'Look closely and you find a whole world of life eating life, a biological orgy recycling the dead back into new life. Healthy soil has an enticing and wholesome aroma – the smell of life itself'.[86] The personification of soil microbes is a common device to encourage engagement, often used by soil educators invoking sensitive soil bodies.[87] Yet identification as a primary route to sympathy tends to preclude the development of

---

84. M Puig de la Bellacasa (n 67) 691.
85. See A Waldow and D Schlosberg's piece 'The Subject of Multispecies Justice: Moving Beyond Individualism with Sympathetic Imagining' in Celermajer et al., 'Justice Through a Multispecies Lens' (n 3).
86. D Montgomery, *Dirt: The Erosion of Civilizations* (University of California Press 2007) 1.
87. See AT O'Brien, 'Ethical Acknowledgment of Soil Ecosystem Integrity amid Agricultural Production in Australia' (2020) 12(1) Environmental Humanities 275.

sympathetic bonds across difference. Instead, respect for alterity and curiosity about difference, as well as the cultivation of a practical willingness to try different ways of being in community, are better preconditions for justice than is identification.[88]

An ethics centring soil as a subject of justice, while a nascent current in the ways in which many farmers and educators describe and justify conservation agriculture,[89] is yet to be sufficiently developed. As such, beyond farming communities, a public reckoning with soil degradation, examining the ways in which violence to soil is institutionalized and upheld by common modern beliefs and practices is still difficult to imagine, at least in the imminent future. Yet as more land-based practitioners learn to protect and promote soil biodiversity, they can demonstrate tangible possibilities for multi-species flourishing and justice to soil, while showing by contrast what can be missing when systemic violence to soil is a norm.

5 CONCLUSION

Taking an eco-centric post-humanist approach to the adaptation of transitional justice to harms committed against more-than-human beings, we have argued for a shift from transformations on the plane of 'ideas' about others and about the norms of justice, to transformations on the plane of practices and embodied relationships. The practices described above provide an intimation of how this shift might occur, even in the absence of an explicitly ethical framework. Nevertheless, one might still ask, can these intimations of change be considered to be anything like transitional justice? Transitional justice in the human sphere typically utilizes the public domain as a space in which injustice can be named, and later, collective self-understandings can be called into question, with ideologies driving injustice problematized. Practices of symbolic reparation (as well as the more full-blown mechanisms like truth commissions) mobilize the tools of the public sphere, including the mass media, as platforms for widening an affectual and ethical transformation in the populace.

With respect to the example of soil that we have discussed in order to illustrate our thesis, even where there are changes, they are overwhelmingly occurring in the private sphere. Witnessing qualitatively different kinds of well-being and abundance on the land, many farmers experience sudden realizations that past practices have suppressed soil and land capabilities. Sometimes these individual experiences move into specialized practitioner groups, which might be seen as constituting types of 'publics', mediated by the internet as well as by in-person gatherings. For the most part, however, such networks do little by way of broader public engagement. Anna Krzywoszynska has written of the limited reach of such 'care networks', and how this reduces their capacity to bring about societal transformation to generate ethical concern for soil:

> While this attentiveness is producing some transformative effects, its potential is limited by the configuration of the soil care network. As long as soil care is configured primarily as farmers' concern [and not a broader societal concern], the potential of attentiveness in generating ethical regard to the needs of soil biota will be limited.[90]

---

88. For an exploration of soil's alterity and ethics, see M Smith, 'Dis(appearance): Earth, Ethics and Apparently (In)Significant Others' (2011) 50 Australian Humanities Review 23–44.
89. AT O'Brien (2020) (n 87) 267–84.
90. A Krzywoszynska, 'Caring for Soil Life in the Anthropocene: The Role of Attentiveness in More-than-Human Ethics' (2019) Transactions of the Institute of British Geographers 1–15.

Yet publics are being forged in unusual ways. There are some budding collaborations between artists and farmers specifically dedicated to engaging larger publics in the transformations taking place through regenerative practices and thereby altering the myths and narratives within which soil is currently located. Simon Mattsson, whose experience is discussed above, has worked with two artists, Lucas Ihlein and Kim Williams, on a chemical-free demonstration plot of sugar cane growing at the Mackay Botanical Gardens, planted and cared for with assistance from members of the Mackay community, and on a musical event – *Sunset Symphony in the Sunflowers*, at his farm. These efforts offer aesthetic enjoyment and community, cultivating a receptive environment in which participants might begin to perceive the interspecies conviviality at work when more soil-sensitive modes of farming are adopted. Although not framed in these terms, these events contribute to the work of justice. In their write-up of the symphony event, Ihlein (one of the artists) and Mattsson state:

> The pay-off (besides the pleasure of the experience itself) is that having the sunflowers there attracts human bodies onto the farm, where they are inevitably prompted to ask the question: 'Tell me again, why did you plant sunflowers in among the sugar cane?' At this point, you've got them! Now a discussion begins about how to farm better for the health of the soil, and who knows where that might lead?[91]

Another project, Earth Canvas, brings together artists and regenerative farmers in South East Australia, and invites members of the public to take part in Open Days where they engage with the farmers, the artists and the practices so as to create a rich shared experience.[92] One of the artists, Jenny Bell, who spent time at Mt Narra Narra station created *Lifeblood*, a vibrant painting expressing the vivid aliveness of what lives as soil.[93] Reflecting on the experience, Bell writes,

> The lifeforce beneath our feet was the hidden force driving this farm ... Lifeblood seeks to celebrate this, imagining a fragment of the world beneath our feet, its microbes, its symbiotic relationship and its interaction with the atmosphere – the interface on which all life on earth depends.[94]

She then describes how the painting includes a portrait of the human farmers, although looking at it, it is difficult to tell which image is them and which the beings of the soil.

Unlike more formal processes of transitional justice, the work here is emergent and oriented towards creating spaces of receptivity in which curious questions lead to deeper conversations. This responsiveness is part of the artists' approaches. Williams states:

> A key thing in conversational work is listening – because it takes a lot of careful, patient and deep listening to form relationships with people and take it somewhere. I guess rather than challenging in a confrontational way, one thing we're doing is showing what's possible in agriculture, perhaps it's more inspiring rather than confronting.[95]

91. L Ihlein and S Mattsson, 'Sunflowers as Agricultural and Cultural Change Agents' in Futurelands 2: An Initiative of the Kandos School of Cultural Adaptation (2017) 21.
92. See Earth Canvas <https://earthcanvas.com.au/>.
93. Photos of *Lifeblood* and work created by other artists can be viewed at <https://earthcanvas.com.au/art-exhibition/#gallery>.
94. Earth Canvas Exhibition Catalogue, Albury Library Museum, p. 12.
95. K Williams, in *Sugar vs the Reef?* Exhibition Catalogue (Mackay Regional Council 2018) 6.

Where recognition of injustice is still not widespread but is nascent, art can function as a powerful bridge and tool of disclosure, connecting the broader public with underappreciated worlds of soil. As Gillian Sanbrook, a farmer and Chairman of Earth Canvas puts it, 'in the same way that regenerative farmers have a symbiotic connection with their land and the animals they raise, artists must attempt to bridge the gap between themselves and the subject of their art'.[96] Such work literally moves people, bringing them physically into spaces where they can perceive in their bodies what it might mean to take soil biodiversity seriously in agriculture.

Our contention is not that these practices of relational care, aesthetic encounter and interspecies conviviality are sufficient to account for the wrongs of the past, nor to provide the foundations for a transformed future. They are rather intimations, openings, suggestive practices that may iterate into larger openings. In the words of Coles, these receptive spaces of community participation generate '[resonant] fields of creative interaction between people and the land', carrying new possibilities for justice with them.[97]

---

96. Earth Canvas Exhibition Catalogue, Albury Library Museum, p. 5.
97. R Coles (n 78) 103.

The practice of multispecies relations in urban space and its potentialities for new legal imaginaries

Teresa Dillon*
Professor of City Futures, University of the West of England

This article explores what it means to enact multispecies relations in urban space. This exploration is rooted in contemporary art practices that create living frameworks through which encounters with non-human animal cultures, histories, rituals and justice are manifested. Such works play with the legalities and categorizations of 'animal' and 'nature' by exposing the nested reasonings and protocols that continue to propagate hierarchical species logics. Consequentially such work, alongside scholarship on earth-bound legalities, looks to how law can foster more just multispecies orderings, which aspire to create more equitable conditions for all. To scaffold such transitions the article makes the case for how a constant, public, educational and social rehearsal that unknots histories of liberal individualism is required in order to shift the ontological position of the human species. This rehearsal is set against the backdrop of climate emergencies and the call for a more expansive notion of the urban commons. The closing reflections point to how the Earth's inviolability must necessarily be placed at the centre of an approach to urban making that is complemented by an intersectional set of innovative cosmologies, actions, manners and ways.

Keywords: *urban, multispecies relations, artistic practices, new legal imaginaries, innovative cosmologies*

1 INTRODUCTION

The impetus for this article stems from an ongoing series of artistic works (installations and performances) engaging with how we encounter (or not) other animals, wildlife and non-human species in urban, as well as from the generous invitation by Professor Anna Grear to contribute to the speaker series 'Imagining the Eco-Social: New Materialist Reflections for the Anthropocene'[1] hosted by the Environmental Justice Research Unit at Cardiff University, Wales. This invitation enabled some of the primary

---

*   I would like to thank Professor Anna Grear for her kind invitation to participate in this series and to her wonderful colleagues and peers, who came together for the 'Imagining the Eco-Social: New Materialist Reflections for the Anthropocene' closing round table event. I would also like to thank Jenny Brindley and Mary Cummins for their support with proof reading and to the journal editors and reviewers for their comments, time and energy.
1.   The speaker series ran over 2018 and 2019, closing with a round table event with Professors Jane Bennett and William Connolly on 10–11 December 2020 <https://blogs.cardiff.ac.uk/environmental-justice-research-unit/2018/08/29/imagining-the-eco-social-speaker-series/ and https://blogs.cardiff.ac.uk/environmental-justice-research-unit/2019/01/18/new-materialist-reflections-for-the-anthropocene-two-new-speaker-events/> accessed 29 November 2020.

interdisciplinary nodes sketched out in this article to be explored. These nodes relate to how we as the human species can move towards more equitable multispecies relationships within urban contexts. Specifically, the primary focus of this article is focused on relationships with animal companions. In supporting this line of thinking several interdisciplinary perspectives are drawn upon, including urban studies, urban and environmental geographies, environmental humanities, post-humanist, materialist and eco-feminist theory, contemporary art, radical politics and ecology. This purposefully expansive cast of theory and disciplines acts as a basis for framing current thinking as well as for the imagining of future refinements and extensions.

For readers of this journal who are familiar with critical legal scholarship, particularly post-anthropocentric legal scholarship, some of the key theoretical points will likely be familiar. As an artist and researcher whose theoretical perspectives normally lie outside of such legal framings, it is necessary to rehearse these points as they are vital to informing new and existing interdisciplinary artistic and academic lines of inquiry, as well as to emerging artistic collaborations with legal academics.

To further support the reader's orientation, in this article the term 'urban spaces' is rooted in sociological understandings of urbanity as the interplay between the amalgamation of diverse people, social roles and relationships within a situated space[2] and the institutional arrangements and social networks that centralize these relationships and enable the accumulation of capital and wealth.[3] Since 2018, of the 7.6 billion people living in the world 55 per cent[4] live in urban regions;[5] this is predicted to rise to 68 per cent by 2050.[6] Humans have therefore predominantly become urban dwellers, with urban space tightly geared towards the service of our species' desires, demands and needs.

Yet, as the economic geographer David Harvey notes, given '[t]he sheer pace and chaotic forms of urbanization throughout the world … [w]e have been made and re-made without knowing exactly why, how, wherefore and to what end'.[7] Given this, Harvey calls for a 'new urban commons'[8] that reflects upon the narratives and imageries that we produce in relation to our cities. Placing Harvey's call alongside the current human or 'Anthropocene'[9] epoch, any attempt towards creating a new

2. H Lefebvre, *The Production of Space* (Wiley-Blackwell 1991).
3. D Harvey, *The Urbanization of Capital: Studies in the History and Theory of Capitalist Urbanization* (Blackwell 1985).
4. <https://www.prb.org/wp-content/uploads/2018/08/2018_WPDS.pdf> accessed 29 November 2020.
5. With urban regions referring most commonly to urban corridors, cities (50,000+ inhabitants), extended metropolitan areas (5 million+ inhabitants) and mega urban centres (10 million+ inhabitants).
6. <https://www.un.org/development/desa/en/news/population/2018-revision-of-world-urbanization-prospects.html> accessed 29 November 2020.
7. D Harvey, 'The Right to the City' (2003) 27(4) International Journal of Urban and Regional Research 939.
8. ibid at 941.
9. The term 'Anthropocene' was introduced by atmospheric chemist Paul Crutzen and environmental biologist Eugene Stoermer in 2000 as a means to distinguish the present era from that of the preceding Holocene. The term, while broadly contested, refers to the effect of human activities on the geology of the planet. An example would be ocean acidification as a result of the pH changes of sea water due to increased carbon dioxide emissions from various human industries and activities or 'plastic islands' that accumulate in the Earth's oceans that can later show up in the composition of the sea floor.

urban commons would seem absurd without taking into account more Earth-bound, multispecies narratives. Yet, as María Puig de la Bellacasa in her book *Matters of Care*[10] notes, the ethics involved in human-non-human symbiosis requires on one hand the decentring of human agencies whilst also 'remaining close to the predicaments and inheritances of situated human doing'.[11] When it comes to urban space and to cities, this tension is at the heart of the matter. For how, in concrete dense urban spaces, can we begin to shift the register from human-centred to multispecies-centred perspectives? This is no small task, yet it is this potential that lies at the heart of the artistic and academic inquiry explored here.

Art and language are tools though which we can begin to shape and imagine new positions. Within cosmopolitical discourse[12] the affective languages of multispecies relations (entanglement, becoming with, coming together, viviality, flourishing, vulnerability) have been pivotal in orientating our view and practice towards more multispecies world making. Exploring multispecies entanglement within the fields of urban and environmental geography,[13] Arcari, Probyn-Rapsey and Singer,[14] in their review of the literature, note how such affective languages often exclude highly commodified and instrumentalized animals (such as cattle, sheep, pigs, chickens) in favour of isolated examples: the unusual, wild, stray or feral (foxes, bats).[15] To address this privileging Arcari, Probyn-Rapsey and Singer call for a more critical approach that questions the 'idealized conception of entanglement and conviviality with "nature", if within that same city other "natures" are still slaughtered, bred, traded, confined, raced, tested on, put to work, abused and killed'.[16] Arcari, Probyn-Rapsey and Singer, while critically sympathetic, for example, to Haraway's[17] call for cultivating and

---

10. María Puig de la Bellacasa, *Matters of Care: Speculative Ethics in More Than Human Worlds* (University of Minnesota Press, Minneapolis/London 2017).
11. ibid at 2.
12. Referring, for example, to B Ulrich, 'The Truth of Others: A Cosmopolitan Approach' (2004) 10(3) Common Knowledge 430–49; M De la Cadena, 'Indigenous Cosmopolitics in the Andes: Conceptual Reflections beyond "Politics"' (2010) 25(2) Cultural Anthropology 334–70; P Descola, 'Constructing Natures: Symbolic Ecology and Social Practice' in P Descolá and G Pálsson (eds), *Nature and Society: Anthropological Perspectives* (Routledge, London 2004); M Nussbaum, *Creating Capabilities: The Human Development Approach* (Harvard University Press, Cambridge 2011).
13. See pp. 6–8 of Arcari, Probyn-Rapsey and Singer's article for an extensive summary of what they included within their review, which first collated articles between 2016 and 2018 that were representative of a 'caring' approach to urban 'nature' and multispecies communities (emerging in Australia), and secondly drew on international research via 'Google Scholar' and university library databases, where searches focused on specific journals published between 2009 and 2019 (book reviews not included), with an emphasis on studies where urban 'nature' and animals – either animals in general or individual species – were located within the city boundaries. Findings from the first search indicated that despite calls for attending with care to neglected things, commodified 'kin' was not included; the second review underscored how 'normalized a limited conception of "nature" has become across the broader urban-focused literature'. P Arcari, F Probyn-Rapsey and H Singer, 'Where Species Don't Meet: Invisibilized Animals, Urban Nature and City Limits' (2021) 43(3) Environment and Planning E: Nature and Space 940–65.
14. ibid.
15. ibid at 12.
16. ibid at 15–16.
17. DJ Haraway, *Staying with the Trouble (Experimental Futures): Making Kin in the Chthulucene* (Duke University Press Books, Durham, NC 2016).

attuning to response-abilities and to Tsing's ideals of neighbourliness as the social relations across differences of both vitality and species (which Tsing considers as essential to good living),[18] warn that the normalization of entangled species relations can lead to a homogenizing language where the practical and theoretical intentions of multispecies thinking fail to be criticized. The authors state that '[i]f urban researchers are not putting human relations with all "nature" under critical scrutiny, then those who draw on this work [such as urban designers and planners] to inform practice and policy are likely to follow suit'.[19]

How then do we attend to addressing the complexity of urban multispecies narratives that on one hand condone the daily mass slaughtering of cattle, sheep and chickens to feed urban populations and on the other privilege nuanced acts of observance, care and attention to others, such as the creatures we define as pets? Attending to this challenge the philosopher, psychologist and animal-human interlocutor Vinciane Despret speaks to the politeness of 'getting to know'[20] another animal. As Despret states: 'if we want to define ourselves as authorized by them to speak in their name, we are required to offer them the opportunity to show what they can do'[21] ('them' relating specifically to animals and in particular to Despret's encounters with ravens).

Placing Despret's suggestion into an urban context – a city for example – requires unpacking if we are to think through how this might work. First, to offer another, be it human or non-human, the opportunity to show their nature in an authentic manner requires making time for slow, consistent, patient and deep levels of engagement. Currently cities tend to be designed for speed, efficiency and density, with the explicit opportunity for contact with other living animal species most often designated to specific areas (supermarkets, butchers, parks, zoos, urban farms, one's own garden or rooftop – if you have such privileged access). While appreciating that there are always outliers to this story, contact with animals in urban spaces is most often predicated upon human-centred sustenance, well-being and/or entertainment.

Even with outlier cases, getting to know another non-human animal is a deeply situated process that is mutually interdependent and tied to emergent ways of knowing that arise from the specificities of that encounter. To be able to speak on behalf of, or to articulate another species' living pathways or life cycle, provides opportunities for expressing their wonder, drama, joys, understanding, or for sympathizing with their suffering or trauma, and requires us to be brought into a sustained communion. For this to happen we need to continually practice modes of encountering and entanglement in urban space that move beyond the given trajectories, while also holding that a multitude of impossibilities and affordances will unfold. If an opportunity for sustained, intentional encountering is provided then we may be in a better position to scaffold the ontological shifts that are necessary to move towards more multispecies

---

18. See A Tsing, *The Mushroom at the End of the World: On the Possibility of Life in Capitalist Ruins* (Princeton University Press, Princeton 2015) 279–80, discussing the work of Lu-Min Vaario and colleagues on the matsutake mushroom and the concept of neighbourliness as the study of difference, specifically mutuality across differences. For further reference see LM Vaario Pennanen, T Sarjala, EM Savonen and J Heinonsalo, 'Ectomycorrhization of Tricholoma Matsutake and Two Major Conifers in Finland – An Assessment of In Vitro Mycorrhiza Formation' (2010) 20(7) Mycorrhiza 511–18.
19. Arcari, Probyn-Rapsey and Singer (n 13) at 16.
20. V Despret, 'THE ENIGMA OF THE RAVEN' (2015) 20(2) Angelaki 57–72, at 62.
21. ibid at 62.

centring – the caveat being that we will need to attend to the discomfort and clashes that such deconstruction and reconstructions will bring. For example, this ontological shift foregrounds a set of intersectional relations which may include those that uphold white supremacy and the logic of animalization as it relates to perceived rights, power and control.

2 PRACTICE-ORIENTED POSITIONS: CULTIVATING MULTISPECIES ARRANGMENTS

Stepping into such framings as an artist whose work sits across the fields of site-based art, critical spatial practice, techno-civic inquiries and collaborative and cooperative learning, the question of cultivating multispecies arrangements and exploring ecological narratives and survival[22] underlies much of my performative and performance-based work. For the purpose of this article, I will draw briefly on the installation 'UNDER NEW MOONS, WE STAND STRONG'.[23] The title of the work, itself part incantation and part poem, evokes the inter-psychological process needed to rise above amplified forms of everyday biometric surveillance and the wisdoms to think beyond its human-centred privileging. The focus of the work was on a particular camera which was positioned at the intersection of Autoroute 40 and Boulevard des Sources, in the West Island of Montréal, Québec, Canada. This camera, deployed to monitor traffic, captured on 3 January 2016 a series of images of a snowy owl in flight. Four days later the images were tweeted by Québec's then Transport Minister, Robert Poeti. The images went viral,[24] turning the snowy owl into an internet star (Figure 1).

Having previously written about the entanglement of this moment in relation to histories of CCTV surveillance, the symbolism of the owl, and the hostility of surveillance infrastructures to avian wildlife,[25] it is worth revisiting some of the points fleshed out in my original essay, as they support the complexities of what it means to move towards more just multispecies urban orderings.

Snowy owls enjoy open, tundra-like terrain. The capture of the owl in flight by the camera was most likely due to the owl seeking a place to perch and search for food. Given the camera's high position, it provided the ideal vista and territorial vantage for the owl, whose initial perching sites (trees) would have been cleared so as to build the motorway. Our enthrallment with the images of the owl, and their subsequent viral spread, produced a number of contradictions, particularly given that surveillance cameras are most often covered in bird spikes or layered with ultraviolet (UV) gels that act as visual and sensory deterrents. Birds can perceive wavelengths in the ultraviolet

---

22. See for example the installation and performance 'A Eulogy to this Ground' (2020) and 'Cleansing Rituals for the Internet' (2020) and the paper 'Liquid Loss, Learning to Mourn our Companion Species and Landscapes' (2019) available at <http://www.polarproduce.org> last accessed 29 November 2020.
23. T Dillon, UNDER NEW MOONS, WE STAND STRONG (2016). Commissioned by the Peacock Visual Arts Centre, Aberdeen, with support from the Festival of Architecture Scotland, 2016 and Seventeen Gallery, Aberdeen.
24. For a summary of the media coverage, see, T Dillon, 'Under New Moons, We Stand Strong: Symbolism and Literacy within an Era of Digital Oppression' in D Bogomir, F Brigitte and Tarasiewicz M (eds), *Faceless: Re-inventing Privacy Though Subversive Media Strategies* (De Gruyter, Angewandte Edition 2018).
25. ibid.

Credit: Ministry of Transport, Sustainable Mobility and Transport Electrification of the Quebec Government

Figure 1   UNDER NEW MOONS, WE STAND STRONG (Dillon 2016)

range and interpret the gel as a threat, altering their course of flight to avoid it. Intentionally, the gels are also imbued with natural oils that aggravate the birds' sense of smell. Such additions to surveillance cameras are examples of 'unpleasant design',[26] also referred to as hostile, defensive and exclusionary architecture – meaning there is an intentional design strategy that uses elements of the built environment to guide or to restrict behaviour. Examples of such design vary according to the behaviour they are intended to restrict or control: from spikes to benches that purposefully block people from sleeping on them, the aim is to discourage loitering, to prevent skaters, homeless people or activists from using the urban space and to ward off anything that is unwanted or goes against the city's dominant commercial norms.[27] The viral celebration of the image of the snowy owl also poignantly illustrates Arcari, Probyn-Rapsey and Singer's previously shared critique. In this case the 'wild' in the form of the snowy owl is celebrated while other birds such as pigeons for example – who are often portrayed as a blight and hindrance to surveillance camera maintenance[28] – are vilified. Deeper analysis of the image also reveals several interlocking sets of human behaviour that need to be challenged. This includes not least the anthropomorphism of the owl, the initial decimating of its resting and eating spots, and the ramifications of such destruction. Revisiting Despret's call to get

26.   G Savičić and S Savić, 'Unpleasant Design' (2013) G.L.O.R.I.A.
27.   See, for example, S Sassen, *Expulsions: Brutality and Complexity in the Global Economy: Brutality and Complexity in the Global Economy* (Harvard University Press, Cambridge, MA 2014); N Smith, *Urban Frontier: Gentrification and the Revanchist City* (Routledge, London 1996); D Harvey, *Social Justice and the City* (University of Georgia Press, Athens 2009).
28.   For example, websites such as Bird·Be·Gone at <https://www.birdbgone.com/bird/pigeon-control/> sell spikes, gels and sonic solutions for repelling birds but is specifically targeted at pigeons, as is Stop-Bird-Pro at <https://pigeon-deterrent.co.uk/> (accessed 15 May 2021) which is a sonic deterrent also focused on pigeons.

to know the animal other, the question then becomes how is this even possible when an encounter is framed against backdrops of anthropomorphism, exclusion, negation and negativity? How does one begin to unravel compounded oversight and neglect? How do we begin to produce the conditions, the sensibilities and sensitivities, to reassess such matters so that we can speak in another species' name and create space that offers them the opportunity to show what they can do?

3 SPEAKING IN THE NAME OF OTHERS

> We lived in a world knowing it was only for us on loan. Everything passed, and we accepted it. The great tides of history arrived to us as streams so small they were hardly noticed. Wars killed us, but so too did space. Food was the same, century after century. Barns were smaller or wider, our companions fewer or more numerous, but the daily routine remained. Birth, grazing, feeding, sleeping. Our centuries were defined by the host breath of a companion in the silence of the shelter, the return to the fields in the days, and by the absence or weight of the plough, sledge, or carriage. We were poor in words for things: our vocabulary was verb-based, built from our doings and those of our companion beings. Our name was given to us by humans. That name rendered us objects. We were so deep inside of history that we did not see ourselves within it, nor did we notice when it abandoned us altogether … We no longer went outside, nor did we sleep within without companions. Now we live inside the factory. It has become impossible to pass on any heritage. Calves are taken from us immediately after being born, and family lines are scatted out of our sight. We do so little that all our culture and habits have faded to nothing. We no long learn from our mothers, but from the machine that tells our bodies how we stand and how to eat. Stuck in the industrial process we live in collective isolation, cut off from all relations that could anchor us to time, history, or culture. For how could we have culture if culture was the transformation of things into objects? How could we have history if history was the weaving together of times from the present moment into the past? We did not even have time, just the monotonous ticking of the clock, the parceling of hours, minutes and repetitions.
>
> So here I am, claiming what is mine and my ancestors ancestors' by law: the history that we so generously gave to you. By incorporating your tongue, we – the foundation, the mute – are pulled into existence, into human thought. But as we approach the threshold of history, we realize that outside language we are still nothing. I can only point to my absence, hoping that in this failure, a hole would emerge through which a cow could enter: But as I leave you now, I do not evaporate into the realm of ideas and imagination. Instead, I melt, I dissolve into your body, as my bovine colleagues have dissolved into the bodies of your family and friends. I remain close, hidden between your concepts, curled into your muscles, waiting to be noticed. And, some day, I will enter.

The above extract was taken from 'The Museum of the History of Cattle' by visual artist Terike Happoja and writer Laura Gustafsson who collaborate on a number of projects under their collective identity Gustafsson & Haapoja.[29] The work premiered in November 2013 in Helsinki, Finland, with the aforementioned text also shared in Davis and Turpin's edited book, *Art in the Anthropocene*.[30]

---

29. L Gustafasson and T Haapoja <http://www.gustafssonhaapoja.org/about-2/> accessed 29 November 2020.
30. T Haapoja and L Gustafasson, 'A History According to Cattle', in H Davis and E Turpin (eds), *Art in the Anthropocene: Encounters Among Aesthetics, Politics, Environments and Epistemologies* (Open Humanities Press, London 2015).

'The Museum of the History of Cattle' forms part of a larger art and research project 'The History of Others', which, as the artists describe, 'investigates cultural histories from non-human perspectives through exhibitions, publications, performances and writings'.[31] Exploring problems that arise from the anthropocentric worldview of Western traditions, Gustafsson & Haapoja seek to 'open paths for ethical ways of interspecies coexistence'.[32] In attempting to speak from the perspective of cattle, Gustafsson & Haapoja's historical analysis provides a way to get to know the animal other. Their work also addresses questions raised in the last section of this article about how one can imagine beginning to unravel compounded oversight and neglect. As containers for other forms of world-making, the historical perspective taken in their installation produces potentials through which sensitivities towards the cultures of another non-human animal species can be discerned. Importantly their work addresses Arcari, Probyn-Rapsey and Singer's call for a more critical approach that questions the idealized conception of entanglement and conviviality with 'nature' by placing emphasis on the lives of cattle whom we so commonly slaughter, breed, trade and kill. In thinking through the histories and cultures of cattle, relaying them, placing them in our most esteemed cultural institutions (museums and galleries) Gustafsson & Haapoja create an active space in which we humans can begin to unlearn and decolonize the centrality of our position.

Another piece by Gustafsson & Haapoja 'The Trial'[33] takes a more performative approach to opening up such potentialities. 'The Trial' is a 90-minute performance in which an imagined juridical encounter – the 'State versus Perho hunters' – was enacted. The performance stages a criminal case concerning 15 hunters from Western Finland, who are put on public trial for killing wolves. During the testimony and cross-examination, the jury hears how the loss of wolves' lives was justified, as the hunters claim they were protecting the community's children and livestock and maintaining public safety. Favouring the prosecution's case regarding the rights of the animals to be protected from unnecessary harm, the judges are asked to give their verdict on the perpetrators' punishment. If found guilty the options play out as follows: life imprisonment for three 'murders' if the destruction of life was premeditated, cruel, or dangerous; imprisonment for at least eight years for the 'slaughter' of three wolves; or imprisonment for four to ten years for the three 'killings' under mitigating circumstances. The judges are also asked to decide whether or not compensation should be given to the Perho wolf pack. In 'The Trial' Gustafsson & Haapoja again turn the tables on our normalized species ordering: the consequence of killing the wolves meaning a life sentence, as it would be if one was found guilty of killing another human with similar implications of culpability regarding intent and similar repercussions and reparations relating to mitigation.

As Haapoja writes:

> Modern law divides the world into two categories, that of legal objects and legal persons. This divide splits the world into two categories of beings, of which the first have inherent rights that are born out of their natural needs, while the latter are destined to only have instrumental value, determined by their use in the service of the first. In today's

---

31. ibid.
32. L Gustafasson and T Haapoja <http://www.gustafssonhaapoja.org/about-2/> accessed 10 May 2021.
33. L Gustafasson and T Haapoja, The Trial (2014–) <http://www.gustafssonhaapoja.org/the-trial/> accessed 29 November 2020.

democracies, every human being is born into the category of legal persons, which is shared with other human-made constructs that can practice ownership, such as corporations, associations or states. The non-human world in all its diversity is destined to stay on the other side of the divide, as merely an object of ownership, exchange and control ... In the face of human-caused environmental crises that are threatening the existence of the majority of the world's species, humans included, it is no longer possible to ignore the tragic consequences of the human-centered traditions of western modernism. Mass extinctions of species and collapses of ecosystems seem to shout out the same protest: 'We are not things. We have agency'. This biological reality is thus challenging the fault at the core of the concept of the modern states, the division of the world into persons and things, humans and non-humans, abusers and the abused. Like groups of people before, the excluded in society, the non-human world that supports all human life, is now becoming visible, declaring its agency and autonomy.[34]

In declaring their agencies, trees, rivers, lakes and animals have been 'calling' for their footing. Stone's seminal paper, 'Should Trees Have Standing? Towards Legal Rights for Natural Objects',[35] several decades ago noted that if animals and other species possess sentience or consciousness they therefore have a subjective good.[36] They have the sort of moral standing that justifies certain inviolable rights: to life and liberty, and in particular the right not to be simply used as means to support human wellbeing. To rehearse here the full scope of the animal rights/welfare debate is outside of the scope of this article, however for those interested: legal scholar and ethnographer Irus Braverman[37] provides a detailed account of such nuances. Drawing on the work of Dayan,[38] Braverman notes how the definition of animalization itself 'serves as a technology of dehumanization, illuminating the fuzziness of interspecies boundaries of law and showing that they are ontologically and politically fraught'.[39] For Braverman 'the project of humanizing law and dehumanizing nature and animality demarcates the boundaries of law: law's sovereignty as dependent on its states of expectation'.[40] Drawing on the work of the French philosopher, Jacques Derrida, who speaks to such demarcations in his works *The Animal That Therefore I Am*[41] and *The Beast and the Sovereign*,[42] Braverman notes how the burden of the beast has weighed down Western law, and, like Gustafsson & Haapoja, calls for its release.

---

34. T Haapoja, 'A Pavilion of Species', in T Elfving and T Haapoja, *Altern Ecologies. Emergent Perspectives on the Ecological Threshold at the 55th Venice Biennale*, Frame Visual Art Finland and Academy of Fine Arts, University of the Arts Helsinki (2015) 14–15.
35. CD Stone, 'Should Trees Have Standing? – Towards Legal Rights for Natural Objects' (1972) 45 Southern California Law Review 450–501.
36. See, for example, the section on 'The Psychic and Socio-Psychic Aspects', Stone, ibid 499–500.
37. I Braverman, 'Law's Underdog: A Call for More-than-Human-Legalities' (2018) 14 Annual Review of Law and Social Science 127–44.
38. C Dayan, *The Law Is a White Dog: How Legal Rituals Make and Unmake Persons* (Princeton University Press, Princeton, NJ 2011).
39. Braverman (n 37) at 131.
40. ibid at 131.
41. J Derrida, *The Animal That Therefore I Am* (Fordham University Press, New York 2008).
42. J Derrida, *The Beast and the Sovereign, Vol. 1* (University of Chicago Press, Chicago 2009).

Exploring the potential for new legal imaginaries in the Anthropocene, Grear[43] (drawing on the work of Kathleen Lennon[44]) notes that encounters with 'alternative imagined configurations'[45] of our subjectivity need to make both cognitive and affective sense. Grear adds that this requires a 'reimagined, liveable way of going-on-corporeally-in-the-world'.[46] Nonetheless, as Grear and others[47] note, the subject of law is currently constructed as a disembodied or quasi-disembodied subject, bound in notions of property and personhood that are also situated and political. Lawful relations are situated within mind-sets whereby humans' 'control' over nature justifies its pillage, along with the peoples of its lands. Such relations are political in that law fails to take into account the inequalities, alienation and violence inscribed within contemporary conditions. Questions of inequality and blind spots are also addressed by the 'inhuman' geographer Kathryn Yusoff, in her book *A Billon Black Anthropocenes or None*,[48] which restates the long-term influences of colonialism on power and the production of relations. She writes:

> The human and its subcategory, the inhuman, are historically relational to a discourse of settler colonial rights and the material practices of extraction, which is to say that the categorisation of matter is a spatial execution, of place, land and person cut from relation through geographic displacement (and relocation through forced settlement and transatlantic slavery).[49]

Speaking specifically to histories of oppression and dispossession, Yusoff reiterates how the categorization of inhuman or non-human, animal or property, is a form of subordination that has been used as a means through which to promote at all costs an ongoing linear and extractive model of living and economics. Such privileging and marginalization, as Grear, Braverman and Favre, to name but a few, have enunciated, leads to a whole host of colonized 'others', including people/s, non-human animals and earth organisms that are to 'differing degrees and varying contexts objectified (and feminized) by a body-politics of privilege and marginalization'.[50]

4 INNOVATIVE COSMOLOGIES

Cities privilege human activity, marginalizing other species by placing them in the service of urban orders that systematically uphold values that currently do not service an embodied multispecies perspective. Art historian and Director of the Center for

---

43. A Grear, 'Legal Imaginaries and the Anthropocene: "Of" and "For"' (2020) 31 Law and Critique 351–66.
44. K Lennon, 'Imaginary Bodies and Worlds' (2004) 47(2) Inquiry 107–22.
45. Grear (n 43) at 351.
46. ibid at 351.
47. B Favre, 'Is There a Need for a New, an Ecological, Understanding of Legal Animal Rights?' (2020) 11(2) Journal of Human Rights and the Environment 297–319; LJ Kotze, 'The Anthropocene, Earth System Vulnerability and Socio-Ecological Injustices in an Age of Human Rights' (2019) 10(1) Journal of Human Rights and the Environment 62–85.
48. K Yusoff (2018), *A Billon Black Anthropocenes or None* (University of Minnesota Press, Minneapolis 2018).
49. ibid at 2.
50. Grear (n 43) at 354.

Creative Ecologies at the University of Santa Cruz, TJ Demos has written on numerous occasions[51] about Haapoja and Gustafsson & Haapoja's work, and has described 'The Trial' as an example of 'innovative cosmopolitics – an experimental way of instituting social relations, establishing commonality, and ordering knowledge about the world'.[52] Thinking through the affective modes of instituting social relations and establishing commonality within the last few years, my own work has explored how ritual, specifically the co-construction of mourning rituals for land and species loss,[53] can support such re-framings. To date this has manifested in a series of works, with 'A Eulogy to this Ground'[54] being the most relevant to discussions relating to practices in urban space. This piece, which was hosted temporarily in a yurt in an urban garden in the western suburbs of Paris,[55] is indicative of the 'hacks' that are required to bring such work into urban contexts. The garden, which had been created by various artists, designers and architects, required intensive soil remediation including phytoremediation, whereby plants are used to support cleaning toxins out of the soil, which had been contaminated and damaged by years of industrial use. Taking the form of a situated ritual and tele-sorcery cast,[56] the yurt (an existing structure in the garden used for various community classes) was transformed into a site for contemplation and reflection. Stripping the yurt back to its basic structure, the floor was covered and kneeling mediation chairs installed around an 'altar' of three interconnected screens. Each screen displayed a projection of an eighteenth-century illustration of the alfalfa plant that played on a loop, which dissolved to black over time and then restarted. This plant, which grows on the site, supports phytoremediation and its history is also interlocked with tales of agriculture, colonization and cattle forage. At set times during the exhibition programme a live, 'tele-sorcery' cast was given. Part story, part incantation and part blessing, this live spoken word text 'projected into the space' and drew on the history of the garden's soil. This history included the flora and fauna that made it their home, or were lost, eradicated or relocated, so that the garden and the site's previous uses and the city surrounds could be built (Figure 2).

Returning to the practices and manners that might enable a regular, public and social rehearsal that consciously unknots histories of liberal individualism, ritual offers the potential for a communal practice that can be shaped to the urban surroundings. Through honouring the lives of other species, ritual creates a temporal structure that brings us into an attentive space through which their lives are foregrounded. In this way, ritual complements Demos' notion of innovative cosmopolitics by instituting social relations, establishing commonality, and ordering knowledge about the

---

51. See, TJ Demos, *Against the Anthropocene: Visual Culture and Environment Today* (Sternberg Press, Berlin 2017) and TJ Demos, *Decolonizing Nature: Contemporary Art and the Politics of Ecology* (Sternberg Press, Berlin 2016).
52. Demos, *Against the Anthropocene* (n 51).
53. T Dillon, 'Liquid Loss: Learning to Mourn Our Companion Species and Landscapes' in V Saracino (ed) (Fall 2019) Screen City Biennial Journal, Volume 2, Ecologies Lost and Found.
54. T Dillon, 'A Eulogy to This Ground' (2020), Installation and video work. Premiered at Nuit Blanche on 3 October 2020 <http://www.polarproduce.org/works/a-eulogy-to-this-ground/> accessed 5 May 2021.
55. <http://www.polarproduce.org/works/a-eulogy-to-this-ground/>.
56. Tele-sorcery was the name given to this form of practice by the artist collective RYBN who supported earlier rehearsals of this work on their radio <https://p-node.org/> during COVID Lockdown 1, Mar–April 2020. It refers to the performative use of spells and chants over network technologies (internet, radio, video chat).

Credit: Martina Cirese.

Figure 2 A Eulogy to this Ground (Dillon 2020)

world. This is the power that art holds. It provides possibilities for conjuring up worlds, which even if they fail, still 'work' as imagery scaffolds through which we can collectively grip onto the ontological changes that are at stake. As acts of imagination each of the aforementioned artworks purposefully attempts to produce framings through which the complex, messy confrontations of multispecies interdependence, relations, privileging and power are played out. As interlocutor strategies, the artworks speak between and towards the instrumental role that legal discourses and their associated orderings 'perform' in order to maintain the status quo, and they begin to destabilize the hierarchical designations bestowed upon nature.

5 CLOSING POINTS

The purpose of this article was to explore what might constitute a regular multispecies practice in urban spaces, while acknowledging cities' human privileging. This question was further contextualized within Harvey's call for a 'new urban commons' and the sympathetic critique of existing entanglement languages and their exclusions. In exploring this terrain I selected examples of artistic practices, which were discussed in relation to their potential for creating imageries that articulate the work required to shift from human-centred to multispecies-centred perspectives. From the images of a snowy owl on a CCTV camera, to histories of cattle and the speculative court trial that brought justice for wolves, to the ritual enactments in urban gardens that tune into the histories of soils, plants and phytoremediation, each endeavour, while existing within a specific timeframe, location and context, drew on a mix of species relations.

Each artwork provides insights into ways to move beyond the hypothetical and theoretical framing of multispecies relations by placing emphasis on what it means to get to know the culture of other species, to mourn and remember them, and to act in a just manner when they are threatened. These 'lived' workings enable imagining what new ontological articulations might look like and address legal scholars' call for more radical material metaphors that allow for 'law's materiality to come forth'.[57] Such artworks can also aide in reimagining law's relation to spatial justice as the struggle of various bodies (human, non-human, non-organic) 'to occupy space at the same time'.[58] Such works also bring us closer to the 'massive' restorative project that is required if we are to heal our relations with other species and the 'natural' world.

By grounding this article in examples from the contemporary arts with a focus on forms of radical participatory engaged practices,[59] the importance of constructing spaces in which species meet emerges as foundational to scaffolding encounters that enable a becoming-with to emerge. Such work also links to what is broadly defined within urban and architectural studies as a form of critical spatial practice, whereby the arrangements that are brought into the frame fundamentally foreground or foreclose certain obligations between species. While one could argue that there are multiple daily moments for reflecting on such obligations, this reflection has to be consciously crafted, carved out, supported, taught and acted upon. This spatial reorientation returns us to Haraway, who in reflecting on her work, *When Species Meet* (WSM)[60] noted:

> The task of WSM is 'becoming with' rather than 'becoming', at every interleaved scale of time and space, in material semiotic places (here, not there; there, not here; this, not everything; attachment sites, not case studies for the general; oxymorons, not examples), all the way down, without end but also without ever starting from scratch and never alone.
>
> All those copulating-words-without-benefit-of-hyphen, all those resignified ordinary words: are they really necessary? Is the trouble they cause any help to staying with the trouble that terran critters, including people, must live? Staying with that kind of mundane trouble requires facing those who come before, in order to live responsibly in thick copresents, so that we may bequeath something liveable to those who come after.[61]

My reading of this is that Haraway, both questioning and reflecting on her own position as to whether language, 'those copulating-words', can 'help', partially answers that it does, in that language is one of the main cultural tools through which we shape our environments.[62] However, words must be partnered with action, interaction and reciprocity. Yet, when it comes to mainstream city and urban planning and architecture (and I emphasize mainstream), there are currently no grounded and direct ways of planning, beyond the tick-boxing mechanisms of bio-diversity accountabilities, which are situated in relation to human benefits – no grounded and direct

---

57. A Philippopoulos-Mihalopoulos, 'Flesh of the Law: Material Legal Metaphors' (2016) 43(1) Journal of Law and Society 45–65.
58. A Philippopoulos-Mihalopoulos, *Spatial Justice* (Routledge, Abingdon 2015) 3.
59. Note these forms of artistic practice, defy easy categorization and are fundamentally transdisciplinary.
60. DJ Haraway, *When Species Meet* (Minneapolis, University of Minnesota Press 2007).
61. DJ Haraway, 'When Species Meet: Staying with the Trouble' (2010) 28 Environment and Planning D: Society and Space 53–55 at 53.
62. L Vygotsky, *Thought and Language* (MIT Press, Cambridge MA 1962).

ways of planning that address the more radical potentials for reimagining our city spaces through multispecies thinking. This article in part continues to look towards the complexities and practicalities of what this means, acknowledging that there are many whose practices recognize the 'need to critically rethink the city–nature nexus',[63] while also trying to create useful bridges between contemporary posthuman legal scholarship and eco-social art practices. In closing, the Australian philosopher and ecofeminist Val Plumwood, in her review of Deborah Bird Rose's 'Reports from a Wild Country' (2005), notes:

> If our species does not survive the ecological crisis, it will probably be due to our failure to imagine and work out new ways to live with the Earth, to rework ourselves and our high energy, high-consumption, and hyper-instrumental societies adaptively. We struggle to adjust because we're still largely trapped inside the enlightenment tale of progress as human control over a passive and 'dead' nature that justifies both colonial conquests and commodity economies.[64]

Mindful of Ernsson and Swyngedouw's warning that we should not 'proceed unheeded through an altered ontological premise' whereby a different storyline masks 'what is really at stake',[65] if we are to break the 'enlightenment tale' the Earth's inviolability now demands that we place it at the centre of all our thinking, doing and decision making.

---

63. Referring here, for example, to A Escobar, 'Habitability and Design: Radical Interdependence and the Re-earthing of Cities' (2019) 101 Geoforum 132–40; D Houston, J Hillier, D MacCallum, W Steele and J Byrne, 'Make Kin, Not Cities! Multispecies Entanglements and "Becoming-World" in Planning Theory' (2018) 17(2) Planning Theory 190–212; and L Forlano, 'Decentering the Human in the Design of Collaborative Cites' (2016) 32(3) Design Issues 42–54.
64. V Plumwood. 'A Review of Deborah Bird Rose's "Report from a Wild Country: Ethics of Decolonisation"' (2007) 42 Australian Humanities Review 1–4 <http://australianhumanities review.org/2007/08/01/a-review-of-deborah-bird-roses-reports-from-a-wild-country-ethics-for-decolonisation/> accessed 10 May 2021.
65. H Ernsson and E Swyngedouw, 'O Tempora! O Mores! Interrupting the Anthropo-obScene', in H Ernsson and E Swyngedouw (eds), *Urban Political Ecology in the Anthropo-obscene, Interruptions and Possibilities* (Routledge, London and New York 2019) at 35.